THE FOOTLIGHTS FLICKERED

Other books by the same author :

THEATRE ROYAL, THE BIOGRAPHY OF DRURY LANE THEATRE
TWENTY SHILLINGS IN THE POUND
CARRIAGES AT ELEVEN
HAYMARKET; THEATRE OF PERFECTION
GAIETY; THEATRE OF ENCHANTMENT
THE MELODIES LINGER ON
GHOSTS AND GREASEPAINT
SHIRTFRONTS AND SABLES
LADIES FIRST
IVOR
AN INDISCREET GUIDE TO THEATRELAND
FORTUNE'S FAVOURITE (WITH D. L. MURRAY)
BACK NUMBERS
NIGHTS OF GLADNESS
PILLARS OF DRURY LANE
MARIE LLOYD, QUEEN OF THE MUSIC HALLS
GIVE ME YESTERDAY
ST. JAMES'S; THEATRE OF DISTINCTION
etc. etc.

THE FOOTLIGHTS FLICKERED

By

W. MACQUEEN-POPE

LONDON : HERBERT JENKINS

First published by
Herbert Jenkins Ltd.
3 Duke of York Street,
London, S.W.1.
1959

Made and Printed in Great Britain by
John Gardner (Printers) Ltd., Litherland, Liverpool, 20.

To my Old and Very Dear Friend
CHARLES SEGUIER BROWN

A Pillar of the Theatre of Enchantment, the Gaiety, in those happy Edwardian Days and who still keeps bright and shining all that was best when Queen Victoria and King Edward VII ruled this realm and when our Theatre, of which he is part, stood at its highest pinnacle of distinction.

Contents

		Page
PROLOGUE		13

Chapter

I	1920—THE DECADE OPENS	25
II	MORE EVENTS OF 1920	37
III	THE MUSIC OF NINETEEN TWENTY . . .	49
IV	VIGNETTE OF A 1920 IMPRESARIO . . .	61
V	1921 SOUNDS THE ALARM	68
VI	VIGNETTE OF A MANAGEMENT	82
VII	1922—AND LITTLE IMPROVEMENT . . .	88
VIII	DOWNHILL WITH 1923	102
IX	VIGNETTE OF AN ACTOR	114
X	1924—AND NOT SO GAY	123
XI	THE SEE-SAW OF 1925	137
XII	1926—AND NEARLY A BLACKOUT . . .	152
XIII	REALLY WEST END	167
XIV	UPS AND DOWNS OF 1927	173
XV	CRITICS, NEWSMEN AND—HANNEN SWAFFER . .	186
XVI	1928—AND THE GREAT CHALLENGE . . .	197
XVII	THEATRE ROYAL ACROSS THE WATER AND SOME OTHERS	210
XVIII	LAST SCENE OF ALL	216
XIX	CURTAIN SPEECH	231
	INDEX	238

List of Illustrations

Facing Page

Ivor Novello's first stage part 16

Owen Nares 17

Basil Gill 17

Marie Tempest 32

Irene Vanbrugh 32

Lilian Braithwaite 33

Binnie Hale 48

Evelyn Laye 48

Jack Buchanan 49

Alfred Lester 64

Godfrey Tearle 64

Marie Lohr 65

José Collins 65

Matheson Lang and Margaret Halstan, Winifred Barnes, Elsie Janis, Ivor Novello and Lily Elsie, Robert Michaelis, Marie Lohr and Sir Gerald du Maurier

Between pages 72 *and* 73

Anna Pavlova 80

G. Grossmith, Jnr. 80

W. H. Berry 81

Norman McKinnell 81

John Gielgud 96

Phyllis Dare 97

Isobel Elsom 97

J. L. Sacks 112

9

		Facing Page
Archie de Bear	. . . .	112
Gus Sohlke	. . . .	113
Julian Wylie	. . . .	113
Laurence Olivier	. . . .	128
Edith Day	. . . .	129
Dorothy Dickson	. . . .	129
Owen Nares and Marie Ault	. . . . . .	144
Leslie Faber	. . . .	145
Lyne Harding	. . . .	145
Gladys Cooper	. . . .	160
Yvonne Arnaud	. . . .	160
Tom Walls and Winifred Shotter	. . . .	161
Lily Elsie	. . . .	176
Margaret Bannerman	. . . .	176
George Robey	. . . .	177
Billy Merson	. . . .	177
Macbeth in modern dress	. . . . . .	192
Jessie Matthews	. . . .	193
Fay Compton	. . . .	193
Back To Methuselah	. . . .	208
Vivian Ellis	. . . .	209
Basil Dean	. . . .	209
Frederick Ranalow and Lilian Davies	. . . .	224
Young Woodley	. . . .	224
Basil Foster	. . . .	225
Henry Ainley	. . . .	225

THE FOOTLIGHTS FLICKERED

Prologue

WHEN the maroons exploded at 11 a.m. on 11th November 1918 and announced the end of hostilities in the First World War, the whole of the country went mad. The War was over. They were the survivors of the conflict. No more of them would be killed—they had come through. Although it may have been sub-conscious, that was the first reaction.

At one swoop, grim anxiety fell away. The British had never considered defeat although they had been perilously near it, had they known all the facts. For many, the greatest suffering had been the daily dread of that telegram from the War Office or the Admiralty announcing the death of somebody near and dear. All that ceased when those maroons went off and Peace came with a bang. Incredible scenes were witnessed in London for the whole of the first week of what was then regarded as Peace, until pitiless rain on the Saturday night put an end to outside revelry. But most people imagined that a New World had been born and they celebrated. They were right, but it was not the New World they anticipated. Those maroons knocked the world off balance just as the guns of 1914 had done.

During the four years and three months of conflict, the British had become inured to a new form of life, which they regarded as purely temporary. They had seen the value of their money— once the highest in the world—sag and wither directly the ill-printed £1 and 10/- notes were rushed out to replace those golden coins. They had seen women invade realms of life hitherto reserved for men. They had seen the rigid code of manners and morality, which had for so long been their standard, swept right away. They had been free people for years—but under the War conditions they were regimented—even their food was rationed. There was actually an Order which forbade them to stand each other drinks, but they would not swallow that; caterers and customers conspired to defeat the law and to gain extras. It added zest to life. "Wangling" came into being. Soldiers soon learnt all about "scrounging" and it became a general pastime, sapping the old ideas of honesty. Despite the vanishing of certain commodities such as whisky, there was nothing approaching the Black Market or the exorbitant prices of the Second World War. There was vast profiteering, but that was directed against the Government rather

than against individuals. And for the first time in its history Great
Britain had become a Military Power. The War took overseas
hundreds of thousands of men who had never left these shores
before—whose longest trips had been maybe to Margate, to
Blackpool or up to London for the Cup. Now they went all over
the globe. The insularity of the British was being broken down.
For many men that War existed in their later lives in the form of
stories to tell in pubs—not of battle or perils, but of strange people
and their doings amongst them in alien lands.

The word cosmopolitan became common. The British at home
met folk from overseas in bulk for the first time. Up to then they
had regarded them as "Colonials," now they found that they had
national views of their own, these men from the other parts of the
Empire, and did not regard themselves as "The Lion's Cubs"—
so beloved of Boer War cartoonists—but as people of distinctive
nations.

London swarmed with them and with French, Belgians, Portuguese,
and Italians as well. The West End at night was rather like a
World's Fair. And the British met the Americans *en masse* for the
first time, too. Their entrance into the War was considerably
delayed—a President of theirs had declared that there was such
a thing as being "Too Proud to fight." That had amused the British,
especially those struggling in the mud of Flanders. So when the
Yanks did arrive, with much éclat, very smartly dressed and tremendously rich as compared with the British Tommy, they were received
not as the saviours which they considered themselves, but as a
schoolmaster might view naughty boys late for school. Although
their speech and manners were understood because of American
plays and American films, the British of those days were still
British enough to regard these Americans as foreigners.

The First World War was of course a social revolution. Men were
snatched from every rank of life and thrust into uniform; they all
went into the melting pot and were shaken up together. Women
who had lived domestic and secluded lives went out into commerce
and into factories doing men's jobs. Wise people foretold that
good would come of this—a better understanding between the
various strata of what then composed society. But that did not
come about.

The World went topsy-turvy. Men who had held subordinate
positions in civil life rose to command. Mere lads became commissioned officers and such was the mortality that they rose to high
ranks at a youthful age. These holders of brief authority sensed
and savoured power. So when the war was over, men who had
been saluted and called "Sir" and who had exacted discipline in
others did not want to be subject to it again themselves. Their ideas

had been shaken up and did not settle down. They wanted that old feeling of peace and security but they wanted to keep their power, too.

The War had changed our commercial status, also. Things which this country manufactured almost exclusively had got into other hands. Germany, our best customer as well as fiercest competitor, was smashed. Russia had gone up in revolution. The shock of the brutal murder of the Czar and his family shook the British but the revolution did not worry them at the time. Their feeling was rather that they had been badly let down by what had seemed a powerful Ally—that Russian Steamroller which only went into action in reverse. They regarded revolutions as the perquisite and habit of foreigners. Their inevitable sense of humour seized on the new word "Bolshevik,"which naturally they recoined into "Bolshie," and they made a joke of it. "Bolshie" always got a laugh. They had forgotten, if they ever knew, that the armies and the might of Napoleon arose out of the bloodbath of the French Revolution. The British never had revolutions—not since the time of Charles I, anyway. They did not realize that they often had them but that here they happened peacefully and by way of legislation. Indeed, they were in the middle of one then—the Old Order was departing never to return again. And the coming of peace was the guillotine on which it expired.

With the Armistice came naturally the desire to get out of the Army and back into civil life. That small but wonderful regular Army which made up the British Expeditionary Force in 1914— the finest fighting force any nation had ever put into the field— had become a swollen mass of temporary combatants. Most things were "temporary" then, like the commissions in the Army. Nothing was secure. But those who had fought were convinced that this had been a "War to End War." They had won, and Freedom was secure. They did not realize that, not for the first time, they had won the war and lost the peace. Their idea was to get out of the Forces, and in their minds was a sort of mirage of all that had been best in the old life, plus the power and authority the war years had given them. But they found that the old world had gone. They woke up to that in 1919. They found that money was tight, prices had risen, and the country was heavily taxed and deeply in debt. It expected to pay those debts out of German reparations, but that did not happen—terrible inflation killed it. Loans to allies were not being repaid. America had become tremendously powerful. Her short spell of fighting had been at long range. She had been continuously productive, and her ideology was spreading, expecially in the Entertainment industry. Jazz and jazz bands predominated, along with American songs and artists. Britain had sacrificed so

much of its own talent on the field of battle that almost two genera-
tions had been lost. But the main idea was to have a holiday and
a good time before going back to work. That was perfectly understandable. The outward and visible sign was the craze for dancing
which swept the land. Everybody danced everywhere and at all
times. Dinner ceased to be a meal and became a mere interlude
in dancing. This craze grew as the 1920's advanced until the Palais
de Danse became a serious rival to the Theatre.

Married men with responsibilites were finding that they had
new problems to face. The younger men did not want to go back
into "the ranks" of civil life. Their sense of value had been distorted.
Many of them had had cheque books for the first time during that
War which seemed to open illimitable wealth. Messrs Cox and Co
knew all about that! Now on discharge they received a gratuity—
a larger sum than they had ever possessed before. Those who still
wanted to be bosses invested that gratuity in businesses which
they did not understand—book-making concerns and motor car
undertakings and often they lost the lot. The steady flow of men—
back into civil life glutted the employment market. Those who
decided that they would go back to the old job often found that it
had vanished; firms had closed down or merged with others. There
were precious few jobs of any kind about. The middle classes felt
the pinch at once, and later it spread to what was still then the
working class. The old aristocracy and the landed gentry were on
the way out. Their manner of life was over. The privileged classes
—so called—felt the pinch, too. Their privilege seems to have been
that they gave their lives to the service of their country for small
reward and small pensions, and new taxation and higher cost of
living were making it a hard fight for them. Into the front rank
was stepping a new stratum of Society whose only standard was
money. They had made their money out of the war which was for
them a gold mine. Even the men and women who worked on
munitions had drawn what were then fabulous rates of pay.

So the early post-war years, which should have been a period of
controlled and careful readjustment, became a great carnival. It is
difficult to blame the people. They firmly believed that war was
now obsolete. There arose an organization known as The League
of Nations. Perhaps it was too hurried in construction. The
Versailles Treaty proved to be a badly patched-up affair made by
war-weary nations anxious to get back to ordinary life and commerce. This League of Nations in Geneva, the heart of neutrality,
was to be the place where all disputes were ironed out—a universal
Court of Appeal which made war out of date. Some people had
implicit faith in it, some had their doubts, many did not think of
it at all. Yet it acted as a kind of mental salve.

Ivor Novello's first stage part in *Deborau*. With him is Madge Titheradge.

Owen Nares. The matinee
idol of the 1920's.

Basil Gill—handsome and
magnificent.

In the meantime, the general idea was a holiday and fun before work. The "Bright Young Things" arose, playboys and girls who tried to paint London red with their extravagant follies with an energy worthy of a better cause. They became "News"—the Press was full of their antics. But the balance of the world had changed, and the people had changed with it. King George V still sat on the Throne; the Prince of Wales was the most popular man in the Empire—alas, the 1920's did him no good; and the Empire itself was bigger in area than ever before—if not greater in reality— swollen with captured German colonies and mandated territories. But the flower of British Youth lay dead all over the world, making some spot "Forever England." With them went what might have been the best of the New World.

Still the bulk of the people did not realize the alteration of life —that although they had peace, prosperity was not just round the corner. They stood on the slopes of a slippery world, a world of brittle ice, from which the old safeguards of solidity, national feeling, home life and domestic discipline had largely gone. The barriers broken down by the war were going up again. That great statesman, Sir Edward Grey, had said on the eve of War: "The Lights are going out all over the world." Indeed he spoke truly.

It may seem strange that so much space has been given to the general state of this country as the 1920's came along, but it is necessary if the condition of the theatre is to be properly understood; for the theatre does to a large extent reflect the conditions of its time, and must conform, in presentation and in acting, to the pre- valent taste and mentality. So to understand the theatre it is necessary to understand the minds of that most important part of it, the audiences. It is also necessary to appreciate what had been the condition of the theatre itself during the First World War. It had experienced its own revolution.

Up to the outbreak of that War, the British theatre had been enjoying its finest hour, and that hour had been a long one, stretching right back into the reign of Queen Victoria. It had started to achieve real quality and glory in 1865 when the Bancrofts, later Sir Squire and Lady Bancroft, took over a despised playhouse in Charlotte Street and Tottenham Street, Tottenham Court Road, London, then derisively called "The Dusthole" and rechristened it "The Prince of Wales's." There by means of inspired acting, magnificent casting, efficient production and the comedies of Tom Robertson— all of the highest quality—they made it the most exciting and fashionable theatre in town and set a new standard in the theatre. In 1871, Henry Irving blazed across the theatrical firmament in *The Bells* at the Lyceum. He became Sir Henry, the first actor ever to be knighted; when he assumed actor-managership at the

Lyceum, he raised the stage to heights it had never reached before in culture, beauty and great acting. Both he and the Bancrofts were actor-managers and it was when the actor-manager held sway that our theatre was at its best and brightest. It was of course, a commercial theatre—but it was something more than that—it was a professionally commercial theatre, which is a different thing.

The actor-managers and manageresses were always essentially "people of the theatre," knowing their job, almost living in their playhouses. They were craftsmen lavishing their personal care and skill on their productions, as Chippendale and Sheraton had done on their furniture, as Reynolds and Gainsborough did on their pictures. They identified themselves with certain theatres and therein they sold branded goods and set a standard beneath which they must not fall. Their productions were expert to a degree and perfectly cast. They did not always have successes, for that is impossible, but they achieved a very high percentage. By their own personalities and talent and by the fact that they followed their own line, they created large and faithful followings who knew what to expect and who got it. They ran their theatres with a policy and they found their following very loyal.

Those were days of stability for players and dramatists; there was a constant market, and every inducement to work. Think of the names of some of them—Sir Henry Irving, Sir Herbert Tree, Sir John Hare, Sir Charles Wyndham and his wife Mary Moore, Sir Johnston Forbes-Robertson, Sir John Martin-Harvey, Sir Charles Hawtrey, Sir George Alexander, Sir Seymour Hicks, Dame Marie Tempest, Dame Lena Ashwell, (Mrs Kendal became a Dame, too), Cyril Maude, Lewis Waller, Fred Terry and Julia Neilson, Matheson Lang and later Sir Gerald du Maurier. It is not a list of stars, it is a galaxy of planets.

To those people, all of whom personally appeared before the public, must be added some producing managers who were also practical men and did their job at first hand and with a policy behind it—George Edwardes, who invented Musical Comedy and filled the Gaiety and Daly's Theatres with romance, sparkle, melody and beauty; Frank Curzon, who had been an actor and who at one time controlled eight West End and suburban theatres at the same time; and Robert Courtneidge, another ex-actor, who knew his job so well and gave London and the provinces so many fine shows. There is another man who must not be forgotten, Charles Frohman, the shyest man the theatre ever knew. He was an American who loved this country, which he made virtually his home, using the Atlantic as a ferry crossing, over which he went to supervise his vast American theatrical empire and back again to his London realm which was based on the Duke of York's Theatre.

He was also a practical man, and one of complete integrity, and he did wonderful service. The First World War took his life. He was drowned when the *Lusitania* was torpedoed and met his death with a brave smile and a quotation from *Peter Pan*, his favourite production, on his lips.

Older people will remember those names though younger folk may not do so. But it is the duty of a theatre historian, himself a practical man of the theatre, to put on record the fact, proved by research and actual first-hand knowledge, that the actor-manager period was the best of all. But the First World War conquered them, by upsetting values. Those men ran their theatres on really economic lines and at a cost which seems ridiculous in these days of inflation. By economy one does not mean cheapness. Well did they know that the last thing you can afford in the theatre is cheapness. But being practical men they achieved their magnificence by knowing just how to do it. They did not look for enormous profits. Few of them had syndicates behind them—they were their own financial backers—and although their earnings would be scoffed at today by young men of small experience and talent who draw such vast salaries, they did very well.

They knew that the real job of the Theatre is illusion and they created it. They and all the players kept themselves aloof; they did not "mix;" they were not "seen about." They lived in a little world of their own; they were people of mystery and not considered respectable by the men and women of the ordinary world. They were definitely not classed as "Ladies and Gentlemen" and, very sensibly, they did not want to be. From the point of view of public attraction, there is no value in respectability—there is too much of it about. But about those stage folk, from the highest to the lowest, there still hung the glamour of "Illusion"—they were still "rogues and vagabonds." They gloried in it. They were stared at when seen in the streets—they provided a thrill. They accepted few invitations—that interfered with their work and their aloofness. And with them work came first. They had no side lines, no radio or television, no recordings, and, for years, no films to provide additional income but to lessen their value by over-familiarity. They had to act and act well, or get out. To them, the theatre was a full-time job, not just a "fill in." Those curious folk regarded themselves as being members of the "Theatrical Profession;" their calling had not been debased into "Show Business" as it is today.

There was a large, prosperous and powerful provincial Theatre, for playgoing was the great recreation of so many people. Those actor-managers knew that, although their profits in the West End might be small, they could make a lot of money in the provinces, either by touring themselves or by leasing their plays to people who specialized in that branch. The provinces had splendid players who never wished to appear in the West End. They were kings and queens in their own realms and wisely they stayed there. And sometimes when the original West End players toured, the provincial audience considered them inferior to those well loved favourites whom they were accustomed to see in such parts.

Some of the "Great Ones" spent more time in the provinces than in London. They brought great Theatre to the provincial cities—people like Julia Neilson and Fred Terry, Sir John Martin-Harvey, Sir Frank Benson, Sir Philip Ben Greet, Matheson Lang and, to some extent, Sir Johnston Forbes-Robertson, too. Tree and Irving by no means disdained the provinces either. There was the D'Oyly Carte Opera Company, which still keeps alive that glorious tradition of Comic Opera. These people brought inestimable value to the theatre. Indeed, the managers of the provincial theatres presented Fred Terry with a magnificent portrait of himself in oils, executed by an eminent artist, as a slight tribute, they said, of the gratitude they felt to himself and his lovely wife, Julia Neilson, for the prosperity that wonderful pair brought to them.

Every city and town had its theatre, often more than one. Touring companies went into the smallest places, taking their "fit up frames" to bring to small halls, corn exchanges and the like the illusion of the Theatre. There were still portable theatres —the most mobile and aboriginal form of all.

It was by touring that actors and actresses learnt their job. For the art of acting—with all deference to the "Methodists"—cannot be taught, but it can be learnt. And the only way to learn it is on a stage facing an audience. They are your enemies, you must conquer them or they will conquer you. No young players expected a West End job at once. They qualified on tour and, when they came to Town, they were expert. The Producer or Director was not then omnipotent. He was there, but he did not teach every inflection, gesture and movement. He was mostly the actor-manager and he would not have chosen his players if he was not sure they could play their parts. Indeed, those players would be asked "How are you going to play it?" They would give their views, which were listened to attentively. There might be a few suggestions but mostly the "producer" kept his company within the framework of the play. He produced the play and not the actors. He brought the play to them and did not force them into it. By that means individuality, power and personality—all of priceless value in the theatre—were preserved and given expression. Nor were there any microphones. If an actor was not heard, he himself heard from the audience . . . and that cured him. There was a standard amongst the audiences, too, as well as amongst the actors. A visit to a play was No 1 "Evening

Out." It was something to which they looked forward and for which they put on their best clothes. Playgoers not in evening dress were unwelcome in the boxes, stalls and dress circle, and in certain theatres those so improperly dressed were refused admission. Playgoing was not a matter of "dropping in"—you did that at the pictures or the music hall—and for those who did not want to "dress" there were the pit and the gallery and the upper circle. The theatre catered for everybody. But mostly the theatre was looked upon as being worth a bit of trouble. One felt, when visiting an actor-manager's theatre, that one was his guest. Of course, there was a little formality at the box office first. There was a very close link of affection between him and his public, ninety-nine per cent of whom never met him in private life but who loved him and his company all the same, bought photographs of them and treasured them all their lives. The theatre was important, part of one's life, a thing of excitement and memories.

Yet, having regard to the fact that players were not considered respectable, right up to 1914 there was still a large portion of the community who considered the theatre with something akin to horror. Not only was it disreputable, it was a place of sin, given over to the Devil. This quite considerable section of the public were decent, law-abiding church and chapel folk, worthy citizens of the highest integrity, in whose veins the blood of the old Puritans still ran and in whose minds old beliefs still flourished. Those people would not go to a theatre on principle. I remember a most worthy man, a churchwarden and a doer of good deeds, whose son was a great friend of mine, saying to me: "I feel I should like to see the great works of Shakespeare performed as I am told Sir Herbert Tree does them at his theatre. But if I went I might be setting a bad example to others weaker than myself who might be led astray." He believed that sincerely, and I respected it. I often wondered how he allowed his son to be friendly with me, for I have always been of the theatre, but he did not object to that. How his objection to the theatre was overcome will shortly emerge. When the year 1914 dawned, the theatre of this land, under the conditions stated, shone and sparkled like a diamond. Then the guns of August 1914 blew it away.

For, when war broke out, it brought a quite unprecedented problem to the people of the theatre. Not since the Crimea had Britain been involved in a European War. All previous wars had been far away and had hardly touched the ordinary life of the people, this was on the very doorstep. Overnight the world changed; there might be invasion, there was the Zeppelin menace—and later they did come and aeroplanes too—and there was a thing called the "Moratorium," which tied up money. The first weeks of war saw a considerable panic in theatrical circles. Young men joined the Colours, everybody talked war, wanted war work. But it was soon discovered that the very conservative British public was still willing and indeed anxious to go to the theatre. Somebody invented a slogan "Business As Usual" and the theatre promptly adopted it. Emergency arrangements were made to carry on. For a short while soldiers and sailors in uniform were admitted free, but that soon became impossible. One or two managements, who should have known better, hastened to put on ill-prepared and badly constructed plays of a patriotic nature, dealing with the war about which neither they nor anybody else knew much at that time. They should have known that the theatre is not the place for topicality, nor is it enjoyed by searchers after illusion. Patriotic sentiments, unless of the past, are the last thing they want to hear when they themselves are involved in such things. It makes them self-conscious; they don't want to think about it, they want much less to hear about it. The great songs of the First World War had nothing to do with it at all, unless they poked fun at it, in the British way. In the Boer War patriotism had been blatant but that was almost entirely a professional war. In 1914 the war was every-body's business. So the public, when it went to the theatre, went there to forget its grim duty outside. It wanted a complete difference; it wanted laughter, colour, romance and sentiment, but not patriotic sentiment. In a very short time those running theatres discovered that and set about providing it. The theatre then found out that, so far from having to struggle for its existence, it was going to have a boom. So it gave the public music, colour, comedy, dancing and girls. Those who dealt in musical productions—Sir Alfred Butt, André Charlot, Albert de Courville, Grossmith and Laurillard and Sir Oswald Stoll—responded nobly, and with profit all round. Revue flourished. So did musical comedy. Oscar Asche hit the bullseye in the dead centre with *Chu Chin Chow* at His Majesty's Theatre, where Sir Herbert Tree had reigned, and Sir Herbert himself made money out of it.

But in England man-power was getting short and all effort went into war work. So America, then far away from the war, moved into the entertainment business. More and more American plays and artists came over here. London, despite its partial blackout, was a gay city, even if the gaiety had a somewhat ghastly ring about it. All ranks on leave wanted to eat, drink dance and be merry, and go to a show. Tomorrow they would be in the trenches, and that meant death at any moment. Air raids came—small matters as compared with those of the Second World War but disturbing enough to a generation bred in peace. The theatre answered this challenge by daily matinées and two early evening shows per week.

Some kept on in the ordinary way. Almost any show could make money, so big was the demand for entertainment and so low the critical taste. The few failures were such awful plays that one wonders how they ever got produced at all. But costs were rising steadily. The Entertainment Tax was imposed in 1916, and that was the only addition which the Theatre made to its prices: the basic figures were still 10/6d for a stall, 8/6d, 7/- and 6/- for dress circle, 5/- and 4/- for Upper circle, 2/6 for the pit and 1/- for the gallery. The tax, of course, was paid over to the Government. So the theatre still ran at pre-war prices when everything else had risen sharply, shortage of materials made productions more costly, shortage of staff and players sent up wages and salaries. But the boom continued and in its wake came speculators from the world of commerce, to whom the Theatre seemed a veritable Tim Tiddler's ground. They put on plays about which they knew nothing, they purchased theatre leases and sublet at steadily rising rents. Some theatres had as many as five or six sub-lessees, all taking a profit and adding nothing whatever for the theatre. Naturally the "Old Order" was doomed, the actor-managers could not compete with this. Death took some, others gave up their theatres and worked on salary in productions for others. It was the end of that dynasty of stability and quality built up during Peace.

Some stable managements held aloft the banner of quality—Sir Alfred Butt, Grossmith and Laurillard, Sir Oswald Stoll, Frank Curzon, Basil Dean and Frederick Harrison, Bronson Albery and Howard Wyndham among them. But there were far too many others out for quick profits through bricks and mortar, caring little what came into their theatre so long as they got their high rental. One theatre, which could have been hired for £25 per week in 1914 rose to a weekly rental of £500. Practical gentlemen on the production side took chances and, if the gamble did not come off—well it was just too bad, for there was no cash to meet liabilities.

There was little or no chance for serious drama or new thought. Those who stared into the face of death all day and night in France did not want that, they wanted glamour, girls and fun. It was quite understandable. Tastes sank and values were submerged. The films boomed and many suburban theatres surrendered to the world of celluloid. The rules about evening dress vanished. More and more theatres permitted smoking, for women smoked now as well as men. Paper was rationed; posters and advertising were reduced; American methods of ballyhoo crept in. But still the boom continued and all sorts of odd characters cashed in—men like Joseph Leopold Sacks, who could neither read nor write— and became quite a power. The old tradition of dignity and polish had gone. It was now a scramble to get as much as possible out of a public hungry for amusement and wishing to escape from reality. So, because it still dealt in illusion, the theatre held on—but not the theatre of pre-war days. Yet one thing happened in its favour: it vastly extended its public. Many of that generation already mentioned, who regarded the theatre as a place of sin, had altered their minds. Their sons had gone to the war. When on leave, they insisted on going to the theatre. They also insisted that their nearest and dearest should accompany them. Those middle-aged folk who had never entered a theatre found it hard to refuse. This might be the last time they could go out with their dear ones; they must do their utmost to please them. So with dire misgivings in their hearts they entered what to them were the portals of the Devil. To their amazement, it was nothing like so bad as they had expected. Indeed, they found it amusing and thrilling; they liked it and they came again and again. That worthy man earlier mentioned who had feared to see Tree was brought by his son to a theatre I was then managing, to see *Where the Rainbow Ends.* We thought this would break him in gently. He trembled as he entered. He stayed to cheer. He said it was as good as a sermon—it showed the triumph of right over wrong. After that he often went to plays. It is a good thing that we had not then reached the stage of frankness and sordidness which reigns today.

The boom went on. Then came the Armistice and the world went mad. Lloyd George, one of the architects of victory, said he would make this a land fit for heroes to live in. He spoke more truly than he knew. It takes a hero to live in it today. But the boom ended; the slumps began, because once again life had altered. The theatre reflected that life in itself. Money was tight; a different age was dawning—the age of speed and of internal combustion. Other forces were arraying themselves against the theatre. The lamps of the Old World were burning again but not with the same steady glow. They wavered, they flickered badly and, by the time that 1920 arrived, the footlights of the theatre were flickering badly, too.

CHAPTER I

1920—The Decade Opens

THE year 1920 ushered in the new decade which followed the First World War. Optimism was prevalent; there was to be a brave new world which was to contain all that was best of the old world which war had swept away and to superimpose on it all the manifold advantages which peace would bring.

It is the job of the theatre to reflect life, and the people of the theatre are the most optimistic in the world; otherwise they just could not exist. They must always be filled with hope and confident of success, and they always are. Their hopes are often dashed into disappointment but their confidence never deserts them. Just as it is always going to be "all right on the night," so it is always going to be "all right next time". The theatre had boomed during the war. Theatrical people even felt some pride in the fact that it now bore direct taxation, for it meant that their profession had rendered national service. But they expected that tax to be removed, as there had been a promise that it would be merely a war-measure. Of course, it did not come off for years—until very recent times—and then only after great agitation. But in 1920 the theatre felt that many restrictions which had hampered it would be removed and that it could spread its wings and do better. Some of its people even thought there was a chance of doing better plays and of achieving higher ideals, not just catering for escapists from the reality of war. Salaries, rents and costs had risen, it was true, but, by and large, business had been wonderful. Now it could soar into the sunshine of peace.

What it scarely realized as yet was that its whole structure had changed; the system of actor-managership, the policy of theatres, had to a large extent vanished. It only hung on here and there. The professionally commercial had been largely replaced by the purely commercial and the anonymous syndicates. The experts were sadly lacking. When an Empire falls it creates a vacuum and outside forces rush in to fill it. That had happened in the theatre and was to become more and more apparent as the decade advanced. The old order of tradition and dignity had almost entirely gone and was to be missed sorely.

Sir Herbert Tree had died in 1917, Sir George Alexander in 1918. Sir Charles Wyndham, long retired, had passed on in 1919, but his brilliant and clever wife, whose stage name was Mary Moore, took an active part in the management of the three Wyndham-Moore Theatres—the Criterion, the New and Wyndham's itself. With her were her own son—now Sir Bronson Albery—and Sir Charles's son, Howard Wyndham. They were very active in the 1920's and kept tradition and quality alive as do Sir Bronson and his own son today. Sir Squire Bancroft was still alive but in retirement. He could be seen crossing Leicester Square on his way to the Garrick Club, the personification of the Old Order, tall, dignified in his silk hat and frock coat, his magnificent white hair and his monocle with the black satin ribbon. Hats were doffed as he passed and he would respond courteously. He always got a special salute from the cabmen on the rank at the northern corner of Leicester Square, for he had given them the shelter which still stands and bears his name. He died in 1926, aged 84. Cyril Maude, that actor of ease and charm, had long since left the Haymarket and the Playhouse where he had reigned as actor-manager but he was still working as an actor and in 1920 was in a big success, *Lord Richard in the Pantry* produced the previous year.

Sir Charles Hawtrey, too, had joined the ranks of the actors who did not manage and was giving superb performances for others. Arthur Bourchier remained an actor-manager. He had left the Garrick where he had been for so long in association with his wife Violet Vanbrugh, and gone to the Strand Theatre, where in 1920 he was appearing, with Kyrle Bellew, in *At The Villa Rose* by A. E. W. Mason, which ran for 126 performances—a success in those days. Marie Tempest was away on a world tour. Gerald du Maurier was still actor-manager at Wyndhams in association with Frank Curzon, but was only just coming out of the Army. The Haymarket, under Frederick Harrison, so long associated with Cyril Maude and an ex-actor himself, kept up its fine tradition. The manager there was Horace Watson and indeed the Watson family still keep that lovely theatre bright and shining. But the old actor-manager régime was now a mere shadow. There were stable managements who carried on pre-war traditions—Sir Alfred Butt, who then controlled the Palace, the Empire, the Gaiety, the Adelphi, the Globe, the Queen's and the Victoria Palace and who, in 1920, became jointly associated with Arthur Collins at Theatre Royal, Drury Lane itself—and Collins was a real man of the theatre. Sir Oswald Stoll was running the Coliseum and the Alhambra as well as his provincial empire. The Hippodrome was controlled by Moss Empires and the Palladium by Charles Gulliver. Charles B. Cochran was amongst the leading showmen and Grossmith and Laurillard led the way in musical comedy. André Charlot and Albert de Courville gleamed in the world of revue. Violet Melnotte owned and ran the Duke of York's Theatre, which she had built herself, and the legendary figure of Joseph Leopold Sacks, who had arisen during the war, was on top of the world. George Edwardes was dead and his lieutenant Robert Evett was making a brave fight to save Daly's the delectable from the grasp of pure commercialism as embodied by the menacing figure of James White, the Rochdale bricklayer turned millionaire. Seymour Hicks, a genius of the theatre, was still active. In such people the tradition of the Past hung on, but they were all finding it very difficult.

There was a new actor-manager, however, in the person of Owen Nares of the Greek profile and matinée idolatry—he was at the Queen's in partnership with Sir Alfred Butt—and there was a new actress-manageress in the charming and talented person of Marie Lohr, who was established at the Globe and had staffed it with stalwarts from His Majesty's. At the St James's Theatre, Gilbert Miller had taken charge and had installed as his star, with the title of actor-manager, the handsome and distinguished Henry Ainley. Nigel Playfair was making history at the Lyric, Hammersmith, an outlying and long disregarded playhouse. That was the position when the curtain went up on 1920.

The year got off to a fine start, for the first play produced in it was a good one—*Mr Pim Passes By*, which opened at the New Theatre on 5th January 1920 and ran, in all, 246 performances, a long time then. It was a charming comedy by A. A. Milne in which Irene Vanbrugh and her husband Dion Boucicault played the leading parts. Irene Vanbrugh was one of the great actresses of our stage and Dion Boucicault was not only a good actor but a fine producer. In the cast was also a young actor named D. Leslie Howard. It was only his fourth part in the West End. As the years went on the initial D was dropped and Leslie Howard became a great star of stage and screen—one of the most sensitive and artistic actors we ever had. His tragic death in the Second World War, when the plane in which he was travelling was shot down by the Luftwaffe, robbed the British stage of one of its great personalities.

There was another "Mister" play in that year too—*Mr Todd's Experiment* at the Queen's Theatre—and here perhaps, as in other cases as the book progresses, that obnoxious personal pronoun 'I' may be allowed to enter, for I was closely connected with it. It was the third venture of the Owen Nares-Alfred Butt partnership at the Queen's. This play is worth remembering because it is an outstanding example of how narrow is the margin between success and failure in the theatre. *Mr Todd's Experiment* was written by Walter Hackett, an American playwright who lived in this country and who shares with Richard Brinsley Sheridan the claim of being the laziest dramatist on record. Yet when he chose he could be very skilful, as Sheridan had been. In his later years, to save himself trouble, Hackett always seemed to write the same play plus a few different twists. He would conceive brilliant ideas and then find himself incapable of carrying them out. Before coming to this country he had been all sorts of things, including a newspaper reporter. He was also a reformed drunkard. Physically he was a huge man, with a large pale face and pale fair hair, and an immense sense of humour. He was also a brilliant conversationalist and raconteur. He had begun writing plays by himself and with others in 1908 and when the 1920's came he had several successes to his credit. He was married to an actress, Marion Lorne, who was a wonderful little comedienne in her own line, vague, astonishing, but altogether charming. She was to the stage what Zasu Pitts was to the films. Hackett knew just how to suit her and always wrote parts for her in his own plays. How he had managed to complete *Mr Todd's Experiment* when he submitted it to Nares and Butt will never be known, but somehow he had done so. Nares, then at the very top of his popularity as a matinée idol, had not been lucky at the Queen's—it was not a very lucky theatre. Nor was he an easy man to fit with plays, although a much better actor than many thought.

Neither of the two first ventures had been over-successful—*The House of Peril*, a thriller, and a piece of American sentimentality called *The Cinderella Man*, in which Renee Kelly had been a delightful leading lady. Despite fine casting and good notices, the profits had been small. But this play by Hackett appealed to Nares; he felt it would give him a chance to act. It was perhaps a bit before its time, for it was a "flashback" and one of the leading characters was a psychiatrist—a type not well known then. The young man played by Nares had sunk into gloom and listlessness because of three unhappy love affairs. By means of flashbacks and aids to memory which started trains of thought, the psychiatrist revived the young man's emotions and then showed him those girls as they were today. Realizing what a lucky escape he had had, the young man pulled himself together and fell into the arms of a little Cinderella-like figure who had been waiting for him all the time. That part was played by Marion Lorne. But one of the girls was quite outstanding, for she was played by Meggie Albanesi—alas, that she should have died so young! This was the most vivid personality and accomplished actress who had stepped upon our stage for years—Irene Vanbrugh and Mrs Patrick Campbell in one small person plus a charm and attraction all her own. But for her untimely death, she would have been Queen of our stage. In *Mr Todd's Experiment* she gave a lovely performance.

All that the finest of casting, acting and modern stage devices could supply was put into *Mr Todd's Experiment*. There was a stage within a stage upon which changes of scene were carried out in the matter of seconds but in complete silence whilst the play went on before them. There was a snowstorm produced by a lighting effect. Holman Clark produced the play and played Mr Todd, both brilliantly.

There was a brilliant first night. An Owen Nares first night then was on a par with those of Sir Herbert Tree when he ruled at His Majesty's. Society, the Law, Literature, Medicine, the Arts, all were represented. And all the famous first nighters were there—Lord Lurgan, tall, handsome and distinguished; the Marchioness of Headfort, who died so recently and who had been Rosie Boote of the Gaiety; Sir Milsom Rees, the great throat specialist; A. E. W. Mason, Lady Colefax, Luigi the famous restaurateur, Lord Farquhar, and many others. Gordon Selfridge, of the famous Store, sat in the front row of the stalls, as always, and not far away from him was Mrs Higson, one of the most regular of all first nighters. A lady of means, although she always said her trustees told her she was ruining herself by theatre going, she had a strong personality. She had a pretty loud voice of great clarity and she would express her opinions very forcibly and without restraint. Her features were aquiline but not so menacing as an eagle's and there was something of the mischief of a parrot there, too. She loved playgoing and called herself "The Old Lady of the Theatre." If she liked a play, she would come a dozen times. If she did not like it, she did not hesitate to say so and give her reasons. I have seen her "telling off" an eminent critic whose opinion differed from hers. If she liked you, you had a good friend. If not, well, you were just ignored. To her friends she was Nell Higson. At first nights she was always accompanied by her daughter, a beautiful young lady with auburn hair.

There was Major "Hoppy" Davies, so called because he was lame. He was very active, slightly rotund and balding, and very popular. He dabbled in theatrical deals from time to time. In a box would be Solly Joel, the millionaire, a bearded figure most imposing when seated but less so when he stood up, for his legs were short. It was generally held that they were hollow, too, on account of the immense amount of champagne he could swallow without turning a hair. In another box was his brother Jack, also a millionaire but of a different type, not imposing at all, seemingly nervous and *staccato*, with his head always sagging on to his left shoulder. In the stalls there was a a rugged, stocky figure, never seeming quite at home in evening clothes, with a brick-red face and deepset piercing eyes with black rings round them. moving through the crowds like a shark amongst minnows and held in awe by many because of his reputed millions; this was James White, a real product of the 1920's and the First

World War. In a stall at the end of the fourth row, which was reserved for him at every first night at every theatre, was Golding Bright, one of the back-room boys. He was a theatrical agent and representative for authors; the cream of the profession was on his books. At any first night it was an even money chance that he had sold the play to the management, represented the author and the major portion of the players. Yet, as soon as the curtain, rose he would sink into a gentle slumber. What did he care? He knew all about it. He was a small, quiet, very well dressed man, of considerable charm, public school and Oxford. Next to his friend Walter Hackett, he was the laziest man in the profession. There was only one place where he was really wide awake and that was the race course. Racing was his real life. His favourite reading was *The Book of Form*. He was very popular and, for all his laziness, very shrewd. He always wore white kid gloves at first nights, which he never removed. He did not wear them to keep his hands warm but to prevent himself from biting his nails, a habit he never conquered.

In the stalls too would be J. E. Vedrenne, a theatre manager and pioneer, and Gilbert Miller, that American who had just taken over the St James's. He loved England because his father, a fine actor-manager named Henry Miller, had been born here. In the days of *Mr. Todd*, Gilbert Miller was a good-looking and charming young man with a most amazing memory which added to his popularity, for he always remembered any complaint from which the people whom he met suffered and would inquire after it with sympathy in his voice. It was most flattering.

Thomas Marlowe, Editor of the *Daily Mail*, was a regular first-nighter—apart from his paper's critic—and he looked exactly what the public expected the editor of an important newspaper to look like. In the stalls, too, was Madeline Cohen, short, dark and stout, without whom a first night was unthinkable. Her father, Edgar Cohen, had put the taxis on the streets of London. She adored the theatre and its people and was a good angel to many of them in time of need. She had a great heart but no looks at all, and she never married. The Cohen home in Hall Road, St John's Wood, was an amazing establishment with an ever-open door and on Sunday nights a constant throng of celebrities came and went in ceaseless flow. Some, however, stayed until the small hours; and one famous man, prominent in the public eye, went there one evening and stayed on for about ten years. There are no such places now.

There were a couple of first-nighters whom every manager liked to have present, if they were disengaged, and if his play was supposed to be amusing. Both of them had amazing and infectious laughs. One was "Scrubby" Ponsonby, who was in the profession after a fashion, a big man with a shock of hair but with a laugh hard to resist, and the other was "Tiny" Turnbull, an actor. He was a very big man and his laugh was as big as he was—it reached the uttermost corner of the theatre. Another famous first-nighter was Louis Sterling, who became Sir Louis. He came here from America with half a dollar in his pocket—thus reversing the usual order—and made a million. Scared about this, he told his fears to his wife to whom he was devoted, and she suggested they should give half of it away. They did so, but more and more rolled in. He continued to give it away up to his recent death, quietly, wisely and without ostentation. He was a great lover of the theatre and always said he would like to die at a first night and he did, very nearly.... But the first-nighters were not limited to the stalls, boxes and dress circles. They were in every part of the house. There was a notable one in the Upper Circle. Theatre managers put her name down on the booking sheet automatically, for the same seat in the Upper Circle—the seat on the middle gangway of the front row, for she was slightly lame. She never had to write in and apply. Her name was Golding Bird. She was a small lady with a very big, booming voice and much given to talking about "My Brother the Bishop", a well known man who held a Colonial bishopric. She was a typical late Victorian, and she adored the theatre. Her means were not ample but she spent all her money on theatre-going. She never missed a first night and if she liked the play she came again and again. She saw *Peg Of My Heart* over fifty times. She had an eye which commanded respect and a way which quelled the most unruly, of turning and regarding other playgoers, who were not behaving as she thought they should. If there was likely to be booing or a disturbance on a first night, she would check such outbreaks in her vicinity by the sheer strength of her scornful regard. She had been known to survey the malcontents of the Gallery, at such places where the gallery lay immediately behind the Upper Circle, by the same method and to reduce all within her range of vision to just muttered growls of disapproval instead of uproar. That is, if she liked the play. If she did not, she let them have their heads but never uttered a sound herself. She just forbore to applaud.

There were two other men who were never missing from a first-night. One of them was Leslie Bloom, who can still be found at the opening of every new play, for he was and still is President of the Gallery First Nighters' Club, the premier theatre club of this country. They do not attend the theatre as a club, however, but as separate entities, and it is not they who lead the booing when such a thing occurs. Inside the theatre they are individuals and express approval or disapproval as they wish. Not all of them sit in the gallery either, some arrive in Rolls-Royces and sit in the stalls. In the 1920's Leslie Bloom actually did sit in the gallery, although during that decade he moved downstairs and invaded the stalls. When that institution, the Press Room, arose, he was in there, too, and of great use as a pourer out of drinks. The theatre is and always has been the great love of his life. At that time he was an interior decorator, and probably the finest in London, his trouble being that his work was so good and enduring that it never needed renewing—it just lasted in its pristine glory. In the theatre he was in a state of constant amazement at what he saw. He was always ready to point out what he regarded as mistakes in judgement and his reiterated cry was "What are the managers thinking about?" During the Second World War he actually entered the profession in a managerial capacity. And now he knows. It is not so easy as he imagined. He still remains the President and pivot of his excellent club, and to be a guest of honour at a G.F.N. dinner is a tribute of which all players are proud.

The other man was to be found in the Upper Circle or standing at the back of the Dress Circle. His name was Tom Scott and he was a barber. He was employed in one of the most fashionable hairdressing establishments for men in the West End, but he was seldom there. He had a very large clientele of his own. Nearly every star and manager was a customer of his. He would go to their houses, flats or dressing-rooms. He never got less than 10/- for a haircut and many gifts of clothes. He knew all the secrets of the theatre and had ideas of his own. When he had those men of the theatre in his chair and under his control he gave them advice—more, he gave them orders. He told them what they ought to do. Many of them listened and paid heed. He was quite outspoken and never pulled his punches. He pervaded the world of the theatre. After a doubtful first night a hasty conference might be called—manager, producer, backer, stage manager, star, all in conditions of great secrecy. But Scott was always there. Nobody asked him, nobody ever found out how he knew, but there he was. Strangely enough his advice was usually very sound. He had his own favourites and to them he was mercilessly frank if he thought they were falling below their standard. His great favourite was Jack Buchanan, and Jack was very good to him. When Scott fell ill, Buchanan, a t his own expense, sent him and his family to the South of France, and Scott never forgot. He did many little kindnesses himself and would help beginners and those whose luck was out with a timely word in the right ear. He had another use. If a management was not quite sure of the chances of a play and wanted laughter and applause guaranteed, Scott was given twenty or thirty seats in the Upper Circle for the first night. He filled them with guaranteed laughers and applauders who behaved most naturally and never overdid it. He was himself the soul of discretion and you would meet this middle-sized, dark, swarthy and

Marie Tempest, Queen of
the English stage.

Irene Vanbrugh, great
lady of the Theatre.

Lilian Braithwaite, who combined charm, talent and beauty.

moustached figure at every first night. His love of the theatre never left him.

In the 1920's the Pit and the Gallery were still institutions of power which held the keenest and most audible of playgoers. It was from those parts of the house that came the full-throated approval or disapproval. As Pit and Gallery were always unreserved, you could not book them. Patrons of them would wait for hours to see a big first night, often for twenty-four hours and on very great occasions for longer.

The queue for *Mr Todd's Experiment* had begun at six o'clock in the morning and had grown all day. I went out frequently and chatted with the patient waiters, all of whom I knew. I sent them cups of coffee and at five p.m. I served them all with tea. This was not intended as a bribe nor did they regard it as such. It was the courtesy of the theatre being extended to those who honoured it by their patronage. "Buskers" entertained them from midday onwards. I saw to it that late-comers were warned that there was no more room. Once in the theatre, these people buzzed with excitement, watched the celebrities enter and pointed them out to each other. They would applaud the actors and actresses who came into the stalls, who were glad and elated thereby, because their presence showed that they themselves were out of work. The pittites and galleryites knew everyone including the Press, an important part of first nights. They watched the arrival of the men and women of Fleet Street. They saw Randal Charlton, "Gossip" Man of the *Daily Mirror*—make an entrance, tall, erect, broad-shouldered, pale of face and clear-cut of feature, immaculately dressed, with fair hair beautifully brushed, and in winter always wearing an astrakhan-collared coat. If not regal, he was at least ducal and looked far more like a duke than many wearers of the strawberry leaves. To be greeted by him proved that you were a celebrity. He stood out in the stalls, he was a prominent figure in the West End. He was seen at the best places, he dropped into the best bars. There came a time when he got married and for about a fortnight he was missing from his usual nightly haunts. Then, suddenly, he reappeared as regularly as ever. Asked if he was happy, he gave a gentle smile. "Marriage is all right," he said, "but it interferes badly with one's fixed habits." He was determined not to let it do so. He had married a beautiful and attractive revue star, but The West End came first.

The critics and first-night Press in those days all wore evening dress and usually had only one ticket, but at the Queen's I always sent them two, which was much appreciated. People sitting in the unreserved parts saw the critical procession enter—St John Ervine, James Agate, (then on the *Saturday Review*,) Archibald Haddon, M. Willson Disher, W. R. Titterton, Henley of the *Daily Mail*, who used a stick and sometimes two, Morrison of the *Morning Post*—only they did not see much of him for he made a bee-line for the manager's office where he spent all the evening—Lawrence Cowan, a small man who wore a dress suit far too large for him and topped it off with a cap—if bored by a play, he produced a pocket chess set and played a game against himself—Florence Roberts, who did First Night Fashions, and stout, smiling Amy Jones, "The Matinee Girl" of the *Evening News*, who was later succeeded by Eric Barker, a famous first-night figure mostly accompanied by a beautiful girl. There were tall, dark and handsome Philip Page, who was "Mr Gossip" of the *Daily Graphic* and later of the *Daily Sketch*, H. G. Hibbert, J. T. Grein, Sir John M. Le Sage, of the *Daily Telegraph*, E. F. Spence, E. A. Baughan, W. A. Darlington, who became critic of the *Daily Telegraph* in 1920 and who also edited the Dramatic Gossip page of that paper from 1926 onwards, and Malcolm Watson the Theatre Correspondent of the *Daily Telegraph*, who liked people to believe he was dramatic critic, too. The entrance of A. B. Walkley of *The Times* was watched with respect. S. R. Littlewood, fresh-faced and smiling and usually a little late but a kindly genial soul, was there, too. Later he was to succeed the fabulous Morrison on the *Morning Post*. One says "fabulous Morrison" because this amazing critic hardly ever saw a play through. Sometimes he did not see it at all. Most, if not all, of his evening was spent in the Manager's Office, from which developed the Press Room, as Press representatives arose in the 1920's. Yet there was always a full column—sometimes a column and a half—about the play in his paper the next morning, meticulously reported, even to untoward happenings. There was much wonder as to how this miracle was achieved and some talk of an understudy in the pit. There was Shelley of the *Daily Graphic*, and an outstanding dominant figure who seldom occupied a stall but lurked at the back of the circle. He wore an antique form of dinner jacket, unlike that worn by anyone else, and a black stock tie round his neck; his face was pale and his hair wiry and bushy; he knew everyone and was feared by most because he did not hesitate to write what he thought and spared none. The outstanding journalist of his day, he had invented the "Gossip Writer" at whom he sneered perpetually. Everyone tried to gauge his reactions. They never succeeded. He was—and is—Hannen Swaffer.

A very different type of man was H. Chance Newton—"Carados" of the *Referee*—a great man of the Theatre. He had been an actor under the banner of Samuel Phelps at Sadler's Wells, he had written innumerable plays, sketches and burlesques and he was one of the best known theatre journalists of his time. His page in the *Referee* was read by everybody on Sundays. No manager or actor-manager ever dreamed of embarking on a new production without giving

"Chance" an interview and the interview usually took the form of a lunch. His impressions would duly appear, couched in the friendliest vein and written in the manner of the 1870's, full of journalese and old-fashioned words. All friends of his were "old and esteemed," all theatre managers were able and courteous. He was the kindliest of souls and loved to praise—and equally hated to condemn. His worst criticism of a play was that it was "Hasty Pudding." He did much to help and encourage young talent, which he had a knack of spotting, and few players of his period but had a good deal for which to thank him. Yet, when he died, I was the only member of the theatrical profession who followed him to his grave at Putney Vale, and there was only one member—apart from the staff of the *Referee*—of the Journalistic profession which he had so adorned—Hannen Swaffer.

A famous American manager was at the first night of *Mr Todd's Experiment*—Al Woods. He had only just arrived in London and Sir Alfred Butt had telephoned to me asking me to supply Mr Woods with two good seats—a pretty tough proposition at the last moment before a smart first night. But I had been trained in a tough school and was always on the look-out for such eventualities. I had a couple of good seats up my sleeve, and the people to sit in them, too, if the occasion arose. So Mr Woods got his seats. He seemed more interested in the theatre itself and the audience than the play, for he hung about in the vestibule and watched me welcome the people, most of whom I knew and whom I treated as honoured guests, for that is how we did things then. When nearly everyone was seated— well after the advertised curtain time as is usual on first nights— Mr Woods came up to me and said: "Say, sweetheart, have a cigar," producing one from his breast pocket. He always seemed to have an inexhaustible supply of good cigars therein. I excused myself on the plea that I was on duty and did not smoke when looking after the patrons. Mr Woods seemed impressed. "Sweetheart," he said, "I been watching you. You smile at 'em, you seem glad to see 'em, You don't puff smoke in their faces and you are polite. Over my side they don't behave that way—they just don't behave at all. I've learnt something tonight. How about coming back with me and managing my theatres? I'd make it worth your while," and he named a sum which made my senses reel. But the curtain was going up. Next morning I refused. I often wonder if I did right.

Those first nights of the early 1920's, of which *Mr Todd's Experiment* is a good example, did not have vestibules full of press photographers flashing off bulbs—flash bulbs had not been invented, They did not have gangs of young men and girls anxiously trying to pick out celebrities whom they did not even know by sight. There was no mass of idle and curious people impeding the entrance, demanding autographs and invading the vestibule and even the auditorium—

although that was soon to come. The audience themselves, although it was a high social occasion, were really interested in the play they had come to see. They had the same marked disinclination to get into their seats as they have now, for they were busy greeting each other and chatting, but they were not avid for publicity, and BBC and ITV commentators had not been dreamed of. Those people were real celebrities and knew it; they were not dependent upon the doubtful and transient fame of the press paragraph. Primarily, they had come to see the play.

A packed house and a distinguished audience, greeted *Mr Todd's Experiment* with cheers and a real ovation for Owen Nares when he made a charmingly diffident little speech; massive Walter Hackett took his bow, smiling expansively. There was a "rave" Press and then . . . no business at the Box Office. The play ran for only 67 performances. Why? That narrow line between success and failure—a vital mistake had been made. When Owen Nares made his first entrance he did so in slovenly dress wearing a beard. There was a gasp in the audience. The beard vanished and suits improved as the show progressed, but both had been there. Comments thereon appeared in every notice, although they praised play and acting. The part Nares played was weak and unsympathetic—Hackett always had trouble in drawing sympathetic characters. The legions who loved Owen Nares did not want to see him in a beard. They did not want to see him weak and vacillating. That is no way for a matinée idol to behave. So they stayed away. *Mr Todd's Experiment* failed and Owen Nares ceased to be an actor-manager at the Queen's.

CHAPTER II

More Events of 1920

IN 1920 some of the old polish and gloss still remained. The decline had not completely set in but it was already nibbling at the edges. There were successes and productions of interest. There was a stage version of *The Blue Lagoon*, that popular novel by H. De Vere Stacpoole, at the Prince of Wales's Theatre. It was dramatized by Norman MacOwan and Charlton Mann, beautifully produced by Basil Dean, and ran for 263 performances, *Brown Sugar*, a comedy by Lady (Arthur) Lever was a success at the Duke of York's and did much to establish the reputation of a rising young actress named Edna Best. It was transferred to the Garrick Theatre.

It is probable that this transfer was on account of that strange woman who had built and owned the Duke of York's, Violet Melnotte. She was a curious character. Her real name was Rosenberg and her antecedents were humble and based on Birmingham. She had been a handsome girl and developed into what was called, in her time, "a fine woman." She went on the stage and although never a success from the point of view of talent she made an impression. She took her stage name, of course, from that old crusted classic, *The Lady of Lyons*. She married Frank Wyatt, a fine performer and charming man, who had been the original Duke of Plaza Toro in *The Gondoliers*. In his family tree were the celebrated and historic figures of the beautiful Misses Gunning. Violet Melnotte annexed them and spoke of them as being her own forebears. She went into management and even had Marie Tempest under her banner, but naturally there were ructions, two such forceful and strong-willed women could not agree. For a while she ran Willis's Rooms, in King Street, St James's, where entertainments and dances were held and where all sorts of people got together. Its reputation at that time was not too savoury, but she made money. Then she startled London by building a theatre in St Martin's Lane, now a good thoroughfare but then, in 1892, little better than a slum. People thought she had taken leave of her senses and nicknamed her "Mad Melnotte." She called her playhouse the "Trafalgar Square" and it did not succeed, so she renamed it the "Duke of York's"—by gracious permission of the then holder of that title who became George V—and luck came her way. She was not so mad, for other theatres grew up around her. She did not exactly live in her theatre but she spent nearly all her time there. Her meals were cooked in a kitchen on the roof level, and the housekeeper had to add this job to her duties. Her office was at the top of the gallery stairs and was a complete example of Victoriana. She sat there in all her glory. In the 1920's she was well up in years but she adopted no new fashions. She was Victorian. Her dresses were elaborate and highly coloured —she liked mauve, petunia and red—and they were all, day and evening, very décolleté; her hats were vast and befeathered. She glittered with jewels wherever she could find room for them; real pearls swathed her neck, diamonds gleamed on her fingers. Her face was dead-white and her eyes too heavily made up. Her hair, white as the driven snow, was piled high on her head, but not much of it was her own; it was mostly a wig. She was quite ruthless and not a little cruel. She trusted nobody. Her theatre was honeycombed with spies; she set everybody to watch everybody else and then had somebody to watch them. She herself watched the master spy. She had one son, Frank Gunning Wyatt, a tall, handsome and very nice young man, who was entirely under her thumb, so he sought solace in liquid form, which was not surprising. He had tried to be an actor and was not too bad, but his mother had him in her theatre again, so that he could be under her watchful eye. He was supposed to have a job there and was described on the programme as "Representative," though of what or whom never transpired. If his view on a matter of business was sought, he had one simple answer which never varied: "I'm in the same position as you are; I haven't got the casting vote;" and would suggest an adjournment to the bar.

Violet Melnotte, who was known in the theatre as Madame—a phrase which exactly described her—never had a home. She said that her dual ambition was to have a house in Brighton and a "bone" at the Opera—a "bone" was a label made of bone denoting the possession of a private box. She never achieved either. She did, indeed, once take a house at Brighton, but before moving in she saw a rat in the garden and departed swiftly, never to return again. When the Piccadilly Hotel was first opened, in the early 1900's, she moved in for a week. She never moved out until she left it in her coffin. She lived between that hotel and the Metropole at Brighton. At the latter she was so well known that once when she signed a cheque (in the purple ink she always used) "Violet Metropole" the bank honoured it. Very tight in money matters, she did not like the prices at the Piccadilly, so much of her food came in from outside. This was done by an unfortunate man whom she employed at the theatre at starvation wages and who, every Saturday afternoon, crept into the hotel laden like a packhorse with parcels slung round him and a large basin of tripe and cowheel—both of which she adored—under his arm. Everybody knew him and pretended not to see him, for he had their sympathy.

She had a little mouse of a woman as a secretary, a very nice woman indeed, whom she oppressed. One day that little lady gave Madame notice, to her complete amazement. She was going to get married, and to a man of means with a town and country house and a couple of cars. Madame had never had such a setback before; it shook her badly.

She was always worrying about her theatre and getting the rent, but the moment she got a tenant she started to make his life unbearable. Nobody would stop there for long. During Charles Frohman's tenancy she had not been able to use the place but as soon as he went she moved in. Warfare raged daily. André Charlot produced a most successful revue but Madame fought him tooth and nail. When fine weather came, Charlot put a notice on the board announcing that the curtain would ring up at 8.30 instead of 8. Daylight-saving had come into force. Madame tore it down and posted one declaring that 8 was the hour. Charlot removed that and said 8.30. Up and down those notices went until Archie de Bear—a great wit, besides being a magnificent publicity man—stuck up a notice of his own declaring that 8.30 was right and that "Melnotte Shall Not Ring Tonight". That settled it. She tried to evict another tenant and her hope lay in locking him and all his employees out of the theatre and refusing them admission. So at a late hour on a Saturday night, with only the fireman in the secret, all the doors were locked and bolted and she waited calmly for Monday morning and the defeat of her enemy. But that secret had leaked. An employee of the tenant hid on the premises and stuck it for the week-end emerging triumphantly on the Monday when Madame's application for an eviction failed. She hardly ever succeeded in her plans but that never stopped her.

She had a succession of managers, but few of them stayed long; she either sacked them for imagined misdemeanours or they went on their own account—and quickly. Her son Frank, getting desperate, asked me to take on the job. I had been trained in a hard school. I knew her well and I took on that problem. And I am happy to say I beat her to it. I always foresaw and forestalled her tricks. She could never sack me and she came to trust me. I used to laugh at her tantrums, kid to her, and invent outrageous bits of gossip to tell her. She would chew over these and, on returning from a week-end at Brighton, forget their origin and tell me what I had told her as something she had picked up beside the sea. Eventually she sold that theatre and Hannen Swaffer said she did so because she could not sack me. I stayed on with the new management, but she took my advice up to her dying day.

In the vestibule, just above the door, she had a large coloured photograph of herself. It was her pleasure to stand underneath it when audiences were gathering and hope to be recognized. Nobody ever did so. But one evening two men stopped and surveyed it; she beamed on them. "Who is that?" queried one. "I don't know," said the other; "Morris Harvey as a Pantomime Dame, I think." Madame never stood beneath that portrait again.

One morning, as soon as the doors opened at 10 a.m., a man sneaked into the ladies' lavatory, just inside the entrance, bolted the door, turned on the gas stove therein and, lying down on the floor, quietly prepared for death. The gas was soon smelt, traced to its source, the door broken down and the man dragged out still alive. He was rushed to Charing Cross Hospital. Madame was furious "Who was to pay for the gas?" she demanded. But nobody had taken the culprit's name and address, nor would the Hospital divulge it. She wreaked vengeance on the staff.

If you were very much in favour, you were invited to come and have a chop with her at the Piccadilly. Whether she only provided chops or not, nobody ever knew, for nobody accepted those invitations. She had not a friend in the world. Sometimes after a first night she would make a splash and go to supper at the Savoy with her son. She would make him go to other tables where sat people whom he knew and ask them to join her. They all found excellent reasons for staying where they were! Life was bearable at the Duke of York's when she was down at Brighton although her spies kept her informed of all that went on. Once a chimney pot fell from the roof into St Martins Lane and fortunately did not hit anyone. Within ten minutes Madame was on the phone from Brighton to find out how it had happened. When she was at the Piccadilly, the only way to get her out of the theatre was to say it was getting foggy. Of that she was terrified. She would demand a taxi to drive her to the hotel at once. It was no easy job to get her a taxi; most of the drivers knew her and that she gave them only the "dead legal" fare. But unsuspecting ones were trapped by the call coming from a theatre and drove up. Then Madame would be bundled in, the cabman given the exact fare and told to drive very carefully and take great care round the corners. It was amazing how many corners they found and how sharply they took them on that short journey. She was bumped about all over the place. Violet Melnotte was an outstanding example of the theatre in the 1920's—and in that particular year she did not make good use of it. She had no less than ten productions there in the twelve months. She will come into the story again.

*   *   *

Plays worth recording in 1920 were a revival of *La Tosca* at the Aldwych, with that magnificent emotional actress Ethel Irving in the title role—it only ran for 32 performances but it was well worth seeing—and James Hackett, the American actor, as Macbeth at the same theatre. A fine comedy by H. M. Harwood, *The Grain of Mustard Seed*, ran—at several theatres—for 222 performances. *The Whiteheaded Boy* by Lennox Robinson came from the Abbey Theatre, Dublin, to run for 291 performances. *The Charm School*, an American play at the Comedy, with Owen Nares, Keneth Kent, Meggie Albanesi and Sydney Fairbrother, ran for 219 nights, and a stage version of that amusing book *The Young Visiters* at the Court scored 105 performances. In the cast was a young actor named Frank Vosper. A play which Owen Nares had been expected to stage at the Queen's, but which he did not do, was produced at the Savoy. It was *Peter Ibbetson*, a version of George du Maurier's famous novel, by John N. Raphael (who was "Percival" of the *Referee*). Constance Collier, that splendid actress and brave and beautiful woman, played Mary, Duchess of Towers.

There was a charming comedy by Gertrude Jennings, called *The Young Person in Pink*. It did quite a little tour of the West End—such things often happened then—playing at the Haymarket, the Aldwych and the Queen's. The young person with a taste for pink was played by a very young actress named Joyce Carey, Lilian Braithwaite's daughter. Whilst at the Queen's this play received the honour of a Royal Visit.

It may not be generally known that, when Royalty goes to the theatre, it pays for its seats, just in the same way as ordinary folk. The management do not invite them as guests. The seats are obtained from one of the big agencies who have acted in that capacity for a long time. Up to the present reign, the Monarch—in fact practically all the Royal Family—have always occupied the Royal Box. They do not come through the main entrance but through a special Royal entrance usually situated at the side of the theatre. They are not the slightest trouble to anyone; their one idea is that no special arrangements should be made, that there shall be nothing elaborate when they come in their private capacity, they just want to be let alone to enjoy the play. They are met at the Royal Entrance by the manager or whoever is deputed for the purpose; he conducts them to the Royal Room, which is immediately behind the Royal Box, where they wait, have refreshments and receive anyone whom they desire to honour. It has always been their custom to wait in there until the houselights are dimmed and the curtain is on the point of going up; then they slip quietly into the box, so that no reception or demonstration shall break the tension between audience and play. Of course, if they are there for a specific purpose in the cause of Charity or a Gala Performance, then they go straight in, because, in a sense, they are part of the show and people expect to see them. They are always most considerate and never want to give any trouble; there is always a lot more pomp and circumstance when the local Mayor turns up than when Royalty attends.

On the occasion of the visit to *The Young Person in Pink*, the Royal party consisted of King George V, Queen Mary and the present Princess Royal. I received them, conducted them to the Royal Room and remained in attendance, as is always the custom, until the moment came for them to enter the box. The door of the box was slightly open and Queen Mary glanced in. "How shall we sit tonight, George?" she asked the King. "Oh, on chairs, as usual," he replied and roared with laughter at his own little joke. Naturally we were all most amused. But he enjoyed the play and laughed to such an extent that the head of the diamond "push-in" stud in his stiff shirtfront sprang out and fell on the floor. I spent part of the interval on my hands and knees looking for it and fortunately found it. At the end, as I was conducting them out, The King said: "The Queen and I thought that Ellis Jeffreys was in this play." "So she is, Sir," I replied, "only she had to go into a nursing home two days ago for a slight operation, which has been performed successfully." "Ah," said King George, "now you send Miss Jeffreys our best wishes and hopes for a speedy and complete recovery, will you? And also, will you let us know when she is back and we will come and see the play again." I did exactly as I was told and they came the second time and received Ellis Jeffreys—that unique actress who has no counterpart today—in the Royal Room in the interval. She had a cup of coffee with them. When they want to see one or more of the cast they always inquire as to which will be the most convenient time, so as not to interfere too much with costume changes and to avoid making the players rush and hurry.

There was a play at the Apollo which had a Royal Visit in 1920. It was *French Leave* which had been transferred from the Globe. At short notice, King George and Queen Mary decided to visit it. The responsible management panicked. They were two young men who had never received Royalty before, so they asked me to help them. I said I would do it with pleasure, but, as I had not done it at the Apollo before, I would come and walk over the course, as it were, between the Royal Entrance and the Royal Box. I did so and found no snags except that there was a door which had to be opened. I put one of the managers on that door. "All you have to do," I told him, "is to open it when you see me bringing them along, and bow as they go by. They will give you a nod and a smile. Then you will just wait until I come back. Simple, isn't it? But we will rehearse it."

And the rehearsal went smoothly. The night came and that young man was on his door. His name was Frank. He did exactly as he was told. When Their Majesties reached the door he opened it with a flourish and bowed very low. They nodded and smiled and passed on. I accompanied them into the Royal Room, waited and talked to them until they went into the box and then returned. I saw Frank still holding the door open—and still bowing. "Come on, Frank," I said, "you don't want to bow now. Loyalty is all right but . . ." "Loyalty be blowed!" he gasped. "I can't straighten up. I've got lumbago." We led him up to his office still bowing. It was probably the longest bow on record. The King and Queen enjoyed that show. Renee Kelly was the star and three young people all destined for a prominent place in the profession—Henry Kendall, Arthur Riscoe and Reginald Denham—were in the cast.

French Leave had left the Globe to make way for a revival of *Fedora*, in which Marie Lohr played the lead and which ran for 112 performances. An enormous success was scored at the Savoy Theatre by a stage version of Gertrude Page's best selling novel entitled *Paddy The Next Best Thing*. The star was Peggy O'Neil, then at the height of her popularity and beauty. She was a toast of the town, songs were written about this red-haired girl with the big eyes, and a brand of whisky was named after her. Publicity blared in all directions. The show was what is theatrically known as a "riot." It had a bitter side for me, however. I had procured an option on it and tried to get Owen Nares to play it at the Queen's. I knew the part was not of the stature he expected but I told him I considered it a sure box office success and that was just what he wanted. He was almost persuaded, especially after meeting Peggy O'Neil, but other councils prevailed. He did *Mr Todd's Experiment* instead. I let my option lapse. The man who took it up made sufficient out of that play to buy a mansion in its own grounds in Bournemouth—to which he retired—and a Rolls-Royce and live in affluence. I still work hard for my living. "Paddy" ran for 867 performances at the Savoy and made fortunes on tour. That is what theatrical business is like.

Other interesting plays in 1920 were *Come Out of the Kitchen* at the Strand; *The Great Lover*, starring that magnificent actor Maurice Moscovitch, at the Shaftesbury; and *The Right to Strike*, which started at the Garrick and did a little West End tour including the Lyric and the Globe. It was a good play by a promising playwright named Ernest Hutchinson, and it dealt with a social problem. Railwaymen came out on strike and, as a reprisal, the doctors of the district affected did the same, which led to dramatic situations. It only ran for 83 performances and deserved to do better. *His Lady Friends*, an

American play, was quite a success at the St James's; it had Charles Hawtrey as star.

Matheson Lang had a most distinguished season at the New Theatre during which he produced *Carnival*, which ran for 188 performances, and then he staged *Othello* for fifteen special matinées. Lang played the Moor and, with the possible exception of Godfrey Tearle, he was the best Othello of recent times. In September he produced one of his greatest successes, *The Wandering Jew*, with himself as the immortal and accursed wanderer, two leading ladies, Hutin Britton (his wife) and Lillah McCarthy, and a many-scened multicoloured production. Lang was then at the zenith of his career, a great actor indeed and the last of them all to possess the "Grand Manner." But during an interlude in that season at the New, there was a play called *I'll Leave It To You*, by a young dramatist who also played in it, named Noel Coward.

Gilbert Miller staged *Julius Caesar* at the St James's with Henry Ainley as Mark Antony and a brilliant cast. It only scored 83. Out at the Lyric Theatre, Hammersmith, where Nigel Playfair, helped by Arnold Bennett, was running a most intelligent and progressive theatre, there was a play called *John Ferguson* by St John Ervine, which had originally been produced by the New York Theatre Guild.

As a patch of gold in 1920, the Haymarket lived up to its great tradition by staging *Mary Rose*. Regarded by many as Sir J. M. Barrie's masterpiece, it made an impression on those who saw it which will never be forgotten. Sophisticated scoffers might call it a "whimsy," but it was a thing of magic beauty to most playgoers and will be remembered by them when many other belauded plays are quite forgotten. It was beautifully cast and played, and the incidental music by Norman O'Neill gave it exactly the right background. Fay Compton's performance in the title role was one of the outstanding things in the British theatre, not only at that time but since. Beautiful of face, figure and voice, she gave a picture which hangs for ever on the Line of Studies in the Royal Academy of our Theatre. It was something to see again and again and something to remember, and many people did—and do—both. *Mary Rose* ran for 398 performances, a highlight of 1920.

Neck and neck with it, but of different texture, was *The Skin Game* at the St Martin's Theatre, where Basil Dean as producer, and in association with Alec L. Rea, was doing the most consistently good work of the entire period of the inter-war theatre. He will cross these pages again and be dealt with in full, as will that splendid work at the St Martin's, where new plays and new artists were discovered, and where beauty of production, mingled with the finest acting and quality, was as high as that of the actor-manager period in which

Dean had been trained. *The Skin Game* was by John Galsworthy and was Galsworthy at his best—keen, penetrative, skilled in character-drawing, telling a story, setting a problem and solving it. I wish that somebody would revive *Strife* in these days of industrial unrest. It is absolutely up to date and it gives an answer to problems still un-solved. *The Skin Game* had a magnificent cast, including Edmund Gwenn, Helen Haye, Athole Stewart, Meggie Albanesi, and young people just beginning to make an impact, like Malcolm Keen and Mary Clare. For many big names of today came from those Dean productions at the St Martin's, where they learnt much. The foot-lights never flickered there whilst Dean was producer.

But the most exciting event of the year did not take place in a theatre at all, but in a twice nightly music hall, the Holborn Empire, one of the few places even then where the pre-war spirit of British Music Hall lived on. This amazing event was provided by an actress named Sybil Thorndike. She was already 38 and had behind her a long and varied career in all sorts of places and all sorts of parts. She was not a star at that time. At the Holborn Empire at a matinée on 23rd February 1920, she played Hecuba in *The Trojan Women* under the management of Lewis Casson (her husband) and Bruce Winston (one of the fattest actors on the stage). The result was a complete triumph. The Press acclaimed it, and the public rushed to see it. Sybil Thorndike also played *Candida*, *Tom Trouble* and *The Showroom*. They were all successes, although only performed a few times. And she played *Medea* and again there was amazing triumph. Her name was famous now, on everybody's lips, and those who loved the theatre and great acting exulted. This led directly to *St Joan* and to the secure foundation of Sybil Thorndike's enduring fame. It started in a twice-nightly music hall, known to its patrons as the "O'burn," and at the begining of what was generally a bad period; but this—and Dame Sybil—were both real theatre. Nothing has spoilt her, nothing can damp her enthusiasm, for which we may be thankful.

In the year of 1920, Drury Lane staged one of its best and most spectacular melodramas. It was *The Garden of Allah* and was a cut above many of its predecessors in quality. A stage version of Robert Hichens's novel of the same name, it was dramatized by the novelist himself and Mary Anderson. Arthur Collins, the mighty producer at that mighty theatre, really let himself go. The play had already been produced in New York (a fact which will surprise many), but Collins made it real "Drury Lane." He put in many touches of his own and nobody knew more about the stage than he did.

There was a splendid cast, the leading people in which were Godfrey Tearle, Basil Gill and Madge Titheradge. Sir Landon Ronald composed the incidental music and conducted the orchestra.

It was the story of a Trappist monk, who broke his vows, came back into the world, fell in love with a beautiful woman and married her . . . and then heard his spiritual side calling again and returned to the monastery. Godfrey Tearle had a speech some ten minutes long in which he revealed himself to his wife for what he was. His delivery of it was a masterpiece of declamatory acting. The story was told in a series of settings which transcended anything in the way of beauty that Old Drury had done before. There was a garden whose cool shadows contrasted with the glare of the sun—with towering palms and masses of tropical flowers. There was an oasis in the desert painted by Joseph and Phil Harker. There were desert scenes, and street scenes brimming with oriental life: dancing houses where quarrels flared up and long knives found their billets. Nothing had been left to chance to get the right atmosphere. Arabs, Moors, donkeys, horses, dogs, sheep and camels had been imported from Northern Africa—indeed, Africa had come to Drury Lane. All Drury Lane dramas, in those days, had to have a big spectacular effect, and *The Garden of Allah* was no exception. It provided a sandstorm in the desert. The curtain rose on what seemed a limitless landscape of undulating sand, created by Bruce Smith. The sky above was vividly blue and one could feel the sweltering, dry heat. Along a sandy ridge passed a caravan, with slow-moving Arabs driving dogs, horses, donkeys, sheep and camels—one of which bore a palanquin. There was even a baby camel, which gambolled about like a true actor and became a great favourite. The caravan halted for the night and camp was pitched. Myriads of stars shone and twinkled with tropical brilliance in the dark sky and a moon shone. Peace should have been there, but somehow it was not.

A sense of suspense arose; the moon and the stars vanished under a pall. The animals showed signs of fear and in the distance wild beasts bellowed and roared. A little wind moaned and then fell into a deep, sudden calm. It was the calm before the storm, for suddenly it broke in all its fury, the desert seemed to take life, pillars of sand rose and whirled like Dancing Dervishes; the wind howled and, with a sound like the roar of the ocean, the whole desert seemed to arise and smite that encampment. Everything was sweeping, driving sand, terrifying, deadly . . . and quite wonderful. Then the storm subsided as quickly as it had arisen, mist enfolded the scene, the moonlight was shadowy, the stars barely visible, and then the dawn came, clear, serene, shining and peaceful. It was a triumph of stage effect.

But on the first night this was not achieved without a mishap. The scene ended an act and had held the audience spellbound. When the curtain fell they came to themselves and applause and cheers volleyed and thundered. Nineteen curtain calls were taken; then the houselights went up. It was then discovered that the first twelve rows of the stalls were sitting there covered in yellow, like millers, or men and women who had fallen into a mustard pot. They had been in the storm, too, and the pease-meal used to represent the sand in the storm had surged over the footlights and smothered them. There should have been a gauze curtain between stage and audience but it was not there. There were no hard feelings; the sufferers were brushed down and took it very well. Indeed the show ran right through the Christmas season and the annual pantomime had to be transferred to Covent Garden Opera House. And, in fairness to the stage manager, even when the gauze was down a little pease-meal seeped through! At rehearsals powdered cork had been used, driven into the air by hundreds of electric fans, but at the dress rehearsal one of the staff had a brain wave and suggested pease-meal. Tried out, he was found to be right; it was lighter, looked more like sand and certainly filled the air more effectively than the cork. Indeed, it over-filled it, but it made a marvellous storm; even the camels seemed impressed and they might well have experienced the genuine article. The whole production was a lesson in the art of illusion which it is the duty of the theatre to purvey. You do not see such things in the theatre nowadays. People say that the realism of the films has killed stage spectacle; that earthquakes, shipwrecks, conflagrations, train smashes and the like in the theatre cannot compete with those of the screen. It is not so really. The public knows that if film directors want trains wrecked or ships sunk they buy real ones and destroy them. Anybody can do that, given the money. What really intrigues the public is to see how near the stage can get to those things by means of illusion. As late as the 1930's, when Ivor Novello did his musical productions at Drury Lane, those spectacles were revived. In *Glamorous Night* a ship blew up and sank. In *Careless Rapture* an earthquake destroyed a seemingly solid Chinese city. In *Crest of the Wave* there was a mighty train smash. And the audiences rose to all those things. If an enterprising manager can find an expert who really knows how to produce these effects, he would have a great success, and that wonderful stage of Drury Lane might come into its own again.

There still remains something to be told of 1920, and that is its musical side. So far only the straight plays have been dealt with and naturally space has been given to successes, in the main. But here in compressed form is the real picture, showing how many plays were produced at each West End Theatre in that year. It speaks for itself. Adelphi, one; Aldwych, eight; Alhambra, two; Ambassadors, three; Apollo, four; Comedy, eight; Court, five; Daly's, one; Duke of York's, ten; Empire, two; Gaiety, one; Garrick, seven; Globe, five; Haymarket, three; Kingsway, seven; Little, six (there was a season of *Grand Guignol*, too), Hippodrome, two; London Pavilion, one; Lyceum, four; Lyric, six; Lyric, Hammersmith, three; New, five; Oxford, two; Playhouse, four; Prince's, five; Prince of Wales's, one; Queen's, seven; Royalty, four; Savoy, two; Scala, three; Shaftesbury three; Strand, six; St James's, five; St Martin's, five; Vaudeville, two; Winter Garden, one; Wyndham's, two.

Seventy-nine plays that year ran for less than 100 performances each; some of them did not get into the twenties. Even allowing for revivals and seasonable productions, and omitting mixed bills such as *Grand Guignol*, it was not too healthy a record.

But where the shows were musical, the footlights burned with steady radiance. And that was a sign of the times, too.

There is one little point worthy of notice about the Drury Lane of *The Garden of Allah*, which concerned the musical side of it. The leader of the orchestra was Albert Sammons and his violin solo was cheered each night. That was how Old Drury did things in 1920.

Binnie Hale. Outstanding comedienne of the 1920's —and after.

Evelyn Laye. A leading lady who reigns today.

Jack Buchanan. The man who was really "West-End".

CHAPTER III

The Music of Nineteen Twenty

THE musical stage of 1920 shone brighter than the legitimate stage probably for the reason that those in charge were for the most part of the older and more experienced generation. Not all the productions were successful, though the percentage was pretty high. But changes were already taking place. During that year Sir Alfred Butt sold his interest in some of the theatres which had been under his control to William Gaunt, a wool merchant from Bradford who had become a millionaire during the war. He was a very pleasant, cheery individual with a strong Yorkshire accent and a firm belief in his own native Yorkshire shrewdness. He professed utter contempt for all Cockneys and never realized that he himself was controlled very largely by his own manager, Horace Fry, who, although a Plymouth man by birth, was a real Cockney by absorption. A sergeant-major in the First World War and with all the force belonging to those of that rank, he graduated into the theatre through the refreshment side until he made himself a position which was quite unique. He was the power behind Gaunt's throne, although the Yorkshireman never understood it. Gaunt, for all his money, never seemed able to find a hat which either fitted or suited him. Bowlers of weird shape and make adorned his head, sitting right on top of it. Along with his contempt for Cockneys he seemed to have a contempt for this new profession into which he had entered. When in the heyday of his power, if anyone approached him to rent one of his theatres, he would spend much time trying to dissuade the would-be tenant from doing so. He would advise them not to dabble in such a hazardous enterprise. They never took his advice—probably he knew that—and possibly his attitude blinded the applicant to the very high rental asked. Gaunt had a partner in some of his enterprises, one William Cooper, an accountant of York. He was a really shrewd man and of great integrity, with a kind heart under his seemingly hard business exterior and his tenacity of purpose. He was rich, too.

Rumour said that Gaunt made his millions by luck. At the outbreak of the First World War he was possessed of literally hundreds of miles of cloth with no likelihood of selling it. But when the war came the Government wanted cloth by the mile and in instant

supply to make uniforms for the great new Army which was spring-
ing up. Gaunt had the cloth, sold it at a very good price and thereby
laid the foundation of his fortune, if indeed he did not build the
entire structure that way. He became very rich as a result. He
invested in theatres as soon as he saw the boom therein. At one time
he had the Adelphi, Gaiety, Apollo, His Majesty's, Winter Garden
and the Shaftesbury. He believed in bricks and mortar and he
purchased woollen mills, which he thought must always be profitable.
But he was to find that the bricks and mortar of the theatre were
only valuable then in relation to what took place on their stages and
that a time was to come when even the woollen mills would be a
liability and not an asset. Eventually he was ruined, but not beaten.
He went back to Bradford and started all over again. He had real
Yorkshire grit.

    His venture into musical plays in 1920 was not one which he
directed himself. He was only a beginner then. So as far as the
Adelphi was concerned, he entered into an agreement whereby the
firm of Grossmith and Laurillard staged the show, which was *The
Naughty Princess*. Grossmith and Laurillard were firmly established
and very experienced. George Grossmith, the senior partner, son of
his famous father who was the comedy backbone of the Gilbert and
Sullivan Operas, was himself a most polished and first-class performer
in musical comedy. He knew all about that kind of show; he had
been right through the mill; he had been star of the Gaiety in its
palmiest days; he had written, produced and adapted many musical
comedies. He had been the right-hand man of George Edwardes
himself and his judgment of a play was as excellent as his judgment
of female beauty—so necessary in musical plays then. His casting
ability equalled both those qualities too. When the Edwardes
Empire broke up on the death of "The Guv'nor", as George
Edwardes was so rightly called, Grossmith joined forces with
Edward Laurillard. Their backing came chiefly from that amazing
manager, (afterwards Sir) George Dance—but he had not been
knighted then—and the new firm soared to success, basing its
methods on the Edwardes tradition. Grossmith, though not handsome, had tremendous charm, a remarkable personality and great
talent, and was one of the best after-dinner speakers of his time; he could
speak anywhere, at any time, and always with the liveliest results.

    His partner, Edward Laurillard, was entirely different. He was
short, whereas Grossmith was tall and elegant; he was stout whereas
Grossmith was slim. Indeed his inclination to stoutness bothered
him, for he was always most immaculately dressed, indeed, slightly
overdressed, He would give every slimming project a chance and
worry his friends for advice. He was often the victim of practical
jokes over this matter, but he did not realize it. So far from having

any ability at public speaking, it was difficult for him to speak at all. He was of Dutch extraction and had been in and around the theatrical profession for years. He had done a bit of everything except acting. He had been a pioneer of picture theatres with a man called Horace Sedger. He had tremendous tenacity of purpose and was very thorough. He often got good commissions to sniff out and investigate likely sites for the erection of theatres—they actually built them then—and he would pursue that aim regardless of any obstacle and difficulty and mostly achieve success. Nothing daunted him, not even physical violence. Sometimes in his negotiation for property, and also in his endeavour to push the claim of an artist he represented, he would so enrage the other side that, quite literally, they would throw him downstairs. He would get up, assure himself that he had suffered no real injury, brush himself down and then, quite unperturbed, enter the office again and renew the attack. He had a pale face with a yellowish tinge and, on beholding him, one's thoughts would stray to those calves' heads which used to be displayed in butchers' windows. His thin, pale yellow hair was turning grey. His face was always devoid of any expression. Nobody ever knew what he was thinking about. It was always difficult to understand what he was talking about, too, although it may be presumed that he knew that himself. He had a thick, guttural voice and a vocabulary so limited that it frequently failed him and reduced him to silence. His manner of pronunciation was entirely his own, and he never got the name of a place right. To him Glasgow was always Glasborough and Edinburgh perpetually Edingow; Greenwood was his idea of Wood Green, which, for him, was clarity itself. You had to be able to speak Laurillardian to find out what it was all about. On meeting you, he always used one phrase: "Well, there y'are, y'see." What it meant, nobody ever divined, but it served as an opening gambit. He would at times make quite lengthy speeches which were quite incoherent and had to be fitted together by the listener like a jig-saw out of the one or two words which had been understood. He was equally confused with personal names. But the brain behind that sallow face was very keen and the mind very astute, Laurillard was not only very knowing at making "deals," but also was a snapper-up of unconsidered trifles arising therefrom which escaped general notice, but which added considerably to his bank balance.

His firm had started operations with a big success *Potash and Perlmutter*, which brought success to the then unlucky Queen's Theatre just when it needed it most; they brought success to the Gaiety Theatre with *Tonight's The Night*, in which Leslie Henson had made his first big success. They had followed that with *Theodore & Co*, providing Ivor Novello with his first musical score. Then Sir Alfred Butt wanted the Gaiety Theatre for himself. So Grossmith and Laurillard betook themselves to a rebuilt and modernized ex-music hall, the Middlesex Music Hall affectionately known as "The Old Mo" in Drury Lane, now called the Winter Garden. And what is more they took the spirit of the Gaiety Theatre with them.

Now they were doing *The Naughty Princess* at the Adelphi with Gaunt. It was produced on 7th October 1920 and ran for 280 performances. The cast included George Grossmith, W. H. Berry, for so many years the resident comedian at the Adelphi, Leon Morton, the droll French comic, Yvonne Arnaud, a young, slim and attractive girl then, Heather Thatcher and Lily St John. When Lily St John married and retired from the stage our theatre lost a real musical comedy leading lady. W. H. Berry played a king—hard-up, of course. He made his entrance in a very bizarre costume with crowns stamped and embroidered all over it, carrying a hunting spear and holding a leash of three hounds. "I'm the King," he explained, "and these are the rest of the pack." It got howls of laughter; that sort of joke was relished in the 1920's. He had a duet with George Grossmith which recalled the best days of the old Gaiety and the Grossmith-Teddy Payne duets there.

W. H. Berry ("Bill") was an excellent comedian, rich, ripe and fruity, and a good character actor, too. He was a remarkably neat dancer and he could really sing. Nobody except Rutland Barrington ever put over a topical song better than he did—and topical songs were still popular in the 1920's. He had started as a messenger boy in a ticket agency, had become a pierrot and been seen at Broadstairs byGeorge Edwardes, who launched him on his theatrical career. He rose to the very top. He was of a very saving disposition and had complete confidence in himself. As time went on, he became completely self-centred, and the world outside his own orbit did not concern him at all. If he was in a "flop," he was scarcely aware of it, his whole attention being centred on whether he, personally, was a success. Maybe it saved him quite a bit of worry and pain. Many people called him a "prop comedian," meaning a comedian who required stage "properties" to make him funny. Well, Bill Berry liked to use "props," but he knew how to be funny with them and there are many "prop comedians" who fail to be as funny as their "props." He could be funny without props, too.

He amassed a nice little fortune and retired. He built himself a bungalow on the northern cliffs of Kent and that bungalow became his entire world. It was a nice bungalow, but to him it was super-perfection. He would not leave it. He hardly ever came to town, so of course he got forgotten. I was one of the very few who ever went down to see him and then he enjoyed himself. He would run up a flag to the top of his flagpole and welcome me in royal style. Then I had to inspect his collection of fuchsias—there were about twelve of them and they were very ordinary, but to Bill Berry they were wonderful. I had to admire, over and over again, his small collection of little jugs made to resemble Dickens characters—Dickens was his favourite author. I was his second favourite author, but only for one book of mine, which mentioned him a good deal. He read this over and over again, rationing himself to a few pages a day to make it last longer. Then there was the model theatre which he had made himself, and it really did resemble Daly's. Beyond that, there was nothing to do except to listen to his talk about himself and to laugh dutifully at his home-made jokes. Yet I went frequently, for he was so manifestly glad to see someone who was a link with his great days. He was a tireless correspondent, too, writing long letters liberally embellished by his own form of joke, which he always explained in parentheses or with the words "Ha, Ha" in brackets. If he ever mentioned Paris, it was always followed by "Naughty, Naughty" in brackets, too. He signed himself "Bilberry" which was typical. He always wrote that he did not expect an answer but, if one did not come pretty quickly, there followed a rather curtly worded postcard, demanding the reason.

He became a complete creature of habits; nothing was allowed to interfere with them. If you called on him, it had to be in the morning. You never got a meal; a glass of sherry and a biscuit were the extent of his hospitality but he dispensed it with the air of providing a Lord Mayor's Banquet. Nobody saw him in the afternoon. Directly he finished lunch he indulged in what he called "a shut eye," which lasted until teatime. Nothing must disturb that. I wrote to him and told him to listen to a broadcast in which I was paying him a real tribute. He was broken-hearted, for that broadcast came in the middle of the "shut eye," so it was impossible for him to listen to it. He never heard it at all. He allowed himself four pipes a day, each lit at exactly the same time, week in and week out. He believed that such a life would prolong his existence and he did not want to die. His memories, his habits and his beloved bungalow filled his entire life. He lived on his capital because he had a rooted objection to paying Income Tax and from time to time he had lucky investments. His capital outlived him in the end. It was as well he died when he did, a few years ago, for since then most of that bungalow and its grounds vanished into the sea during a landslide and that would have killed him, anyway. An old, curious and, perhaps, not a lovable man; still he had some sterling qualities. He had been a very fine comedian who never gave a bad performance, exhibiting a sense of character seldom found in what were then called "low" comedians, and never did he utter a vulgar line or crack a blue joke. He could be funny without that.

His greatest performance, of many fine performances, was as

Nisch in the original production of *The Merry Widow*, a splendid bit of rich comedy acting. He could use his face, he understood gesture and by-play. He had in his time played opposite to all the other great comedians of his day, including George Graves and George Robey, and had held his own. He was delightful in *The Naughty Princess*.

Daly's Theatre, that delectable place in Leicester Square, was a battlefield during 1920. When George Edwardes died, Robert Evett, a leading tenor in his own right and a chief staff officer of "The Guv'nor," took over the management, decided to resist all comers and to keep the flag of the Edwardes tradition flying high. For a time he did so nobly. Big business, in the person of James White, was after Daly's. Evett scored a victory with *The Maid of the Mountains*, with the superb José Collins as his star. It was an entirely all-British show and it ran for 1352 performances. On 15th May, 1920, Evett produced *The Southern Maid*, which he hoped would have similar success, but you can seldom "do it twice" in the theatre. *The Southern Maid* was an excellent musical play but was always overshadowed by the fame of its forerunner. The title role was an exact fit for José Collins with her dark, rich beauty, and her amazing voice which would have enriched Grand Opera, and gave full scope, too, for her considerable talent for acting. *The Southern Maid* kept the serried ranks of James White at bay for 306 performances but it did not inflict the shattering defeat caused by *The Maid of the Mountains*.

At the Lyric Theatre, Hammersmith, Nigel Playfair followed up his production of *John Ferguson* and a revival of *As You Like It* with a full-scale revival of *The Beggar's Opera*. This was really a work of art. Frederick Austin reset the old airs without detracting from "period," but made them doubly acceptable to audiences of the day. Nigel Playfair himself added something to the score. The costumes and scenery designed by Lovat Fraser were a delight to see. All London flocked to the Lyric, Hammersmith, where the revival ran for 1469 performances—pretty good for a play first produced at Lincoln's Inn Theatre in 1727, which was actually the first English musical play, or comic opera.

The London Hippodrome had a successful revue called *Jig-Saw*, staged by Albert de Courville, who also wrote part of it, his co-authors being Wal Pink and Edgar Wallace, who had not started his meteoric career as writer of stage thrillers and eventually manager, too.

Charles B. Cochran produced *London, Paris and New York* at the London Pavilion (the erstwhile music hall) on 4th September, 1920. Staged by Frank Collins, it ran until 30th July 1921, 366 performances, and was one of the best shows of Cochran's 1920 vintage.

The Lyric Theatre, Shaftesbury Avenue, had a musical comedy called *The Little Dutch Girl*, the book of which was written by Seymour Hicks and Harry Graham (who also did the lyrics), and the music composed by Emmerich Kalman. Opening on 1st December, 1920, it ran for 207 performances, well into the following year. Jack Hulbert made a big success in it. There was a revue at the Queen's, on 13th December, 1920, in which that very great American star Elsie Janis appeared, fresh from her previous triumphs at the Palace. She came over from America for this show and, of course, "her mother came too." The two were inseparable. Elsie Janis herself wrote the book and the lyrics, and Herman Finck, the celebrated composer and conductor at the Palace Theatre, did the music. The Palace Girls were there, too. The title of the Revue was *It's All Wrong*, and that title was nearly all right. Elsie Janis was at the height of her fame and yet, with so much to recommend it, *It's All Wrong* never really made the grade. What Elsie had done was to construct a Palace revue and stage it at the Queen's. Environment means a lot to a production; what would be a success at one theatre will fail at another. That is what was the matter with *It's All Wrong*.

Mrs Janis, the redoubtable, was the prototype for all stage "Mothers." Handsome in an aquiline way, she had piercing black eyes and a will of iron. Nothing deterred her, nothing stopped her, she swept aside all opposition. The word "impossible" for her did not exist. During the First World War she brought into this country a couple of dogs and a parrot, just when quarantine laws were at their strictest. But those laws wilted before "Mother," as we all called her. The parrot was reputed to be able to speak French, but nobody except Mrs Janis ever heard it do so. The dogs were strange, ratlike little creatures, which were always getting trodden on. When one crossed the Janis apartment in the Carlton Hotel there would be a succession of yelps, for the dogs had burrowed under rugs and were out of sight, although there was always a litter of cutlet bones on which they had regaled themselves. Apart from the livestock, the Janis entourage consisted of Frank, the chauffeur, who persistently drove on the right-hand side of the road as in America— how he and the occupants of the car escaped death is a miracle— and Hallie, the coloured cook, who made up her face heavily with rouge, but whose cooking, especially fricassees, was heaven. They always stayed in the same suite at the Carlton (now vanished). If anyone was in occupation when they wanted it, out they had to come, whoever they might be. The closeness of understanding between Elsie and Mother was unique and a little frightening. Mother, although she might be miles away, always knew what Elsie had said in her absence, and on her return would praise or blame, according to how she felt about it. She would do this immediately she came into the room. Nobody had told her. Elsie never went into a shop, Mother did all that. And they had a means of thought transference of which I, who always looked after them, had ample proof. That suite at the Carlton was always filled with celebrities and a most constant visitor was F. E. Smith—Lord Birkenhead. Mother once petrified the assembly, when a meal was being served, by telling the waiter to "Pass the Lord the butter." "F.E." was the most amused of us all. He said it was the greatest compliment he had ever received. But not even Mother could make *It's All Wrong* a success, It struggled along for 112 performances.

During 1920 the Vaudeville Theatre had two revues: *Just Fancy* and *Jumble Sale*. The former ran for 332 performances and the latter, in which Binnie Hale made a success, for 176, running into 1921.

The firm of Grossmith and Laurillard were producing their own shows at The Winter Garden, to which rather outlying theatre they had taken the true Gaiety atmosphere, including W. H. (Billy) Dawes, one of the Gaiety's best and most popular managers. The chief comedian in the outfit was Leslie Henson, almost the last of the great comedians of musical comedy, who died so recently. The 1920 production was a musical version of a well tried farce entitled *A Night Out*, in which Stanley Holloway also played. It was a resounding success and ran for 309 performances.

The Prince's Theatre had two musical productions. One was *Pretty Peggy*, in which Charles Austin, a great star of the music halls —his creation of Parker. P. C. will be remembered—ventured into revue and had with him Lorna and Toots Pounds. *Pretty Peggy* ran for 168 performances. The other, *Oh, Julie!* was a musical show transferred from the Shaftesbury, with Harry Welchman, one of the best leading men the musical comedy stage ever had, and Ethel Levey in the cast. In all it ran for 143 performances.

The old Alhambra Music Hall in Leicester Square—now a cinema named The Odeon—had become a theatre by 1920, as had its great rival, the Empire. At the Alhambra, in 1920, there was a musical play called *Medorah*. It was presented by a strange little man named Bernard Hishin, who was backed by James White on occasions, and who had started life as a "tiger" at the Theatre Royal, Nottingham. In his switchback of a theatrical career he had many ups-and-downs, and *Medorah* was certainly one of the "downs." He gave it a vast production. It was a jumble of America and the Far East and described as an "Eastern-American Musical Romance." Ada Reeve played the title role, a star of every form of stage entertainment, who still brightens the world and works with all her old vivacity and force. But she could not save *Medorah*. It was soon clear to Mr Hishin that his financial resources would not stand the strain and that he must immediately raise some money wherewith to pay

"Treasury" as the salaries of the artists are called. He sent to all his friends, and many mere acquaintances, telegrams asking for help and explaining his awkward situation. I got one. It ran into twelve pages. Now I was at the Queen's, not five minutes walk away from the Alhambra. The telegram was reply-paid, so I replied, regretting my inability to help. It seemed to me that the money he had thus spent might have gone quite a way to helping the Treasury to function. But Hishin was like that. A small man, he did everything on the biggest possible scale. He used the longest polysyllabic words he could discover; he once began a conversation with me by saying: "Has it ever occurred to you, my dear Popie, in the course of your peregrinations through the devious mazes of this terrestial orb which we inhabit as it whirls through space . . ." He never approached anything in the simple way. He always made a speech at curtain fall at his first nights, whether demanded or not; and they went on for so long and were so involved that the audience had departed long before he had finished and the artists had changed their attire, taken off their make up and were on the way home, too. He was afflicted with bad health arising from some mysterious complaint no doctor had ever been able to diagnose. His friends noticed that it was always acute and chronic in times of financial stress but seemed to depart when fortune smiled. He died not long ago; his last jobs were as a money-taker at the Adelphi and also at a provincial theatre—a comedown in position which he shared with other once quite well-known managers.

The other 1920 production at the Alhambra was a very different thing. It was *Johnny Jones and his Sister Sue* described as "A Robey Salad." Naturally it was a vehicle for George Robey, and with him was Phyllis Bedells, one of the finest prima ballerinas this country ever possessed, who still flourishes and imparts her art to the rising generation. George Robey was then at the very zenith of his amazing powers. He was quite at home at the Alhambra, where *The Bing Boys* had been produced, and for a long time he spent his life between the Alhambra and the London Hipprodrome. Well did he deserve his title of "The Prime Minister of Mirth." But he could play Shakespeare with the best of them, and was a very notable Falstaff. It was an ambition of my great friend Julian Wylie and myself to stage *A Midsummer Night's Dream* with George Robey as Bottom. It would have been wonderful but we were never able to achieve it though once we had hopes of Drury Lane. *Johnny Jones*, produced at the Alhambra on 1st June, 1920, ran until 26th February, 1921, 349 performances.

The Empire in Leicester Square had also returned to its original status of theatre and, like its old-time rival, the Alhambra, is today a cinema. In 1920, it was staging musical plays. On the 18th February, its offering was *Sunshine of the World*, described as an operette in three acts. It was a most elaborate production and its sponsors had high hopes. One of them, a most experienced manager and a Colossus of touring companies, announced that its purpose was to educate the public into the sort of entertainment they ought to see and support. He should have known better. The public in search of entertainment will fly from anything which endeavours to educate them. Despite its good value and its colour—it had an Indian setting and, although that background should be attractive theatrically, it always seems very difficult to put over on the stage—*The Sunshine of the World* only contributed 49 lessons to the British public in its mission to raise their standard of taste. It deserved a better fate.

The Empire's second venture was entirely different. This was an American musical play imported into this country by that strange and now legendary character, Joseph Leopold Sacks. Its title was *Irene*, which it pronounced "Ireen," in Yankee fashion. It had some new stage tricks: it ended its scenes by means of wings closing in rather like the cut-off of a cinema camera. But *Irene* did not depend on stage tricks for its success. It was a first-class show with no educational nonsense about it. It started in the poorer districts of New York and ascended into the highest circles. It was a variant of the never-failing Cinderella story with plenty of contrast and even suspense. This was not surprising as it was adapted from a comedy called *Jane O'Day from Broadway* by James Montgomery, a leading American dramatist, and a charming man who never wrote a failure. The music was by Harry Tierney. Tom Reynolds produced it in London and as conductor there was Frank E. Tours, a most accomplished musician, a Londoner born who made a firm reputation in this country before going to America, and who is one of the nicest men who ever waved a baton. He still flourishes in the States.

Irene was presented by J. L. Sacks in association with Sir Alfred Butt, It had a fine cast although the leading lady was totally unknown in this country before her appearance in *Irene* on 7th April, 1920. Her name was Edith Day.

That first night was a most memorable one. It was a night of triumph for all concerned, but especially for that unknown leading lady. Everyone did well, especially Robert Hale, that great comedian and character actor, who that night scored the biggest hit of his long and distinguished career. He played Madame Lucy, a fashionable man-milliner. His study was based on that celebrated character, Willy Clarkson, the costumier and perruquier, who sat in the stalls applauding loudly and said he was "'ighly delighted with Robert 'Ale." But it had many touches of its own and it stood right out as a character study, to be always remembered by those who saw it. Bobbie Hale got an ovation.

And what of Edith Day? Well, she began quietly, but impressed the audience by her grace, her undoubted charm and her dark beauty. As the play moved along, she moved with it and seemed to grow in stature. The people warmed to her, she fascinated them. She sang a song which has become a classic, "Alice Blue Gown," and sang it with such a lovely voice and such great artistry that she stopped the show. One thought she could never "top" that, but she did. There came a number, with the chorus, called "Irene" and she not only sang that but danced, too. Danced? She hardly seemed to touch the stage; it was gossamer on a dawn breeze. And then, she did a back kick, actually touching the back of her head with the sole of her foot, not once but several times. The audience went mad. It stood up and cheered and cheered. Again the show stopped dead; it seemed that it would not be allowed to start again. But it did, and it swept to a triumphant end. The noise and cheering were more like what is heard at a very exciting Cup Final than a West End first night. People were standing on the seats in the stalls, yelling for Edith Day. Calls innumerable were taken. Speeches were made.

Now, his friends had told Joe Sacks that he would have to take a call if *Irene* was a success. He had never wanted the limelight; all he required was money and success. But so insistent were his friends, notably my great crony, Tom Reynolds the producer, and myself— and we were really pulling his leg—that he yielded. He had a special evening suit made, in a vivid blue material and he went on. None of the public had ever seen him, although by virtue of his successes like *The Lilac Domino* and *Going Up* and many more his name was well known. That odd little figure in the weird blue clothes ambled on, his hair trimmed, his pronounced "widow's peak" very prominent, his face close-shaven and nearly as blue as his suit, his lower lip sagging and his nose plunging into it, his eye scared—and he made a shambling bow, There was a great burst of laughter and then cheers, but the laughter was the loudest. Joe fled to the wings and never took a call again. But what did he care? Here was success, tremendous success. And head and shoulders above all the rest stood the graceful figure of Edith Day, with the magnificent voice, the dramatic ability, and the dancing of a prima ballerina. That night she became the Toast of the Town and a Queen of the Musical Comedy stage, to reign there for years and to be remembered with pleasure and gratitude now that she is in retirement, but still the same charming Edith Day.

Irene, although pronounced "Ireen," was also pronounced success. It ran right into 1921, 399 performances, and might have run longer but for internal dissension. It was easily one of the best and brightest of all the musical productions of 1920—indeed of many years—presented by J. L. Sacks, that amazing little illiterate whose own story is one of the most exciting, romantic and amazing ever known in the Land of Illusion which lies behind the footlights. Up to that time those footlights had never flickered for Joseph Leopold Sacks.

CHAPTER IV

Vignette of a 1920 Impresario

JOSEPH LEOPOLD SACKS, who started his life as a boy in a circus in South Africa in the 1890's, rose to be a leading impresario in the great and growing country, invaded London and conquered it, and at one time had no less than five plays running in the West End simultaneously, was never able to read or write.

He had no education at all as a child and he was never able to learn when he grew to manhood. So he lived in a strange world of his own cut off from the advantages of literacy. Yet such were his brain, wit and mental power that, with nothing but his own intelligence to help him, he bestrode the world of the theatre like a Colossus. He reached the dizziest heights, and a change of luck cast him down. He did not bemoan his fate; he got up and started all over again, with that indomitable optimism which never deserted him. He never changed. He was the same in prosperity and poverty. He was a keen judge of men and women, and about the best judge of a musical play on either side of the Atlantic. He had an unswerving loyalty to his very few friends. He loved children, although he never had any of his own, and they loved him, and he loved birds and animals. Such things endeared him to the few who really knew him and even those who felt reason to be aggrieved would smile and say "Poor Old Joe." His very simplicity awoke sympathy; yet that was something for which he never asked. What he wanted was achievement. If he never forgot a bad deed or an insult levelled at him, he never forgot a kind word or a favour. His greatest joy was to see, in lights across the front of a theatre the words "J. L. Sacks presents." He could not read them but he knew what they meant.

Joe Sacks was never quite sure where he was born but he thought it might have been in Grodno. He was taken to Johannesburg via London by an uncle when he was a small child. That uncle sent him to school when he was about seven years old but that sort of humdrum life did not suit little Joe. He went to see a circus and, when that circus moved on, he went with it. His uncle does not appear to have worried very much.

He was only a child but he worked hard. He cleaned the caravans, he sold tickets, he was a Boy Clown and did all the odd jobs. When the show was not in progress he sold oranges, bananas and trifles around the side shows and the menagerie. His will to rise was indomitable. He had no interest in the distractions which appealed to other boys; for him life contained only work, for he saw that as the ladder which would take him to the heights. At the age of fifteen, he became assistant manager of that Circus.

Very shortly after he found himself in London, for Frank Fillis, the circus proprietor, had contrived a great show called "Savage South Africa." It came to the Earl's Court Exhibition as part of "Greater Britain" in 1899. It was presented there and greatly enlarged by Imre Kiralfy, the master showman. The basis of it was "Major Wilson's Last Stand" against the Matabele and, of course, the eventual victory of British arms. It was a huge success.

Whilst that mimic war was in progress at Earl's Court, the Boer War broke out. Earl's Court closed down, Fillis took his show on tour but had to close it with great loss. He managed to get back to South Africa with the natives he had brought over, but he had only six schooled horses left out of five hundred. He was ruined.

Joe Sacks was out of a job but he did not care. He did not go back to South Africa at once—war had nothing to do with him. He had saved about £3400, and he treated himself to a holiday in London and Paris. He saw all the sights and shows and he got ideas and dreamed dreams. Then, after three months, he, too, went back to South Africa. There was war there, but war might mean business, too. He landed at Cape Town in March 1900. He found that city full of soldiers. Martial Law prevailed, the whole of Cape Colony was an armed camp. How was he, a showman, to earn a living? But he saw that the population of Cape Town was swollen beyond the normal, and that there was no sort of provision of entertainment for most of the troops. There was the Opera House, but that was high-class and expensive. He decided he would fill the gap.

He met a man in a bar who said he knew all about entertainments. They formed a partnership and put up a capital of £1500—£750 each. They found a disused hall in Plane Street. At a cost of £1250 they made it into a well equipped little theatre or music hall. Sacks soon discovered his partner knew little or nothing, but he himself had the knowledge required. He got together a variety company of four men, three girls and a pianist. They were all music-hall folk and adaptable. Joe sorted out the acts and arranged a routine. He ballyhooed the Plane Street Theatre around town. It was a great success; it was a gold mine. The salaries were £65 a week, the total running expenses were £95 a week. For three golden months Joe and his partner netted a profit of between £600 and £700 a week.

Troops from all parts of the Empire continued to pour into Cape Town. A large detachment arrived from Canada, full of patriotism and high spirits. They had come to fight and they started fighting before they met the Boers. They decided to paint the town red and succeeded. One of the ruddiest bits of work was the Plane Street Theatre—they broke it up entirely.

Joe Sacks was in a quandary. He had lost his source of income, he had a company on his hands, but he was not down and out. He decided somebody should pay and that somebody should be the army, or Her Britannic Majesty's Government. He went straight to the fountain head. He demanded to see the General Officer Commanding, Cape Town. Anyone who has ever tried to do such a thing knows the difficulties, but they did not daunt Joe Sacks. He could not fill up forms because he could not write, but he made himself so persistently annoying by his continued presence, by his pestering and importuning, and his threats of messages to the War Office itself, that eventually the General was persuaded to see him.

This was an ordeal, but Joe braced himself. He was shown in and there was the General before him. That imposing figure, the product of public school, Sandhurst and the Army, faced this odd-looking, uncouth, entirely illiterate young man, unprepossessing of appearance, speaking hardly understandable English. Joe stated his claim, and it was fair and just. Maybe that General had a sense of justice; maybe Joe understood human nature; and perhaps that wonderful smile of his, which transformed his ugly face and was like the sun breaking through stormclouds, helped a bit, too. He won. The General probably wanted to get this out of the way. He knew how such things got troublesome if they reached the War Office. He deducted a few items—which Joe had added for the purpose of taking them off—and settled the claim for £1250. He was glad to see the back of Joe Sacks when he left the office full of thanks.

But he had not seen the last of him. For Joe that was only the first round. He was back again with another claim—who was to pay his company? True the damage to the hall was settled, but there remained the claim of the company thrown out of work because of military action.

The General stormed and raved. Joe stuck to his guns. All right, he must bring the whole affair before the War Office. That quietened the General, he did not want that. What did Mr Sacks suggest? Joe was ready. All over South Africa, he said, were troops with no entertainment. Let the General give him permission to take his company to supply that need and all would be square. The General could not do that, but he compromised by giving Joe a document which recommended him to the local commanders, and he put his own official stamp on it. Joe had won again.

He secured a couple of saloon railway coaches in which to travel. Joe went on ahead and his partner managed the company. They worked out a tour. As soon as Joe arrived in a town he showed his pass and made arrangements with the Town Major. There was always one snag: under the wartime curfew everybody had to stop at home after dark. Joe suggested that a ticket for his show should be the equivalent to a pass. The Town Majors agreed. So he would take the largest room in the town, often in a hotel, and sell tickets in advance. He always sold at least four times more tickets than the hall would hold. Few wanted to come to the show but they all wanted an evening out. And the show played to capacity all the same. It was a good show, for Joe believed in quality. The artists were fêted everywhere, especially the girls. Round and round they went. Eventually they got to Port Elizabeth, where they played for three nights. Then they went to Durban, where Joe got rid of his partner, whom he did not trust. It was now December, 1901. They shared out and Sacks's share was £18000. He took the company out again.

The dawn of 1902 showed signs of peace. Negotiations had started. The British High Command was at Waalstad, on one side of the Vaal River, the Boer High Command on the other. Joe turned up with his show. The British High Command, being gentlemen, asked their now beaten enemies to attend a Gala Show given by Mr Sacks and his company. They knocked down the wall of a room in the hotel to make suitable accommodation. The Gala Show was a triumph. Money simply rolled in. The Boers, not to be outdone in courtesy, asked Joe to play a Gala for them with the British Generals as guests. They were all there, including Botha and De Wet, whom the British could never catch, but Joe Sacks's show caught him. Again, a triumph. And a lot of money.

Peace was signed at Vereeniging and Sacks disbanded his company. They went home rich. They had boxes of golden sovereigns, pillow cases and stockings filled with them, too, and the girls glittered with jewellery. Joe had made £28,000 but he said the company had done better than he did. He sent them home from Cape Town and went back to Johannesburg. He did a deal over a hotel and made about £32,000. Also he fell in love with the daughter of the man who managed it for him. Something broke the romance. He never married anyone else and he never forgot that girl. He would always find work in his shows for any girl who resembled his lost love. He came to England, he made contacts, he imported British shows into South Africa. He also played variety. In 1907 he decided to build a Music Hall in Johannesburg, which met with violent opposition from the management of the one already established. The proprietor of this accused Joe of all sorts of crimes and said he would stop him building. Joe said he would drive his opponent out of town in five years and would build his hall. And in five years, despite all

Alfred Lester, the great comedian who specialised in gloom.

Godfrey Tearle. The outstanding actor of the 1920's.

Marie Lohr. Leading lady
and actress-manageress.

Jose Collins whose force and personality flamed in the 1920's.

sorts of difficulties, he had done so. He built and opened his Hall, the Palladium, and drove his opponent out of business.

But there was a vast organization in South Africa which was up against Joe Sacks, too strong for even his wits to scatter. He carried on for a while and made many important contracts, but eventually he was defeated. He left Johannesburg with hardly £100 in his pocket, but there was something there worth far more than that. It was a contract whereby Harry Lauder, then on top of the world, agreed to appear under his management in South Africa, where the great Scots comedian had never been. Joe went straight up to Lauder's home in Scotland with a proposition. Would Lauder take the same money to appear in a revue in the West End instead of going to South Africa? Many people had tried to lure the wily Scot into such an engagement but they had all failed. Joe succeeded. Lauder saw the advantage and agreed. The result was *Three Cheers* at the Shaftesbury. The First World War was on. For some time the show was a success, and then Joe sold out.

He decided to go to New York and see what he could pick up. The night before he sailed he had dinner at the Piccadilly Hotel with a friend who was to look after his affairs whilst he was away. That friend had another man with him, a stockbroker. Joe talked about his schemes and his ideas. The stockbroker, who had never seen him before, suddenly said: "You don't know me, Mr Sacks, and I don't know you, but I think we would get along together. If you'll allow me, I will invest £500 in this enterprise of yours." Joe did not actually need the cash but it went against the grain to refuse money. He told the man it was a great risk, but the stockbroker laughed and said he got his money that way—by gambling. He wrote out the cheque then and there and Joe took it. That £500 cheque produced £35,000 for that stockbroker.

In New York Joe was listening to some scores being played when his eye fell on some published music lying about. He could not read what it said but he liked the colour used on the covers—it was lilac, his favourite hue. He bought the show from which that number came. It was *The Lilac Domino*. He met a composer he knew who was working on a new score. Joe heard some of it played and said he would buy it. The proposed show had the stopgap title of *The Aviator*. But publishers were involved. They would not agree unless Joe bought another show called *King Fu*. So he bought that, too, to get *The Aviator*.

When *The Aviator* was eventually produced in New York it was called *Going Up*. It was a tremendous success. London managements who knew nothing of Joe Sacks cabled to their representatives to secure it. Back came the answer, it already belonged to J. L. Sacks.

Little Joe came back to London. He brought with him an entire production of *The Lilac Domino* and a full company, too, ready to open at once. But theatres were at a premium in 1918. Managements with plays were queuing up. Joe could not get one.

Now he knew one person in London, beside the friend who was looking after his affairs and with whom, for reasons which need not be gone into, he had quarrelled. That person was myself. He had met me when he came over here to negotiate the Lauder deal. I had at that time a great friend in Johannesburg who kept writing to me about the amazing Joseph L. Sacks, so when a queer-looking little man sent in a rather dirty card to the Globe Theatre one day and wanted a seat, curiosity compelled me to see him and show him courtesy. He interested me very much. In fact, I could not shake him off until he vanished again to America.

Now he was round to see me again. He wanted a theatre for *The Lilac Domino*. I knew all about that play. I was then with Sir Alfred Butt, who had read the play and turned it down, but there was a new revue at the Empire which was of little use. I had an idea. I knew Sacks had bought *Going Up* which Butt had wanted to get, like everyone else. I knew, too, that we very badly wanted an attraction for the Gaiety. I discussed a proposition with Joe Sacks and he agreed. I took him round to Sir Alfred Butt's office and told him to wait outside. He could hardly contain his anxiety. I saw Sir Alfred at once. I suggested he should let Sacks bring *The Lilac Domino* into the Empire. Sir Alfred, who had no opinion of the play, demurred at first and then quoted very difficult terms. "That would be no good to him or to you, Sir Alfred," I said. And then I played my trump card: "Don't forget Sacks has *Going Up*. If I could arrange that he would let you have that for the Gaiety, where we want a show badly, would you give him reasonable terms for the Domino at the Empire?" "Where is he?" asked Sir Alfred. "He's outside," I said, "jumping on and off the kerb with excitement. I'll bring him in. Now you don't know him and have never seen him. If you were a judge and he was the prisoner, you would probably say: 'Stop the evidence. Guilty.' But it's not as bad as that. And don't forget he cannot read or write." Sir Alfred laughed. I brought in Joe Sacks. The deal was done. *The Lilac Domino* was produced at the Empire—in the afternoon because of air raids—on 21st February 1918 and ran for 747 performances. *Going Up* was produced at the Gaiety on 22nd May, 1918, and ran for 574 performances. Both theatres got successes they badly wanted, Fortunes were made and Joe Sacks was on top of the world. I was the only person who got nothing out of it, except kudos. That is what usually happens to me.

King Fu became *Shanghai* and was played at the Theatre Royal, Drury Lane. And Joe turned out success after success.

He bought a big car and had it painted lilac; its claxon horn played the first few bars of "The Lilac Domino Waltz." He himself was lost in that car but it gave him immense pleasure. Soon he had five shows running in town. He took offices in Gerrard Street and his headquarters were known as "Liberty House"; the whole place was upholstered and painted in lilac. He had a mansion at Maidenhead and a motor launch which was lilac, too. He rode an enormous horse and looked like a little monkey on it, with an enormous cap on his head. He smoked the biggest cigars he could find. He never spoke proper English but like Laurillard, whom he despised, a lingo of his own. To him a "show" was always a "saow." He could be ruthless and cruel to those he did not like. He would immediately destroy airs and graces if arrayed against him. In his office he sat alone. He had a machine which connected all the other offices and he would switch it on and listen to what they were saying about him behind his back. He learnt a lot that way. His manager drew a salary of £20 a week which was paid to him in cash on Fridays, and every Friday evening, as regular as clockwork, that manager, an inveterate but unlucky gambler, lost that £20 to Joe Sacks, who put it back in the safe again, for use the following week.

Joe had that wonderful smile which redeemed his plain, not to say ugly, face, his drooping upper lip and his nose which went down to meet it. He also had the knack of being able to cry like a child whenever he so desired. In later years it stood him in good stead.

In 1920 a play was produced in New York which every London management wanted to secure. They or their representatives attended the first night and at the end met the American management to make their bids. Then they were told they were all too late. Joseph Leopold Sacks had bought it before production, just as he had done *Going Up*. That play was *Irene*. Joe met with disaster later. He died not long ago, down but not out, and always in pain because of a wound during an air raid in the Second World War. But always he fought on and always he hoped to see once again those words he loved so much in lights "J. L. Sacks presents." He did not live to see them. Maybe the Hereafter will be kind to a very brave, if very odd, little man.

CHAPTER V

1921 Sounds the Alarm

IT was the year 1921 which really struck the note which was to govern most of that theatrical decade. Most of the post-war excitement and extravagance had ended in 1920 but the dancing craze continued unabated. It was, in general, a time to settle down, take stock and begin again. But that was not so easy, old habits had been broken and new ones not yet formed. Conditions were bad all over the world. When bad conditions obtain in the life of the community the first trades and professions to feel it are theatres, restaurants, and all kinds of entertainment. The British do not consider entertainment essential, or they did not do so in 1921. Now, of course, it is laid on to their houses like gas and water, in the form of Television and Radio.

In 1921 there were forty theatres in the West End, if the Victoria Palace, which did plays at Christmas time, was included; and there was also the Everyman in Hampstead, which had been opened by Macdermott in 1920 with excellent results, presenting new plays and notable revivals. But when dissection of the theatrical results of the year is made, a gloomy picture is presented. In a remarkably short time the theatre had tumbled from booming prosperity into a grim position.

As a rule, the people of the theatre, and even those who criticize it, take a benevolent view and confine their remarks to a few specific cases. But there was a man who really let himself go about 1921. He was Archibald Haddon, who was deeply interested in the theatre, dramatic critic of the *Daily Express*, champion of rising talent—he was loud in praise of Sybil Thorndike—and he became the first regular broadcaster on theatrical matters.

He saw the plays and if, as a critic, he never got very much below the surface, he got news for his paper and understood the general picture. This is what he says: "It was one of the worst seasons in living memory, artistically as well as financially. The principal causes were the coal stoppage, the drought, restricted train services, unattractive plays, and general maladministration." In some of those things he was right, but the drink restrictions and increased prices of admission, which were negligible, had little to do with it, and anyway could not have affected the artistic side. He continues:

68

"At the height of the slump, only half a dozen of the forty West End Theatres were making both ends meet. One ordinary summer evening there were only six people in the stalls of a certain theatre which accommodates two thousand." [He means that was the total capacity of the theatre, not of the stalls.] "Many other houses had from twenty to thirty stalls occupied, not all of them paid for." And he is right: things were like that in 1921.

Mr. Haddon cites an instance of drink restrictions harming the theatre: "An American, on his arrival in London, booked two stalls for the Gaiety. The piece was *Faust On Toast*. He went out for a much-needed refresher. The bar was closed. Next morning he called on the ticket agent who sold him the tickets. The only printable part of his diatribe was "I'm off to Paris at once." Well, bars closed at 10. p.m. in 1921. That American has my sympathy but, if he had the strength and courage to sit out *Faust On Toast* until that hour, he must have been a pretty tough and determined man. For *Faust On Toast* was a real flop. It was taken off after 14 performances, reconstructed, put back and removed again when it had run, in all, 34 performances. I think it was more the play than his inability to get a drink which drove that American to Paris. In those days most Americans carried hip-flasks, anyway.

As critic, Mr. Haddon put amongst his failures of 1921 a play called *Heartbreak House* by George Bernard Shaw. He writes: "A freak play by Mr. Bernard Shaw, called *Heartbreak House*, was pluckily produced by Mr. J. Bernard Fagan at the Court Theatre. Its performance lasted a few minutes short of four mortal hours—but it seemed like years—during which period an excessively intelligent audience was by turns tantalised, obfuscated, flabbergasted and amused. Nothing happened until the final moments but talk, talk, talk." Mr. Haddon did not like Shaw or his play, but later, on a second visit, he had to admit that he found "it alive and kicking, or rather chinwagging" to a laughing, applauding and crowded house. He decided there had been some clever "cutting." Maybe Bernard Fagan was a better judge of a play than Archibald Haddon, but in justice it must be admitted that he was not the only critic to denounce the play.

Haddon was a Puritan at heart and railed against what he called "the cynicism and sensuality" of many of the plays. He said this was one of the causes of the bad state of theatre business. He attacked one called *Up In Mabel's Room* and demanded to know "where in it was the quality of greatness which should distinguish the work of the London stage?" It must be admitted freely that there was no such thing in *Up In Mabel's Room*. This came from America and was produced at the Playhouse. Charles Hawtrey, Isobel Elsom and a

young lady named Beatrice Lillie were in it. It was described as a
"Frivolous Farce in Feminine Foibles," and that was enough to kill
any play. It only ran for 37 performances, so very few people had
their morals contaminated. I wonder what Archibald Haddon
would have thought of some of the plays of 1959.

It is best to pick out the highlights of 1921 before dealing with
the darker side. At the Aldwych there was a production of *The
Tempest*, sponsored by Viola Tree, Sir Herbert Tree's clever if
erratic daughter. Henry Ainley played Prospero and gave one of
the best renderings ever of this often dull and pompous part,
Francis Lister, then just beginning his real career, was Ferdinand
and Louis Calvert, a magnificent all round actor, was Caliban.
Viola Tree, who had played Ariel in her father's production—but
had not been very aerial—contented herself with Juno. The scenery
was a joy to look at, and the revival ran for 46 performances!

A really outstanding play was *The Faithful Heart*, by Monckton
Hoffe, produced at the Comedy Theatre. It was a beautiful piece of
work and it had a message which was delivered well and truly by
Godfrey Tearle. The character he played had learnt this lesson in
the late war—"To do the things you can't explain, because it is
right." Most skilfully produced by Leon M. Lion, it gave Godfrey
Tearle a chance to put up an outstanding performance. It made him
indeed the Actor of the Year—and he had many triumphs in this
period. Tearle in *The Faithful Heart* lingers in the memory. That play
ran for 194 performances.

Another outstanding 1921 success was *Ambrose Applejohn's
Adventure*, written by indolent Walter Hackett, who seemed to have
really made an effort. Produced at the Criterion Theatre on 19th
July, 1921, it ran until 19th August, 1922, 454 performances. It
gave Sir Charles Hawtrey one of the best parts of his long brilliant
career, and one will never forget him as a pirate in the "flashback"
portion. *Ambrose Applejohn's Adventure* is too well known to need
description. It became a sort of mascot to Hackett, and in every
play which he wrote afterwards he always had a character named
Ambrose. He bestowed it, too, on an Irish terrier which he was very
fond of, but had not the slightest idea how to treat. The poor thing
never got any exercise. Hackett would take it out in his huge
Daimler car, which had a silver bison as a mascot looking very
much like Hackett himself, and they would go into the country to
give Ambrose a run in the fields. But they never stopped anywhere
to give Ambrose that run, and so the poor dog got none.

James Bernard Fagan, whom Mr Haddon regarded as plucky,
did some very fine work at the Court Theatre in 1921—practically
up to the old Vedrenne-Barker standard. His productions there
included *Henry IV; Mr Malatesta; The Playboy of the Western World;*

John Bull's Other Island; Heartbreak House (in which was a rising young actress named Edith Evans); *She Stoops to Conquer;* a Christmas play called *The Great Big World*, and *Othello*. Godfrey Tearle was the Othello. That was memorable.

Tearle had made a tremendous impact in *The Garden of Allah;* the mishap with the sandstorm on that first night had not blinded the public to his merit. They "called" him; the theatre resounded with shouts of "Tearle, Tearle, Tearle," a wonderful tribute. His performance in *The Faithful Heart* further endeared him to the public and now he was to triumph as Othello. He became a star, as they are called nowadays.

It is not always wise to use the word "great" to describe a performance; that status is rarely achieved, but at any rate Godfrey Tearle's Othello stood on the very threshold of it, with one foot inside the door. He looked every inch the warrior. Tall and handsome, he made up with an olive complexion, a short beard and a moustache, all of which threw into relief his flashing eyes and teeth. He used his voice wonderfully; every syllable told, and he came near to the silver chimes of Forbes-Robertson, who had perhaps the most musical voice the stage ever knew. Even at the height of his rage and fits, every word was audible and articulated. When his jealousy struck him he might have been a furious tiger; he moved like one and there was a deep growl of rage. He leapt at Iago's throat like a tiger, too. He held his audience spell-bound. Just a little more force of personality and this might have been a really great Othello, but it was a splendid one, all the same. Of course, it challenged comparison with that of Matheson Lang. Lang adopted a different make-up. He was much darker than Tearle, and he was not so neat or well-barbered. His hair was long and straight. But he looked every inch the man whose arms had spent "their dearest action on the tented field." Lang was the complete soldier. His great voice rang out, his articulation was as clear as Tearle's; not a word was missed. His rages were just a bit more frantic and behind the whole character was that immense strength of personality which Lang possessed and which made his Othello better than Tearle's. It can be safely said that Lang's was a great Othello.

Miss Nell of New Orleans managed to scrape together 122 performances, with Irene Vanbrugh in the name-part, partly at the Duke of York's and partly at the Garrick. At the Gaiety, a strange venue for such a thing, was Maeterlinck's *The Betrothal*, sequel to *The Blue Bird*, which ran for 111 performances. In the cast were Bobbie Andrews, Winifred Emery, Una Venning and Gladys Cooper. *The Edge of Beyond*, adapted by Roy Horniman and Ruby Miller from Gertrude Page's best-selling novel, achieved 194 performances at the Garrick. Another best seller adaptation, *The Knave of Diamonds*

by Ethel M. Dell, scored 185 performances between the Garrick and
The Prince's with Violet Vanbrugh in the cast.

At the Globe, an American play called *Woman to Woman*, which
included Willette Kershaw, ran for 116 performances, and at the
same theatre *The Truth About Gladys* by A. A. Milne, with Norman
McKinnel, Irene Vanbrugh and Dion Boucicault in the cast, ran
for 124 performances.

A play by Somerset Maugham, called *The Circle*, actually got the
bird at the stately Haymarket. A certain portion of the audience
booed it lustily. They had been exasperated by the inaudibility of
some of the performers, whom they had repeatedly advised to
"speak up" and not to mumble. A little of that sort of thing would
not be amiss in 1959. *The Circle* was followed by a revival of *Quality
Street*, which scored 344. The Maugham play ran for 180 despite the
hostile reception.

There was a strong drama at the Lyceum called *The Savage and
the Woman*. In this Philip Yale Drew, called "Young Buffalo," made
a hit. Later he figured in a real life drama which was just as exciting.

At the Lyric a Jewish actor (recently passed on) whose name was
Harry Green made a big success in *Welcome Stranger*. With him was
Margaret Bannerman. Its run was 224 performances.

Matheson Lang did a season at the New Theatre and gave an
outstanding performance as Christopher Sly in Forzano's play, he
also had a success with *Blood and Sand* in which he played a
matador.

At Wyndham's the real actor-manager with a theatre as his home
reasserted himself. Gerald du Maurier was back with a bang in a
good thick-ear melodrama with no nonsense about it, *Bull-Dog
Drummond* by "Sapper." Although du Maurier is looked upon today
as a most artistic actor with a penchant for high comedy, he was
always at his best in melodrama. Despite the understatement of his
method of acting and that great restraint which people took for
"naturalness," he knew how to play drama. If he did not rant and
roar, his face, his eyes, the whole of his body acted all the time. His
Raffles was as good a piece of work as our stage ever saw, and his
Arsène Lupin matched it. His revival of *Diplomacy* was a classic and
the famous "three men scene" was never better performed than
when he, Norman Forbes and Arthur Wontner played it. This art of
his shone in *Bull-Dog Drummond*.   He was not physically suited to it
but he made you believe that he was. The result was a run of 429
performances. His flair for casting also showed, for in the company
were Ronald Squire, Basil S. Foster and many other front-rank
people. He kept the flag of actor-managerial quality flying at
Wyndham's.

Lord Dunsany had a play at the Ambassadors called *If*. It ran for

Matheson Lang, the finest "Othello", with Margaret Halstan as "Desdemona".

Winifred Barnes, popular leading lady in the musical comedies of the 1920's.

Elsie Janis, one of the greatest stars America ever sent us.

Ivor Novello, who rose to fame in the 1920's, and Lily Elsie, one of his leading ladies.

Robert Michaelis, musical comedy star and idol of the ladies.

Marie Lohr and Sir Gerald du Maurier, two outstanding figures
of the 1920's.

178 performances with Henry Ainley and Gladys Cooper in the leads. Playing two small parts—"doubling" as it is called—was a young actor named Leslie Banks.

The Duke of York's had a dreadful year and found only one play which ran for any time at all—*The Wrong Number*.

The Little Theatre staged a very successful season of *Grand Guignol* which included such classic shockers as *The Old Women*, *Shepherds' Pie*, etc. There was a resident company including Lewis Casson and Russell Thorndike.

Abraham Lincoln played at the Lyceum and the Scala. Then Godfrey Tearle had yet another success in *The Sign on the Door*, an American play by Channing Pollock. It ran for 306 performances, right into 1922. In it with Tearle were Gladys Cooper and Leslie Faber.

Sarah Bernhardt made an appearance in London at the Prince's in *Daniel*.

Robert Courtneidge's production of *Out to Win* ran for 121 performances at the Shaftesbury, with that delightful actor George Tully in the lead. A mixture of the younger and older generation provided *Polly With a Past* with 110 performances, the younger generation including Noel Coward, Henry Kendall, Edith Evans, Edna Best and the older players, Donald Calthrop, Aubrey Smith and Paul Arthur, with Claude Rains as perhaps the "middle age."

Ian Hay had a success at the Strand with *A Safety Match*, in which actor-manager Arthur Bourchier and Kyrle Bellew played. There was also a young actor named Clifford Mollison, who was making great strides.

Those were all the plays of 1921 which ran for 100 performances and more, except one to be dealt with later and some musical productions. But they were by no means the only plays of quality or with a useful purpose. There was, for instance, *Deburau* at the Ambassadors. Despite Robert Loraine and Madge Titheradge, it only ran for 28 performances, but there were some youngsters in it destined for high rank—Robert (Bobbie) Andrews, Leslie Banks, Jeanne de Casalis—whom so many will recall as Radio's Mrs Feather—and another who was playing his first part on the stage and whose name was Ivor Novello. So far as acting goes, he belongs to 1921, although his music was already widely known. A play called *Will Shakespeare* has not been forgotten, as those who read on will discover.

That is not a long list of successes or brilliant plays. The other side of the picture should be examined. Here follows a résumé of what was happening in 1921: the Apollo, *Don Q* 86 performances; Duke of York's, (amongst others) *Lonely Lady* 16 performances, *Tartan*

Peril 5, *Pilgrim of Eternity* 10; Garrick *The Fulfilling of the Law* 69; *Count X* 94; Globe, *The Hour and the Man* 27; Kingsway *,The Heart of a Child* 50, *Hunky Dory* 76 (including transfer to the Apollo); Playhouse, *Hanky Panky John* 24, *Love* 19, *M'Lady* 28, *Up in Mabel's Room* 37; Prince of Wales's, *Nighty Night* (including transfer to Queen's) 73; Queen's, *The Hotel Mouse* 36; Shaftesbury *Sweet William* 21, *Timothy* 7. *Timothy* is worthy of notice for another reason. It came from America, its authors were the great David Belasco and W. J. Hurlbutt, and its star was the greatly beloved Cyril Maude, who had reigned for years as actor-manager at the Haymarket and Playhouse. It was received in dead silence. There was no disturbance at the end and no booing. The whole audience just dispersed in dead silence. Maybe they were stunned. It was the custom to do this in America so perhaps this was a tribute from a 1921 audience in London to an American play they did not like. It had never happened before, and has never happened since.

There was one play at another theatre which almost equalled it. This got worse and worse as it went on. Early applause died away into grim silence. The curtain fell on an audience which seemed unable to make a sound. Even the "gods" sat there motionless and dumb, but there arose a man from amongst them maybe stronger than all the rest. He stood up in his place and put on his overcoat. In silence he ascended the stairs to the back of the gallery. Then he turned and faced the stage. He said, very quietly and with great clarity: "Well, goodnight, all!" He put on his hat and departed on tiptoe as if from a chamber of death. It was the only possible epitaph . . . and the most deadly ever known.

To resume the failures of 1921. Royalty, *A Social Convenience* 71, *The Cinema Lady* 3, *Two Jacks and a Jill* 22, *The Speckled Band* (revival) 20; St James's, *Daniel* 45, *Emma* 22, *Threads* 28, another revival of *The Speckled Band* 98, (all those were staged by Lyn Harding, a magnificent actor but unfortunate when he tried management, his performance in *The Speckled Band* was always amazing); Strand *The Trump Card* 61, *The Thing That Matters* 30. All those plays had excellent casts. There were two more short runs which will be dealt with when a period of the management of ReandeaN comes under review.

Now, as to musical productions—again the story is brighter, but there are some bad patches, too.

The redoubtable recruit to theatreland, William Gaunt, produced his own musical show at the Adelphi, dispensing with the help of Grossmith and Laurillard. W. H. Berry was still resident comedian which was an asset, and there was also Robert Michaelis, one of the best romantic heroes musical comedy ever had, with Thorpe Bates and Sylvia Leslie. The music was by Ivor Novello and the play was called *The Golden Moth*. It ran for 281 performances, a short run as compared with those scored by the Butt musicals at the same theatre such a little time previously. The story was a version of *Robert Macaire*. Ivor wrote a beautiful song for Thorpe Bates called "Dear Eyes that Shone".

A Pinero play was adapted to music—one of his best farces, called *The Schoolmistress*. Its musical title was *My Nieces*, and it was played first at the Kingsway and then at the Aldwych. The leading parts were played by Ralph Lynn and Binnie Hale, who made a big success. She was then only about 22 years old. *My Nieces* ran for 171 performances.

Robey en Casserole at the Alhambra ran for only 108, as against the 349 of *Johnny Jones* which had preceded it.

Daly's kept the flag flying with *Sybil*. This play had been on the shelf for a long time, for George Edwardes had originally bought it in Vienna. It suffered because its music had been played by orchestras all over London. But with José Collins, Harry Welchman and Huntley Wright—back in his old home—it ran for 347 nights.

The Empire made a bold attempt to stage light opera in the form of *The Rebel Maid*. The music was by Montague Phillips. It was "costume" and so the comedy was difficult, and the "book" was very involved. It had a fine cast, including Walter Passmore, Thorpe Bates, Hayden Coffin and Clara Butterworth, who had made a big success at the Empire in *The Lilac Domino*, but it only ran for 111 performances. A public now intent on dancing had not a great deal of use for rather heavy light opera. But Thorpe Bates sang a song in it which stopped the show and is still popular, called "The Fishermen of England," and how well he sang it!

At the Gaiety there was the disaster of *Faust on Toast*, which has already been mentioned. It was an attempt to revive the old form of Burlesque and it failed utterly, but it introduced to the Gaiety a man who was later to bring back success when it was sadly needed; his name was Firth Shephard. Even the production by George Grossmith and the presence of Jack Buchanan and Robert Hale in the cast could not save *Faust On Toast*.

Albert de Courville produced a revue called *Pins and Needles* at the Royalty and later took it to the Gaiety. Edmund Gwenn and Alfred Lester—the never-to-be-forgotten "Peter Doody" of *The Arcadians* —were in it but it did not succeed. It ran for 204 performances between both the theatres, but business at the Gaiety was so bad that de Courville stuck up a notice at the stage door; "Abandon Hope All Ye Who Enter Here." Yet such a short time before the Gaiety had been the brightest place in London.

This bad beginning had worse behind. *Pins and Needles* was followed by a musical comedy from the French entitled *The Little Girl In Red*.

It had a first-class cast and lovely Margaret Bannerman in the lead.
Yet, despite some very good stuff in it, it only ran for 33 performances.
The story behind that play was fantastic. It had everything which
one reads about in novels dealing with theatre and a good deal more.
Its initial trouble was that it was under-capitalized, and the man who
managed it, despite heroic endeavours, could never catch up with
the demands made upon it. He worked nobly to that end and did his
best to avoid disaster. I remember a cheque for £2,000 being handed
over by a backer at a coffee stall in Piccadilly at 2 a.m. After the
first night a supper party was given at a nearby hotel. It was just as
fabulous as the rest of the story. The party was given, ostensibly, by
a rich young man about town, though there are doubts as to whether
he ever knew he was the host. The girl in whom he was interested did
not attend the party; she went off with another swain. That cast a
damper, to say the least of it. However there were lots of celebrities
there and champagne flowed like water. Everybody made speeches,
some clear, some incoherent. One girl began to speak and then after
a few words, said "Oh, golly, I feel Uncle Dick!" She was hurried
from the room. In the small hours two of the guests who disliked
each other had a fresh quarrel and fought it out with chairs. I have
always wondered if the hotel ever got paid for that party; the odds
were against it.

In 1921 *Chu Chin Chow* ended its record run at His Majesty's
theatre. People could hardly believe it; it seemed part of the established order of things. Double prices were charged for the last performance and the theatre could have been sold out ten times over.
When the announcement of the withdrawal was made, a lady came
to see Oscar Asche at the stage door and was shown into his dressing-
room. "Mr Asche," she said, "my son and I were at the first night of
Chu Chin Chow. He was, of course, in the Army then. Whenever he
came home on leave we came to see this play. I booked two seats for
the last performance, despite the fact that my son was killed in
France in the last week of the war, but I shall sit in one stall
and my son's cap will be in the other. I think he will be there,
too . . ."

Oscar Asche made a big fortune out of *Chu Chin Chow* but spent the
lot. He decided to do another Oriental show and wrote it himself
with music by Percy Fletcher. Frederick Norton, the composer of
Chu Chin Chow refused to write any more after that phenomenal
success; he was too terrified of Income Tax. This new play was
called *Cairo* and was described as a "Mosaic in Music and Mime."
Asche played in it himself, as did his wife, Lily Brayton, and
there were many of the Chu Chin Chow favourites in the
cast.

It is never easy to do the same thing twice in the theatre, *Cairo* ran for a mere 267 performances, as against the 2288 of its predecessor. It had not the stable background of "The Forty Thieves," which was really the story of *Chu Chin Chow*. Asche put almost everything possible into the production and to the eye it was a thing of beauty; perhaps he put in too much. But it was far too near its record-breaking rival. However, there was one scene which, for splendour of setting, lighting and production, brought the audience to its feet, cheering. In an old and ruined Egyptian palace, the villain of the piece gave a party, saying it was probably a place wherein "Cleopatra and her countless lovers, ages ago did carouse, disport and sin." A line of flickering, flaming braziers competed with the moonlight which drenched the scene. All was silence. Then a perfect tidal wave of humanity, half-naked, howling, singing, laughing and shouting broke over the stage. The brass blared, cymbals crashed and drums thundered and throbbed as that mob went seemingly crazy. Everything was bizarre, fantastic, utterly uninhibited. Women who seemed almost nude were raised aloft on the shoulders of men, to be dragged down and embraced in abandoned attitudes by other men. Girls like Furies, with flowing hair of green, red and all other hues, hurled themselves on the villain who sat enthroned like a Prince, smothered him with lascivious caresses and fought for his favour. It was wildly virile, a very whirlpool of colour, noise and ceaseless movement. When the orgy was at its height, the curtain fell so suddenly that it took the audience by surprise. Then almost immediately it rose again on a picture which left them breathless. The noise, the movement and the music had gone. There was silence. The crowd of revellers worn out with excess were strewn about in heaps everywhere, utterly exhausted. It was like a picture by Doré. As an example of the power of contrast, it was unique. Then came the cheers. 1921 was a bad year, but that scene has never been excelled.

The Chauve Souris did a London season and became popular, largely through their originator and compère, Balieff, and his quaint manner of rendering his quainter English.

The London Hippodrome staged *The Peep Show*, which ran for 417 performances. This fine, colourful show was produced by that great man of the theatre, Julian Wylie, who had succeeded Albert de Courville as producer in chief at the Hippodrome. It was full of good things. The dances and ensembles were devised by Gus Sohlke, a curious little man from some unspecified part of Middle Europe, who looked like a little Buddha. Gus never completely mastered the English language, but he was very fond of the sound of words and, if he heard one which appealed to him, he would use it irrespectively of its meaning. I remember him saying to the dancers to whom he had been teaching a most intricate routine: "Girls, dat's better. But I

want dat you should do it again, and dis time, do it with impunity."
They understood him. He worked with Julian Wylie on the pantomimes, too, and Julian was King of Pantomime. He did a dozen or
so every Christmas, and one at the Hippodrome while he ruled
there. Gus Sohlke went around the provincial cities to do the dances,
but he never knew the names of the places or the pantomimes. To
him, Newcastle was always "Newcastle on the Rhine," "Babes in the
Wood" became "Babes in the Boots;" "Puss in Boots" became
"Puss in the Woods;" "Dick and der Vittington" was a great
favourite of his. He went for a holiday once in the West Country and
was enchanted by the scenery. On being asked which place he liked
best he replied at once "Comelli." Comelli was the name of a famous
dress-designer but Gus's friends understood him to mean Clovelly.
C. B. Cochran, the master showman, was in charge at the London
Pavilion. In 1921 he staged there *Fun of the Fayre*, which ran into 1922,
with 230 performances. Evelyn Laye played the lead and dear old
Arthur Roberts appeared, too, nearing the end of his long life but
nowhere near the end of his gags. There were also the Dolly Sisters,
those amazing ladies from Hungary. Cochran always liked a dash of
the Continent in his shows and he had a large dash in this one, for,
besides the Dolly Sisters, there were the Fratellini Brothers, clowns
who were the rage of Paris and who excelled in the circus ring. They
were only a moderate success in *Fun of the Fayre*. There was also
"Trini," who was, Cochran claimed, the loveliest girl in the world.
He had found her in Madrid. She really was something to look at.
Those Cochran revues at the London Pavilion were highlights of the
1920's. He was a master of publicity and did everything in excellent
taste. He preferred, however, pastel shades and undertones when it
came to décor. The humour of his shows was never his strongest
point, and that was where he sometimes fell down. He would, on
occasion, let his love of the Circus bind him to the more intimate
requirements of the stage.

His first nights, to the end of his life, were great social events.
They were positively choked with celebrities and to attend one con-
ferred quite social status. It is not always wise to have such an array
of brilliance all gathered together at the same time in a theatre. P. L.
Mannock, for many years dramatic and film critic of the *Daily
Herald* and also a wit, put this in a nutshell. "At every Cochran
First Night," he said, "there are always two shows—one in front of
and one behind the curtain. And it sometimes happens that the one
in front is the more brilliant of the two."

In 1921, Cochran was riding high. He had for some time been
ruling the old Oxford Music Hall, which he had made into a theatre.
In 1921 he had it rebuilt and altered beyond recognition and staged
a revue there called *The League of Notions*, a palpable hit at the

League of Nations. It ran for 357 performances. At Christmas 1921, he staged a pantomime at the Oxford, *Babes in the Wood*, in which The Dolly Sisters and the Fratellinis appeared. It was rather an odd pantomime.

There was a delightful musical comedy at the Prince of Wales's entitled *The Gipsy Princess*, with music by Emmerich Kalman. There were back-stage ructions, however, for the capital was insufficient for the purpose. Writs poured in. The manager of the show was quite unperturbed. He sat at his desk as solicitors' clerks brought in these unwelcome documents. "What, more of them?" he would say "Just put them on the table, my dear fellows, wherever you can find room." *The Gipsy Princess* transferred to the Strand Theatre and scored in all 204. It deserved a longer run, but internal dissension killed it.

Charlot reigned as a king of revue, one of the best of them all. There have been few managers with a greater flare for spotting talent than he. He stands second only to the great George Edwardes in that respect. He had a revue at the Prince of Wales's in 1921 which was one of his best. It was called *A to Z* and, indeed, it contained almost everything, including the Trix Sisters, Gertrude Lawrence and Jack Buchanan. Most of the music was by Ivor Novello in his best light manner, and a song of his gave Jack Buchanana great hit—"And Her Mother Came Too." It is still sung.

A to Z was not only a fine show, but it did something of value. It gave that unique artiste Gertrude Lawrence her first leading part in London. She had been on the stage since she was a child. Lee White and Clay Smith, two celebrated revue artistes, saw her on tour in a play called *Money for Nothing* and spoke to Charlot about her. He brought her to town in 1916 as a dancer and understudy to poor ill-fated Billie Carlton in his revue at the Vaudeville called *Some*. She played that part on the subsequent tour and in 1917 she was back at the Vaudeville as principal understudy in *Cheep*. She played for all the "leads" on various occasions. She played Beatrice Lillie's part in *Tabs* for two months in 1918 and she was also in another Charlot show called *Buzz Buzz*. In 1920 she became leading lady in the cabaret at Murray's Club, London's first real cabaret show, and she toured in "The Midnight Frolics," but that Christmas found her understudying again, this time for Phyllis Dare in *Aladdin*, Julian Wylie's pantomime at the London Hippodrome. Then followed a music-hall tour with Walter Williams. Charlot then judged her ready for stardom, and she became leading lady in *A to Z*. She conquered London and the show ran for 433 performances.

A musical comedy from America came to the Queen's called *Mary*. Despite tuneful music and the presence of Evelyn Laye and Ralph

Lynn it only ran for 90 performances. But that was superb compared with a revue called *Fantasia* which followed it at the same theatre. That was so little to the public taste that after eight performances it was taken off, remodelled and reproduced under the title of *Put and Take*, a gesture to a game which was the craze of the moment. But the public did not put their money down or take to the show. It only lasted for twenty performances under its new name. It is worth remembering that in the cast was Eric Blore—destined to be a film star, and a wonderful "butler" in Hollywood pictures—who died so recently. He never acquired an American accent; English was good enough for him. That celebrated war-time Concert Party, "Splinters" filled the Christmas gap at the Queen's.

There was a show at the Royalty which was inspired by great success of *The Co-optimists*, but it fell between two stools. It was neither a full-sized concert party as was *The Co-optimists* show, nor a genuine revue. It hovered and did not succeed, yet it was a good show as far as material went, and full of stars. In it Laddie Cliff featured "Coal Black Mammie." During its run a young man named Douglas Furber was added to the cast as a raconteur. He was an amateur and it was his first stage job. He became one of the most successful and prolific writers of musical-play libretti and also of revues. It was called *Ring Up*.

Charlot was at the Vaudeville in 1921, as well as at the Prince of Wales's. At the Vaudeville he staged three revues, *Puss Puss*, *Now and Then*, and *Pot Luck*.

The firm of Grossmith and Laurillard, as such, had ceased to be. Laurillard had left the combination and his place was taken by J. A. E. Malone, a far more experienced and knowledgeable man of the theatre than "Laurie". Indeed he had been right-hand man to George Edwardes. The new firm celebrated its entrance at the Winter Garden by presenting *Sally*. This had music by Jerome Kern, one of the best American composers of the period, and there was a Butterfly Ballet the music of which was by the great Victor Herbert. *Sally* was a first-class show and a big success, running for 383 performances. Playing the lead was an American girl from Kansas City, who had been seen in London once before, dancing with Carl Hyson in Cochran's *London, Paris and New York* at the Pavilion in 1920. She was married to Carl Hyson and had started as an exponent of ballroom dancing. George Grossmith snapped her up for the Winter Garden. She was so pretty that the audience gasped when they saw her and broke into applause. She danced divinely, she could sing and she could act. On the first night of *Sally* she captured London. Her name—Dorothy Dickson. With her in *Sally* were George Grossmith and, of course, Leslie Henson.

When the proportion of successful musical shows is contrasted

G. Grossmith, Jnr.

Anna Pavlova, the peerless.

W. H. Berry as Christian Veit, the Court Glass Maker, in *Lilac Time*, the popular operetta.

Norman McKinnell, one of the most powerful of actors.

with those of straight plays in 1921, it is easy to see in what direction lay the taste of the public. It should also be borne in mind that when failures occurred they were mostly because of inexperienced management. Success lay firmly in the grasp of the Old Brigade. But new blood was making its mark, as will soon be seen.

CHAPTER VI

Vignette of a Management

AMONGST the welter of inexperience and mediocrity which had come into the theatre during the First World War and immediately after it, there was one management which, although new, aimed at and achieved a very high standard indeed, as high as that of the actor-managers, and yet succeeded in being modern without being cheap and vulgar and looking to youth as much as to experienced age. It was called ReandeaN—that being a combination of the names of the two men who controlled it, Alec L. Rea and Basil Dean.

These two men, complete opposites in manner, had one great bond between them, a genuine love of the theatre and what it stood for. They had come together first in Liverpool in 1911. Dean had been with Miss Horniman in Manchester at her famous theatre, the Gaiety, where he played many parts and learnt a great deal. He had gone on acting after he left there, had written a play or two and was then invited by Miss Darragh, a celebrated actress who had done excellent seasons of Shakespeare and good plays in Manchester, to come to Liverpool and help in founding a theatre movement there. In this a good actor named Charles Kenyon was interested. So was Alec L. Rea, son of the Rt. Hon. Russell Rea, M.P. Alec Rea was engaged in business in Liverpool as a ship-owner and merchant, and he loved the theatre. He was also a man of considerable wealth. Basil Dean joined this group and the result was an experimental season at Kelly's Theatre; from that arose the Liverpool Repertory Theatre, of which he became a Director with Rea, who was also Chairman.

Dean worked there, doing remarkable things, until he went to Birmingham to be technical adviser in charge of the construction of the now famous Birmingham Repertory Theatre. In 1912-1913 he was associated with Sir Herbert Tree at His Majesty's Theatre. The War came in 1914 and Dean joined the Cheshire Regiment, being gazetted Captain in 1916. In January 1917 he was transferred to the War Office and appointed Head of the Entertainment Branch of the Navy and Army Canteen Board (NACB). He built garrison theatres, toured plays for the troops and organized the first proper entertainment an army ever had. It was to serve as his foundation for the creation of ENSA in the Second World War.

When peace came, Dean entered into a partnership with Alec L. Rea under the title of ReandeaN Ltd. This firm, which was to provide one of the brightest pages of theatre history between the two World Wars—it may well be the brightest—commenced operations in 1919 at the Aldwych Theatre with *Sacred and Profane Love*. Dean produced every play ReandeaN presented. There followed *The Blue Lagoon* at the Prince of Wales's in 1920—a big success. Then they leased the St Martin's Theatre and really began operations.

It seemed to be, and was, an ideal combination. Rea was a business man and rich and adored the theatre. He was a smallish man of very quiet habit. He never shouted or raged. He had wide-open eyes and on his very pleasant face was always an expression of anticipated happiness. Perhaps that happiness was realized, although it cost him a good deal of money. He dressed well and in good taste and was given to wearing spats. He had a kindly nature and charming manners, which made him popular with everyone. He would do very nice things for people when they were in need of help and make no fuss about it. He had no drive or attack and perhaps not a very strong will. But in those respects the firm was well served by Basil Dean, who had them in full measure. Rea was Chairman of the Company and held the purse-strings, but he was always a bit in awe of the masterful Dean and could seldom, if ever, say "No."

There was another man in the outfit, and he was a genius. This was George W. Harris, who supplied the artistic side. He designed and painted the scenery, did the décor and gave advice. He was a wonderful craftsman and artist. He always caught the atmosphere of any play and seemed able to give the players an aura which was exactly right for them. Some of his scenes were worthy of the Royal Academy, yet they were always perfectly practical for stage use. Much of the success ReandeaN achieved was due to George Harris. His settings for *Hassan* and *Will Shakespeare*, exactly right in every respect and filled with atmosphere and beauty, will be remembered by all who saw them. He died all too soon.

The business manager of ReandeaN was E. P. Clift, who is still in the forefront of producing managers today. A man of experience, he had served with Dean in the NACB wartime organization; he had actually managed the very first Garrison Theatre and so he joined the new set-up.

In 1921, ReandeaN presented and Basil Dean produced *Just Like Judy* at the St Martin's. It was a comedy by an experienced dramatist, Ernest Denny, but it only ran for 18 performances. It was done with polish, style and a first-class cast, included in which was a young actor named Clive Brook, who became a great film star and flourishes today. Their next production, *Over Sunday*, by William Hurlbut, only ran for 20 performances. Everything possible for it in the way of production was done by Basil Dean and in its distinguished cast was a young actor named Malcolm Keen, then at the beginning of a long and brilliant career. These two initial failures did not daunt ReandeaN, for they already had *The Blue Lagoon* to their credit at the Prince of Wales's and at the St Martin's they had done *The Skin Game*, which was Galsworthy at his best and ran for 349 performances.

In 1921 they were steadily making their mark. At the St. Martin's, in 1921, Dean produced *The Wonderful Visit*, notable because it was the work of H. G. Wells and St John Ervine, adapted from H. G. Wells's story about an angel who came to earth. The trouble about this play was that, although it was a fine story in novel form, it wavered a bit in stage medium. It was by turns comedy, melodrama and high morality. A vicar had been decrying the cruelty of mankind. He said they would shoot an angel if one appeared. And, of course, it happened. The vicar dozed off. Darkness fell, a great rhododendron bush suddenly sparkled with fairylike lights, strains of unearthly but melodious music filled the air. Out from the bush stepped a beautiful youth in a silvery tunic, bare-armed and bare-legged, with shining silvery wings. The vicar believed in his angelic visitor and invited his parishioners to meet the visitor in his vicarage. The rustics were not impressed. They guyed the phenomenon, they had no belief in angels at all. A titled lady, who should have known better, was the ringleader. The poor vicar "lost face" and there was much moralizing—it must be confessed of a rather obvious nature. And, of course, the angel got shot and wounded. It was naturally the duty of every sportsman to take a pop at so strange a bird. The angel went back to Heaven and the vicar woke up.

This may sound banal in the telling but the play had some moments of queer beauty, most of which were supplied by Basil Dean and George Harris between them. Lighting and scenery were lovely and imaginative. The angel, using a War Memorial as his platform, appealed to Heaven for guidance. The sky lit up as if indeed Heaven was shining through. It was a touch of magic. The eventual departure of the angel in fire and flame, which might so easily have resembled an exit of a pantomime demon, was so well contrived that it had the grandeur of the Old Testament and Elijahs's chariot of fire. The stagecraft made a deep impression because of its gifted imagination.

There was a magnificent cast, with J. H. Roberts as the Vicar, Miss Compton—and there is not her counterpart on the stage today —as Lady Hammerglow, young people like Malcolm Keen and Moyna Macgill—a lovely girl and sensitive actress then just emerging from the understudy stage and given a chance by Dean—and Harold French as the angel. At that time he was a young actor who had played parts at the Liverpool and Birmingham Repertory

Theatres, and a few others elsewhere, and had been with ReandeaN in *The Blue Lagoon*. He had a chance here and he took it, playing a very difficult part splendidly. Only Owen Nares, at that time, would have been an alternative. So ReandeaN continued their encouragement of youth. *The Wonderful Visit* played only 28 times at the St. Martin's, but it made a mark, all the same.

Then Basil Dean produced for the firm, at the Aldwych, *Love Among The Paint Pots* by Gertrude Jennings. It ran for 73 performances. Also at that theatre, for a matinée, they produced *The New Morality* by Harold Chapin and did it well. At another matinee they did *The First and the Last*, a drama in three acts by John Galsworthy, with Malcolm Keen, Owen Nares and Meggie Albanesi in the cast. Dean's capacity for work was prodigious.

At their own theatre they had done a noteworthy job by producing a play by a new dramatist, Clemence Dane, called *A Bill of Divorcement*. That was on 4th March, 1921. It was an instantaneous success and a new dramatist was acclaimed. The calls for the author were the most enthusiastic heard in a theatre for years. Miss Dane had, indeed, written a fine play .Her theme, divorce, was very much in people's minds owing to the findings of a Royal Commission on suggested alterations in the divorce laws. Two of the recommendations had just become law, those sanctioning divorce after five years of incurable insanity or three years of habitual drunkenness. The action took place on Christmas Day 1932, so she went forward eleven years in time, but she would have pleased Dickens's Mr Curdle, for the unities were strictly observed. The play is too well known for its story to be told. That original production was superbly acted by all concerned, especially by Lilian Braithwaite as the wife, Malcolm Keen as the returned husband, Aubrey Smith as the husband-to-be and, Meggie Albanesi as the daughter of the divorced couple. The scene in which the ex-lunatic husband made his appeal to the wife who had divorced him will never be forgotten by those who saw it. Malcolm Keen and Lilian Braithwaite rose to the greatest heights and swept their audience with them. Meggie Albanesi gave an inspired performance too. Basil Dean's production was masterly.

Clemence Dane (Winifred Ashton to her friends), born in London, is the complete mixture of all the arts. This is not a case of being Jack of all Trades and mistress of none, for she is a leading dramatist, novelist and poetess, a splendid painter and first-class sculptress. Until she left the stage she was also a very good actress, playing under the name of Diana Cortis. That practical stage experience explained the excellence of her technique as dramatist. She loves the district of Covent Garden, where she lived for years, and her name Clemence Dane derives, of course, from the church of St Clement Danes in the Strand nearby. In the Theatre Royal, Drury Lane, amongst the great ones of the historic playhouse, stands a bust of Ivor Novello which is her work. Through *A Bill of Divorcement*, in 1921, she took her place amongst the dramatists who matter, and she has held it ever since.

She had another play produced that year, presented by ReandeaN at the Shaftesbury Theatre on 17th November, and called *Will Shakespeare*. This did not repeat the success scored with *A Bill of Divorcement*. It was a very different sort of play. Miss Dane let her imagination loose on the great figure of Shakespeare and also on the only slightly lesser figure of Christopher Marlowe. She presented a picture which was a challenge to all Shakespearean students, for in her play Shakespeare killed Marlowe in a fit of jealous rage over Mary Fitton, whom Miss Dane identified as the Dark Lady of the Sonnets. Nobody can ever be quite sure about the mysterious details of Marlowe's death, but this was a very startling theory. Indeed, the Swan of Avon did not show up too well all through the play. It ran for 62 performances and deserved more, for it was a good strong drama, well contrived and with some real purple patches. Miss Dane knows how to write parts which give the players a chance and she did so in this play. Although it did not reach its century, it deserves its place as a notable dramatic event of 1921. Dean produced it and gave it a fine cast, with Philip Merivale as Shakespeare, Moyna Macgill as Ann, Irene Rookes, a wonderful actress, as Mrs Hathaway, Arthur Whitby as Henslowe, a most characteristic performance and the best of all for "period." Haidee Wright, that amazing and sensitive actress, was a vivid Queen Elizabeth, Mary Clare, then just starting her career, was Mary Fitton, and Claude Rains was Kit Marlowe. Playing a tiny part in a vision-scene, that of Queen Margaret, was a very young actress indeed, named Flora Robson. *Will Shakespeare* was scenically beautiful, thanks to George Harris, and the production of Basil Dean was most imaginative. It was a play of which any management might have been proud and it shone amongst the welter of mediocrity which surrounded it. Perhaps it was before its time, and the times themselves were out of joint in 1921. Miss Dane has written many successes since then, and remains the same gracious lady, full of love for the theatre.

The ReandeaN partnership already shone like gold in the dingy tapestry of the 1920's. The only pity was that it did not last for much longer, but in 1921 there were still several years ahead of it.

Perhaps it was not possible for this partnership between Rea and Dean to be enduring, although they always remained friends and were to come together later. Even then, Basil Dean was not the easiest man in the world with whom to work. He is still, and justly, a figure of distinction in the world of the theatre. He has vast experience, he can spot talent when it is only just sprouting and, when it comes to actual stage work, he is a skilled craftsman. Somewhere within him is a poet, a disciple of Beauty. But he is a lone wolf. He does not make friends easily. He wears about him armour which can be pierced and his humanity beneath it laid open, but few people will risk the task of finding those chinks. His personality is very strong; he is a fighter and cannot brook opposition. He will attack, head down like a bull charging; yet so often a strategic approach would win the victory which a frontal attack fails to achieve. He has tremendous force which he has never tried to harness. He sees what he believes to be his way and that is his path to follow, come what may. One of his troubles is that naturally he is a shy man with a sensitive nature, and has covered that up with his armour of force until he cannot shed it. Very few people really know him He is a tremendous worker and the job in hand swamps everything else and limits his outlook. To him that is all that matters and he goes at it, hammer and tongs. The object he has to create, the play he has to produce—those are all that matter. The people in it become to him mere puppets which must respond to his direction. He is a hard master to serve, though he is probably quite unaware of it. As this story shows already and will show still more as it proceeds, many of the leading players of today have much for which to thank him. It is doubtful if they ever did so. He himself never bestows praise at the time, although he is perfectly conscious of where it is due and, if opportunity arises, will give it in full measure later on. But praise at the right and critical moment is of such great value.

A really keen sense of humour would have saved him so much trouble in his brilliant, if difficult and adventurous, career, but he has little time for present laughter: one must drive on. Basil has done fine service to the theatre and was doing it in full measure in the 1920's, when such service was badly needed. He has his failings and nowadays he probably realizes many of them, but his theatre qualities are beyond reproach. ReandeaN in the persons of Rea and Dean kept the theatre tradition in the forefront when it was nearly dead. Both of them, in their own way, loved the theatre and believed in it—Alec Rea until he died. Basil Dean does so still.

CHAPTER VII

1922—and Little Improvement

IF 1921 had been a bad theatrical year, 1922 showed little improvement. Apart from one or two successes which had lasted on from the previous year only forty plays out of all those produced in London that year ran for 100 performances or over. And, of those, fifteen were musical. All the same, there were some important beginnings, and a steady rise of new names. There was a big proportion of short runs—no less than forty-two plays failed to reach fifty performances—and in that rather deplorable total revivals and seasons such as *Grand Guignol* are not counted. The only satisfaction was that some of the plays which succeeded in running were good, but others which ran were not so good.

The dancing craze did not diminish; it increased. New forms of dance bands came into being, the first of them being The Dixieland Jazz Band. Before long bands were to be top-line attractions—ousting individual stars. The most serious menace to the theatre, however, was not a band, but a new production of science and mechanism. This was Radio. In the year 1922 the British Broadcasting Company came into being and this new form of entertainment was open to everybody. It was something different and to most people it seemed like a miracle. Tens of thousands started to "listen-in" and found it an all-absorbing hobby.

The British Broadcasting Company began to make its own stars at once. They were not so much performers—although there were those, too—but announcers. The voice became all-important. These ghost voices invaded hundreds of thousands of homes, becoming unseen personalities of great power and attraction. They became friends, although invisible. Listeners fiddled with the crystal set, found the sensitive spot on the crystal on which to place the cat's whisker, and then through their earphones heard music and voices. Children's Hour was a great delight to the youngsters; here was something which came into their own homes especially for them. The aunts and uncles of Broadcasting became beloved; perhaps most beloved of all, by listeners of all ages, was the voice of Uncle Arthur, who was Arthur Burrows. One would say he was the outstanding personality of 1922.

This new force certainly made the footlights flicker. Many pooh-

poohed the whole thing as a mere craze. "It won't last," they said. "People will soon get tired of sitting at home, crouching over their sets and just listening." But that did not happen. More and more became converted to this new thing. Then the big names in the entertainment world lent their talents and their voices to it, led by George Robey. The Marconi Company put a crystal set *de luxe* on the market. Far from being a craze, broadcasting became part of everyday life and listening was a necessity. The newspapers gave it great prominence, for no payment. It was News. This was the most serious menace the theatre had ever faced, worse than the cinema. But that was not as yet realized.

However, the theatre went on. Those plays which succeeded in passing the century mark should be examined. *The Way of An Eagle*, dramatized by Ethel M. Dell herself from her own best-seller, ran for 150 performances at the Adelphi with Godfrey Tearle in the lead. There was a good play called *The Wheel* at the Apollo by James Bernard Fagan which lasted for 137 performances. *Quarantine* by F. Tennyson Jesse at the Comedy just managed to touch 102, with Owen Nares and that rising young actress Edna Best in the cast. At the Criterion things were a bit better. There *The Dippers*, by Ben Travers—his success as a farce-writer just around the corner—put up a run of 175 performances, with Binnie Hale and Cyril Maude in it.

The Theatre Royal, Drury Lane, had closed after the long run of *The Garden of Allah*, so that its auditorium could be remodelled and reconstructed, and the beautiful result can be seen today. It re-opened on 20th April, 1922, with *Decameron Nights*, a sort of musical drama. It was a Decameron story told as only Drury Lane could tell it, with great colourful scenes, vast crowds, dazzling costumes, sword fights and big effects—a drama reinforced by music. There was quite a sensation in a scene which showed some monks rescuing an apparently nude woman from the sea, while the waves roared, dashed over rocks and burst into spray around them. Sir Alfred Butt now reigned at Drury Lane with Arthur Collins; J. L. Sacks had an interest in that show, too. Herman Finck, who had left the Palace Theatre to be musical director at Drury Lane, wrote the music which included a striking item, "The March of the Crusaders." *Decameron Nights* gave the new Old Drury a fine start with 370 performances. Amidst a perfect welter of failures the Duke of York's Theatre found one success, an American play called *The Broken Wing*, which was a novelty, as it concerned an aeroplane which had crashed. Later it was done as a musical play under the title of *Silver Wings*. But *The Broken Wing* was remarkable for the performance of Thurstan Hall and of a young actor named Francis Lister, who played the airman who had crashed and gave a fine study of a man struggling to control his shattered nerves. This play ran for 119 performances and deserved to do more.

The Empire did not have much luck. It managed to get 129 nights out of a revue called *The Smith Family*, which had a sort of story running through it and in which Harry Tate played.

The incomparable and irrepressible Seymour Hicks produced and played in *The Man in Dress Clothes* at the Garrick Theatre. He gave a superb performance and the younger generation always identified him with that part. There was a portrait of him in that character in the Royal Academy. Despite a good Press, it started very slowly, but it boomed into success by a special method. One evening Lord Northcliffe, the mighty Press Lord, went to see it and was much impressed. Hicks told him they were having a bit of a struggle and Northcliffe said he would help. He issued instructions that there must be a "story" in the *Daily Mail* every day drawing attention to *the Man in Dress Clothes* and its merits. "This," he said, "MUST go in." Later this sort of thing became known in Fleet Street as a "Must." *The Man In Dress Clothes* was the first "Must." As a result it ran for 232 nights, a long time in that unlucky year, and was later frequently revived.

The Globe got 164 performances out of *The Laughing Lady* by Alfred Sutro. It had a fine cast including Godfrey Tearle, Violet Vanbrugh, Edith Evans—steadily rising to the top—and delightful Marie Lohr. On 7th June there was a play produced at the Haymarket which ran until the January of the following year, 267 times. It deserved to do so for it was *The Dover Road*, dramatist A. A. Milne at his best. Henry Ainley played the strange gentleman who altered the course of some married lives and Allan Aynesworth his no less strange butler.

ReandeaN had two productions that year, one at His Majesty's, as it was then called, and one at the St Martin's, their home ground. The play at His Majesty's was a really noble effort. It was *East of Suez*, by Somerset Maugham. It brought the mystery of the East to the theatre, full of drama, menace and excitement. Basil Dean's production was a masterpiece. In *East of Suez* Meggie Albanesi gave a very beautiful performance, one of the best of the many bests that glowing young actress provided. She was a curious girl, wrapped up in her calling, living on her nerves and always dissatisfied with herself. She always thought that she could have done better and would dissolve into tears of disappointment. Yet she had held her audience enthralled and nobody save herself was conscious of a flaw. She loved rehearsals, they could never be too long or too arduous for her; she was theatre through and through and she owed much to Basil Dean, and admitted it with pride. She had a beauty all of her own, curious dark, silent beauty which compelled. *East of Suez* was worthy of the traditions of the theatre in which it was produced and a feather in the cap of ReandeaN. It saw the year out at Her Majesty's, running for 214 performances until 3rd March 1923.

That management did as well at the St Martin's in 1922. There they produced a double bill, made up of *Loyalties* by John Galsworthy and *Shall We Join the Ladies?* by J. M. Barrie. Two plays, by the most distinguished dramatists of the time—that shows what sort of work ReandeaN were doing in that undistinguished year of 1922.

Loyalties was a drama in Galsworthy's best manner, familiar today because of revivals on stage and television. It made a deep impression on the playgoers of 1922 with its impeccable casting, and production by Basil Dean. Two small parts in the play were performed by two young actors, Clifford Mollison and Ian Hunter; indeed, the last-named doubled as "A Constable" and "A Young Clerk." Both of those names are famous today. *Shall We Join the Ladies?* was one of the best and at the same time most tantalizing of Barrie's plays. It was in one act and the dramatist poised that eternal problem of the thriller—"Whodunit?" A murder had been committed. There was a group of people round a dinner table, on each of whom suspicion fell, but what the answer was nobody ever knew, or ever will know. Whether this was a deliberate trick by this brilliant but whimsical dramatist, or whether he really set out to write a thriller of the approved style, but embellished by his wit and imagination, could not be discovered. He just left it in the air. It is believed by those who should know that he never finished it because, when he tried to do so, he could not. His own mystery beat him, or very likely he did not see his way to making such a story as Barriesque as would be expected of him. Anyway, he left the mystery unsolved for ever. How that intrigued people and what discussion it caused! And what an impact it made on those who saw it in 1922—and still does on those who see it today.

There was a good deal of sparring between Galsworthy and Barrie as to whose play should open the evening. It was solved by Leslie Faber, who was appearing at the Playhouse as well as in *Shall We Join the Ladies?*; that play went on second to give him time. Those two productions shone like a torch in the gloom in which so many theatres were immersed.

At the Lyceum, Edmund Gwenn played *Old Bill M.P.* and got much fun out of his performance of that famous creation of Bruce Bairnsfather, with the House of Commons as a background. It ran for 159 performances. Matheson Lang had a season at the New Theatre, his usual London home in those days. He revived *Mr. Wu*, his most famous part, and got 114 performances out of it. But he did not have success with *The Great Well* by Alfred Sutro, which was performed only 70 times. It was a modern play and Lang's admirers preferred him in costume.

Gladys Cooper and Dennis Eadie played *The Second Mrs Tanqueray* at the Playhouse, with Miss Cooper as a splendid Paula and Dennis Eadie the best Aubrey Tanqueray since George Alexander. The run of 222 performances shows its success. *Lass O' Laughter* at the Queen's scored 121, with its author, Nan Marriott-Watson, in the cast. And starting at that theatre before transferring to the Globe was one of the outstanding successes of the time, *Bluebeard's Eighth Wife*, adapted by Arthur Wimperis from the French of Alfred Savoir. This play really made the name of Hugh Wakefield, who had started on the stage as a child and played all sorts of parts. He had joined the Royal Flying Corps in 1914, was demobilized in 1920 with the rank of Major, and went straight back to the stage. He had played in revue, musical comedy and straight plays, but *Bluebeard's Eighth Wife* enabled him to exploit his rich talent. The play ran for 478 performances.

If Four Walls Told, by Edward Percy, played at both the Royalty and the Savoy. In it that delightful actress Louise Hampton gave a lovely performance and some young people enhanced their rising reputations—Reginald Bach, Francis Lister, Roger Livesey and Moyna Macgill. Another Royalty production to pass the century was *The Green Cord* by Marion Bower and Anthony Ellis.

It is, however, a sign of the poor quality of many of the plays produced that revivals of older successes did very well. *Ambrose Applejohn's Adventure*, revived at the Savoy, did a further 139 shows, and *Paddy The Next Best Thing* returned to its original home to make its total up to 827. At the Shaftesbury an American thriller, *The Cat and the Canary*, did pretty well with 182 performances.

Arthur Bourchier produced a stage version of *Treasure Island* at the Strand for the Christmas season, with himself as Long John Silver and Frederick Peisley as Jim Hawkins. It was a success and has been constantly revived ever since.

Wyndham's was only saved from a very bad year by a revival of Barrie's *Dear Brutus*, which ran for 258, as against its original 365, performances.

There was an interesting season at the Court Theatre under the direction of Leon M. Lion, a distinguished actor and producer, and J. T. Grein, critic, journalist and theatre-lover, who had done splendid work for the theatre in many ways, especially in connection with the Stage Society. His presentation of Oscar Wilde's *Salome* by that club involved him in a libel action with an extraordinary character who flashed across the world in the First War period, and whose name was Pemberton Billing. He, as defendant, conducted his own defence and Grein was awarded one farthing damages. The case should never have been brought.

Jack Thomas Grein deserves his meed of remembrance. He was born a Dutchman but became naturalized here. In his time he was critic for many newspapers and he was immensely Gallic in manner and appearance; he had the courtesy of a French nobleman of the old days and addressed people whom he knew and who worked in literature or the theatre as "Cher collègue." His Independent Theatre really brought Ibsen prominently before the public. He staged *Widowers' Houses*, the first Shaw play to be seen in London. Indeed, it was from the Independent Theatre that the famous Vedrenne-Barker management arose at the Court, which almost revolutionized our Drama. And now, in 1922, Grein was at the Court himself, loving every moment of it, his round, fresh-complexioned face suffused by smiles, his silver hair gleaming and his moustache bristling with eagerness. His partner, Leon M. Lion, although born in London, was also very French in appearance and manner.

These two men at the Court in 1922 presented *The Silver Box*, *The Pigeon*, *Justice*, and *Windows* all by Galsworthy, and revivals: *The Rabbi and the Priest; Mr Garrick* by Louis N. Parker. Leon M. Lion played in most of the plays himself. Probably no money was made, but it was excellent theatre.

The Little Theatre, now bombed out of existence but which stood in John Street, Adelphi, housed a most exciting and successful *Grand Guignol* season. It had indeed become the Horror Theatre of London. Lewis Casson and Sybil Thorndike were in it.

A glance at the year's record of the theatres is a good pointer as to the state of things, and here is a list of how many plays each theatre staged. Adelphi, 2; Aldwych, 8 (some of them transfers from elsewhere); Ambassadors, 8; Apollo, 8; Court, (the J. T. Grein-Lion season) The Swedish Ballet, and revivals of *When Knights Were Bold* and *Alice In Wonderland;* Criterion, 1; Daly's, 1; Drury Lane, 1; Globe, 5; Comedy, 3 (and one of them notable as will be seen); Duke of York's, 7 (amongst them a play by Pinero called *The Enchanted Cottage* which only ran for 64 performances); The Empire, 4; Haymarket, 1; His Majesty's, 1; Kingsway, 10 (there was, however, a young actor there named Ivor Novello who already had fans waiting at the stage door); Little, 3 and the *Grand Guignol* Season; London Hippodrome, 2; London Pavilion, 1; Lyceum, 3; Lyric, 2; New, 5; New Oxford, 2; Palladium, 2; Playhouse, 2; Prince's, one short season of the Guitrys in French plays; Queen's, 5; Regent, 3; Royalty, 8; St James's, 4; St Martin's, 1; Savoy, 7; Shaftesbury, 5; Strand, 9; Vaudeville, 1; Winter Garden, 1; Wyndham's, 3 (one of them by A. E. W. Mason, called *Running Water* only lasted 28 performances). Not quite so bad as 1921, but not so good, either.

Some short runs were *A Prodigal Daughter* (Aldwych) 5; *My Son* (Ambassadors) 11; *Husbands Are a Problem* (Ambassadors) 19; *The Secret Agent* (Ambassadors) 11; *Nuts in May* (Duke of York's) 15; *Pomp and Circumstance* (Duke of York's) 18; *Destruction* (Royalty) 8; *Sarah of Soho* (Savoy) 12; *In Nelson's Days* (Shaftesbury) 3; *Nighty Night* (Shaftesbury) 17; *Angel Face* (Strand) 13. And there were many which only got to the 20, 30 and 40 mark.

Two things of merit still have to be dealt with. One of them was *Secrets* at the Comedy, a very lovely play indeed by that fine dramatist, Rudolf Besier, and May Edginton. In this Fay Compton gave an exquisite performance. She was on the stage almost all the time, portraying a woman at varying stages in her life, starting as an old lady, going back to a young girl in the full bloom of her youth, then to a young wife, and then a middle-aged mother, and ending up as an old lady again. As she changed her costumes, make-up and wigs, so she changed her character. She hit every note dead in the middle, everything was in perfect tune. Very seldom is such a *tour de force* as this to be seen and it must linger in the minds of all who beheld it. *Secrets* was definitely one of the best plays of its era and it ran for 374 performances.

The other notable event was something of a very different nature. It was a farce. It was more than that, it was the opening chapter of a big theatre adventure. It was called *Tons of Money*, written by Will Evans, a famous comedian, and "Valentine," a man who knew a lot about the theatre and wrote excellent lyrics and libretti. However, *Tons of Money* was despised and rejected of all managements. Nobody would have anything to do with it. Then a manager in a very small way—albeit he was an enormous man—named Bannister Howard, sent it to Leslie Henson, with the suggestion that he should read it with a view to making it into a musical comedy. Henson did not think much of it, but he had just embarked on a joint managerial venture with Tom Walls, Walls and Henson Ltd, and their capital was very limited indeed. Henson gave it to Tom Walls, who handed it over to the business manager of this young and not very strong firm, whose name was Reginald Highly. He read it and rather liked it. He got Tom Walls to read it, too. Tom was a man of quick decisions. "I think we'll do this in Town," he said to Henson. That comedian, who had faith in Tom's judgment, agreed, with the proviso that they must get Ralph Lynn for an important part. Lynn was then in the front rank but mostly played in musical comedy and revue. He was approached but he had another job offered. That held things up. Then the other job fell through and he joined the little outfit. They got to work. They scraped together £3,000. They sent it on tour for a few weeks and it went very well. They approached Grossmith and Malone, hoping to get them interested financially, but failed. Tom stuck to his guns. The Shaftesbury Theatre was rented—and it was not renowned for its luck. A cast was assembled which included Tom Walls (who did not appear until Act 2); Ralph Lynn; George Barrett; Ena Mason; Mary Brough (whom everyone loved); Yvonne Arnaud (slim, clever and attractive); Willie Warde; a young man named J. Robertson Hare (who even then had a furrowed brow and worried look); Madge Saunders (who was Mrs Leslie Henson and so pretty that, when she was at the Gaiety, an Eastern Potentate tried to buy her for his harem); and Sydney Lynn.

They opened the play at the Shaftesbury on what is considered, theatrically, the worst night of the year—the Thursday before Good Friday. But it was also April 13th and 13 was Tom Walls's lucky number. Henson and Tom were standing at the back of the circle, waiting for the curtain to go up. Their hearts were in their mouths. Down below, in the orchestra pit, a small band was playing under the baton of a young man named Jack Hylton, whose first London theatre band that was. Just before the curtain rose, Highly the business manager arrived with a cheque which the two directors must sign. They did so and asked what that left in the bank. "Oh, about three pounds fifteen" was the answer. And up went the curtain. The feelings of those two men can be imagined. Was this going to be lucky, or were they going to be ruined? Anything could happen . . . and it did. They sold the option on the American rights for £1,000 in the second interval and, when the final curtain fell, nothing mattered any more. *Tons of Money* was going to live up to its name. As the run proceeded, signs of success were not lacking. Tom Walls bought a Rolls-Royce; Lynn, much more careful with his money, a better car than the one he had been using; and Highly discarded his push-bike for a motor-cycle. The show was boosted. Pocket wallets bursting with what looked like £1 and 10/- notes were given away, until the authorities stopped it, and then little gilt coins resembling the vanished sovereigns flooded the town. They turn up in odd places even yet. *Tons of Money* transferred to the Aldwych on 30th October, 1922, and proceeded to make theatre history by running for 737 performances. It did more than that. It enabled those Aldwych farces to be part of the theatre for years—run on the old actor-managerial system—and that series of farces lasted for thirteen years. Only one play a year was needed. *Tons of Money* was a very bright spot indeed in 1922's chronicle.

The pivot and mainspring of the whole thing was Tom Walls. He shared the leads with Ralph Lynn and they were that wonderful combination, complete foils to each other. Tom was the producer of the farces and one of the best producers the stage ever had. He possessed not only foresight, but courage, and he always had complete confidence in himself. He was an extraordinary man. Maybe he was born a hundred years or so after his time. He was the last of the Regency Bucks, the Corinthians. He was of that stock entirely and he would have loved to live at that time. He was a man in whom sport and gambling always held the upper hand and even exceeded his very real love for the theatre. If any big sporting event was on, Tom was certain to be "off" that night, not playing in his own show. It had been so even in his young days when he was with George Edwardes playing "old men" superbly—he and O. B. Clarence were the best "old men" of the stage. He was one of the very few men who ever realized all their ambitions. He was born in Northampton, of a good family. As a boy he made up his mind to be an engine-driver, as did so many other boys when steam locomotives ruled rail traction. When he was about to leave school his father asked him what he wanted to be. Tom told him, with quiet determination. No arguments by his father could shake him. Walls senior was a sensible man. He had some friends who were officials of the railway at Northampton and to them he explained the difficulty. It was decided to give young Tom a job on the railway and the dirtiest job possible. He was put into the sheds and made to grease and oil the engines. He did not like that. He wanted to drive engines, not grease them. The explanation that a long apprenticeship was necessary before such a thing was possible did not impress him at all. He was Tom Walls—of course he could do it. One day his chance came. He was left alone with a big, new engine, which had steam up. He leapt on the footplate and drove that engine some distance down the track, to the horror of all beholders. He managed to reverse it and get it back into the shed again. Then he leapt off and ran for his life. He left that hated job. His ambition was fulfilled—he had actually driven a engine. His next ambition was to be a detective. Here he found stupid regulations which made it necessary to be a uniformed police constable first. He chafed at this but he joined the Metropolitan Police and patrolled around the actual district in which the Aldwych Theatre stands. He did not like being "on the beat," it was too slow for him. Again a chance arose. As a humble P.C. he was able to detect a small crime and bring the criminal to justice. That ambition, too, was achieved. He left the Police. Then he wanted to be an actor, and he became a very good one and liked it. He wanted to be a film star, and a film star he became. Up to his dying day he "stole" most of the pictures in which he played. He wanted to be a jockey, but physique and weight were against him. But he rode winners as a "gentleman rider" and often won at "Point-to-Points." He had

John Gielgud, beginning his career in the 1920's, as "The Baron" in *The Three Sisters* at Barnes. Beatrix Thomson as Irena.

Phyllis Dare, leading lady of the 1920's who shines today.

Isobel Elsom, star of musical plays and drama, too.

always loved and understood horses and now he wanted to train them. So, despite his theatrical activities, he also became a trainer and had some successes. But his overwhelming desire was to own and train a Derby winner. The world knows that he achieved that—with "April the Fifth."

The name of that horse brings up the matter of superstition. Ninety-nine per cent of theatrical people are superstitious and Tom was no exception. So are sportsmen as well. He had a great belief in the number 13. It might be unlucky for some but not for him. There were thirteen letters in his own name of Tom Kirby Walls. *Tons of Money* was produced on Thursday, April 13th. He always, from then on, produced his shows on the 13th unless it happened to be a Sunday. That managerial career lasted for thirteen years and produced thirteen plays. There were thirteen letters in the name of Robertson Hare, and he was in all of the farces. As a final test, there were thirteen letters in the name of April the Fifth. It is hard to find an answer to all that.

Tom was quite fearless. He cared for nobody, but many people cared for him. That caring for nobody applied only to his enemies and opponents, for he was the best friend a man could have. I was part of that Aldwych outfit and he was a very old and dear friend of mine. I hold his memory in deep affection.

Money meant little to Tom Walls, it was something to spend, to gamble with and to give away to those who needed it. But achievement meant a lot to him. Although his money bank balance was nearly always in a parlous state, his account of achievement was brimming over. Nothing worried him. His greatest fault was being absent so often from performances on account of his love of sport. He could play any game; he could use his fists, he rode to hounds, he hunted stags, which did not increase his popularity, and he loved winter sports. He was a sportsman in the best sense of the word, a generous winner, a good loser, and every inch a man. He will cross this chronicle many times, but 1922 saw the beginning of his greatness.

Now let the Musical plays enter. There the record is a bit better, though there were some failures. A musical play called *Jenny* flopped badly at the Empire, despite Edith Day and a fine cast. *The Curate's Egg*, a revue by Arthur Wimperis with music by Herman Finck and Vivian Ellis (a new name just entering the lists) and a good cast could only exist for 83 shows. Another revue which made its appeal on topicality and was called *Listening In* only survived for 26 performances at the Apollo.

The Duke of York's went in for grand opera with a version of *The Merchant of Venice* composed by Adrian Beecham, son of Sir Thomas; it was only sung 32 times. *Love's Awakening* at the Gaiety, music by

Kunneke and produced by Austen Hurgon, a king of revue who knew his job, petered out after 81 performances; and *Angel Face*, despite music by the great Victor Herbert, died after 13 shows.

Better things happened, however. *The Island King* at the Adelphi (W. H. Berry was still there) ran for 160 performances, which was not so bad, though well below the usual Berry vintage. But Daly's Theatre had a real success and well deserved it. This was *The Lady of the Rose*, which many will remember. The book was by Frederick Lonsdale, who was later to make an epoch of his own, and the music by Jean Gilbert. In the leading parts Harry Welchman and Phyllis Dare showed how romantic musical plays or light operas should be performed and sung. Phyllis Dare gave a performance of great beauty in every way. Her appearance at the top of a staircase, down which she passed like a queen, beautifully arrayed, left the audience breathless. There are no entrances like that now, since the death of Ivor Novello, and more's the pity, for they are real theatre. Phyllis Dare was the complete leading lady. She could act, sing and dance. Her Mariana in *The Lady of the Rose* was one of the best things this accomplished actress ever did.

Harry Welchman had, for him, an unusual part, for he was the villain, but he invested it with such charm and with such romance that even the dirty work won sympathy in a way which was quite remarkable. Yet he never stepped out of character, although it must be admitted that the villainy he practised was of the dashing and romantic brand. But Harry Welchman, besides being a fine singer and handsome man, was—and is—also a good actor. And in *The Lady of the Rose* he was remarkable and always received an ovation. This play ran for 507 performances, despite the fact that Robert Evett had been driven from Daly's by James White. It was a real Daly's play, for old Edwardesians had produced it for the new master. And if Evett had been driven from Daly's, he was not defeated, and he hoisted his banner on the other half of the Edwardes Empire, at The Gaiety. He did not attempt to revive the old Gaiety style; he took the atmosphere of Daly's with him and he had José Collins as leading lady. There he produced a musical play called *The Last Waltz*. with music by Oscar Straus and book by Reginald Arkell and Evett himself. Never had José Collins been in better voice, more vibrant or more commanding. Her leading man was handsome Bertram Wallis. José had been Queen of Daly's; now she become Queen of the Gaiety, for 288 nights passed before *The Last Waltz* was played for for the last time. It made history in another way, too. It was the first musical play ever broadcast from a theatre. Broadcasting headquarters were next door to the Gaiety then, in Marconi House; some of the sound effects and music used therein had leaked in through a fault in the studios during rehearsals. They gave Evett the idea which led to the first joining of hands between stage and radio.

Another very big musical success was *Polly*, an adaptation of the Gay opera which was the sequel to *The Beggars' Opera*. It was produced at the Kingsway and transferred to the Savoy running for 324 performances. The title role was played by Lilian Davies, a lovely woman with a lovely voice, whose early and tragic death robbed our stage of an ideal leading lady.

The Little Theatre produced *The Nine O'Clock Revue*, a concession to new habits on the part of the public who spun out dinner-time so as to be able to dance. It was a success too (385 performances) and in the cast were Mimi Crawford (who became the Countess of Suffolk) and incomparable Beatrice Lillie.

Julian Wylie staged one of his very best revues at the London Hippodrome, called *Round in Fifty*. This was based on Jules Verne's famous adventure story *Round the World In Eighty Days*, but as a concession to the growing trend of speed they knocked thirty days off it at the Hippodrome. All sorts of devices, including films, were used to carry on the story at top speed. It was written by Sax Rohmer, an experienced writer who gave the world many thrillers including *Dr Fu-Manchu*, and by Julian himself and his brother Lauri, who was a genius and wrote sketches of classic quality. The music was by Herman Finck and James W. Tate. George Robey was the star and the memory of him in Sing-Sing, a prisoner himself running an entertainment for the other prisoners, is one which lingers gratefully in the locker of laughter. *Round in Fifty* ran for 471 performances. That story of Jules Verne seems to bring luck, for in film form it was phenomenal.

Cochran's 1922 contribution was *Phi-Phi* at the London Pavilion. It was adapted from the French. Arthur Roberts was still there, so was Trini, and there were Woicikowsky, and June, with Evelyn Laye in the lead. Cochran got 133 performances out of it and had more comedy than usual, thanks to Walter Williams, Stanley Lupino, Jay Laurier and the aforesaid Arthur Roberts.

Whirled Into Happiness was a big musical production at the Lyric which ran for 246 performances. Billy Merson once again left the music halls to play in West End revue and his success started an ambition in the heart of that quaint little red-nosed and red-wigged comedian, who sang such popular songs as "The Spaniard Who Blighted My Life" and "On the good ship Yakihickidula." It inspired him with a desire to go into West End management himself.

The other show at the Lyric was one of those things which shows how much luck enters into the life of the Theatre. It was a musical play based on the life of Franz Schubert and the music was all from

Schubert's pen. There was a delightful production with the real atmosphere of Vienna and a fine cast. Courtice Pounds played Schubert. But despite good notices, the show hung fire. The management which had presented it got cold feet and another management took over and held on. The result was that *Lilac Time* became the rage and ran for 628 performances. It made fortunes on tour, is often revived and is played by amateurs all over the country. It just shows that in the theatre, you never know. That other celebrated light opera *Dorothy* was just such another case.

Cochran had a show at the Oxford, as well as *Phi Phi* at the Pavilion. This was *Battling Butler*. In it Jack Buchanan scored a very big personal success. There were also two real pugilists, Messrs Alexander and Hurley. It lasted for 238 "rounds."

The London Palladium presented a vast revue called *Rockets*, staged by Charles Henry, who still does the big shows at the Palladium and takes television in his stride. Its stars were Lorna and Toots Pounds and Charles Austin.

There was a different sort of production at the Regent Theatre, which had been a music hall and is now a cinema. There the Birmingham Repertory Company presented a very beautiful thing called *The Immortal Hour*, a music drama by Rutland Broughton. A special success was made by Gwen Ffrangcon-Davies. It ran for 216 nights; smart London found the way to the Euston Road and *The Immortal Hour* is now a classic.

The Vaudeville had a success in a revue called *Snap*, in which was the always delightful Clarice Mayne. It ran for 230 performances.

Grossmith and Malone, at the Winter Garden, presented *The Cabaret Girl*. It had a wonderful cast, although Leslie Henson was absent. In it was a young lady called in the programme Enid Taylor who later rose to fame as Enid Stamp-Taylor. Delightful Dorothy Dickson was the leading lady, opposite to George Grossmith himself. No wonder it ran for 462 performances.

But the combination of Gertrude Lawrence and Joseph Coyne failed, however, to make a musical comedy at the Garrick, *Dédé*, lasted for fifty performances.

There was one other notable event in that year, which left a gap not to be filled. On 7th October, 1922, Marie Lloyd died and a light went out in the world of entertainment never to be kindled again. Marie Lloyd was unique. She was just "Our Marie." Some may wonder why her death, Queen of the Music Hall though she was, should find a place in a theatre history. The answer is simple. Sarah Bernhardt, years before, was guest of honour at one of the distinguished supper parties which Sir Henry Irving gave on the stage at the Lyceum and which were attended by all sorts of celebrities. Somebody, who should have known better and had not much tact, asked

Bernhardt whom she considered the best actress on the English stage and the company hushed for the great Sarah's reply. It came without hesitation and with the greatest conviction. "Marie Lloyd," she said. And she meant it, too. Nor was she far wrong. When that light went out, a nation mourned.

CHAPTER VIII

Downhill with 1923

AS the 1920's progressed, values and standards of all kinds were descending in level, and that was true of the theatre, too. There was still a surface of hectic gaiety but it was mere scum on the top of the pot; and what was underneath it was to boil over before many years had passed.

The financial situation of the country was bad and that was reflected in the box offices of the Theatre, for in that way the Theatre reflects life, far more than in the nature of its plays. The box office is the only true test of prosperity or otherwise.

The theatre of 1923 had lost most of its great names, names which had given it stability. New people were on the way but their power had not matured; it actually was never to mature in quite the same way as that of their forerunners. There were no new dramatists of real stature coming over the horizon—here and there a successful play, but nothing which showed real greatness. It is by means of its personalities—players and playwrights—that the theatre prospers. The "star system" is often derided and condemned by a minority—sometimes a noisy minority—but it is the system which keeps the theatre alive. Wise Dr Johnson knew that well when he wrote his famous prologue for David Garrick's reign at Drury Lane. And it is the public alone which makes the stars. They arise by popular demand; they are the people whom the public want to see. Managers may try—and have done—to thrust their choice upon audiences but unless the playgoers agree, that flickering star dies away.

In 1923 there were very few names which could drag the public into a theatre, and they were mostly the older generation of tried favourites. This was one of those intermediate periods which occur in our theatre history.

A great player or a great dramatist can revitalize the entire situation. Shakespeare made the English theatre-conscious; the arrival of Tom Robertson brought a new school of comedy to the stage; the impact of Ibsen from abroad and Pinero at home had widened outlooks and opened new fields. That remarkable period at the Court Theatre had popularized Shaw, a new force, a man whose genius lay in making a play of ideas also a play of action. He was still there in 1923; so were Galsworthy with his trenchant reforming pen, Maugham's social comedies of insight and satire, and Rudolf Besier, who could write almost anything from high comedy like *Don* and *Secrets* to blank verse tragedy. Barrie was there also to give a touch of charm and whimsicality, and Lonsdale was shortly to emerge. But, with him as the exception, the dramatists were of the Old Brigade.

There is always a bone of contention as to which matters most in the theatre, the play or the players. There is really no argument at all. The theatre is really the art of acting. Without that it does not exist. It does not need brick walls and a stage; wherever there is acting, there is the theatre. A good play is a tremendous asset, of course, but it is merely words on paper until the art of the actor brings it alive. When you get both good plays and good acting you get great theatre. Yet many of the finest phases of our theatre have been when the actor was completely in the ascendant and the dramatists only complementary. In those days, when the classics were the stable fare, the public would flock to see their favourite players in familiar parts. When they played a classic role for the first time, it was a tremendous occasion. Right up to the first world war an indifferent play which contained some first-class performances, or even one outstanding performance, would draw the public.

In 1923 the theatre, like the world outside it, was in a very fluid state; there was no thickening in the soup and very little "stock" either. It is true that our theatre had, for many years, drawn largely upon French plays, but they had been not only translated but adapted and anglicized for native palates. Often their original authors must have been hard put to it to recognize them. The World War had dried up that French source to a large degree. Managerial eyes now turned more and more to America. There they spoke our language, or at least an understandable variant of it, and in 1923 the American speech was nearer to English than it is today. The English understood American. Films had accustomed us to the American way of life, or what we believed it to be. American plays needed no adaptation; they could be staged right away, so many managers bought American ready-made goods, instead of trying to obtain home goods made to measure. That is not much use to a theatre which should be primarily national in appeal. Nobody wishes to exclude foreign plays; it is right that the public should see them. But it also has a right to see its own, if it can get them. And in the 1920's the men who controlled the theatre were taking the easy way.

The menace of broadcasting also grew and grew. Its personalities began to shoulder out the stars of the stage. "Uncle Rex" (Rex Palmer, who is still with us) became a tremendous and well deserved favourite. The radio showed its power in many ways. In 1923, for the first time, the Premier's Speech at a Guildhall Banquet was broadcast. Tens of thousands stayed at home to listen in. There was another menace, not realized then. That was the microphone. People were becoming accustomed to it. Those who broadcast—and more and more people of the theatre were doing so—began to rely on it. Today it is omnipotent and is one of the main destructors of the illusion of the theatre and the magic of the human voice. It is the victory of the phoney over the real. I would like to see it barred from all theatres. If actors and actresses cannot make themselves heard without it, they have no place on the stage; they should remain in broadcasting studios. The trouble is that a public nurtured on mechanism accepts the microphone as an attraction. That is what makes the outlook so grim.

The position in the Theatre in 1923 was that only forty-three plays managed to pass the 100-performance mark, several of them being revivals and twelve being musical. Only a few straight plays were in any degree outstanding. *The Lilies of the Field,* by John Hastings Turner, ran for 273 performances at the Ambassadors. Hastings Turner could turn out neat workmanlike plays. It was a ReandeaN production, with Basil Dean in charge, and in a fine cast were two outstanding young actresses of the period, Edna Best and Meggie Albanesi. E. Temple Thurston, novelist and playwright, had *A Roof and Four Walls* at the Apollo, which ran for 132 performances. In the cast was Frank Freeman, who is now Chairman of the Board of Directors of the Royal General Theatrical Fund and does yeoman work for his fellow professionals. At the same theatre there was a revival of Barrie's *What Every Woman Knows* (269 performances), with Godfrey Tearle playing John Shand; Tearle was the outstanding actor of this period.

Drury Lane struck a bad patch. An extraordinary play called *Angelo*, which not even the stage genius of Arthur Collins could make palatable, ran for only 29 performances. In it was Maurice Moscovitch. Maybe it was before its time. Nor was *Ned Kean of Old Drury*, based upon the life of Edmund Kean, much more fortunate. It had that powerful actor H. A. Saintsbury in the name part. It was melodrama—and too much "melo" for the "drama." It is impossible to depict that blazing genius, Edmund Kean, adequately on the modern stage. There was an attempt by a publicity device, which had a grain of truth in it, to prolong the run of this play. When its withdrawal was announced a gentleman named Greenlees, connected with a famous firm of whisky-distillers, rose in the stalls and said that rather than see such a fine play perish, he would finance it himself for a time. He was loudly cheered, especially by the company and staff, and he was as good as his word, but for all that *Ned Kean* was only played 61 times.

But a real Drury Lane melodrama saved the day. It was called *Good Luck* and it lived up to its name. This was the real thing—Drury Lane drama as it should be with spectacular scenic effects and all. It had been written by Ian Hay but Arthur Collins did not think it had the breadth and stature which Drury Lane demanded. He called in that master of theatre craft, Seymour Hicks, who took the script away with him. About a week later he returned and came along the corridor towards Collins's office whistling cheerfully. "Here it is, Arthur," he said. "I think it's all right." "What have you done?" asked Collins "Oh, put in a fire in a prison, a shipwreck and Solly Joel's bathing pool at Maiden Erlegh,"replied the irrepressible Seymour. "We'll do it," said Collins. And they did. It ran for 259 performances, and that is a long time in that immense theatre. It had a real Drury Lane cast including Edmund Gwenn who was to play a Jewish bookmaker. "I can't play this," said "Teddie". "I've never played a Jew." So he turned it into a Cockney. *Good Luck* was basically a racing play and the horse race in it occasioned a bit of bother on the first night. Drury Lane had had horse races before, notably in that vast success *The Whip*, and had got away with them, despite a bad hitch on the first night of *The Whip* when the horse so named did not win the race as he should have done. In *Good Luck* no chances were to be taken. The public was not to see the winner passing the post, but a section of the race presented in a different way. Real race horses were to thunder straight at the audience, as if about to gallop over them; they would thus experience the thrill, if thrill it be, of infantry facing a cavalry charge. It was perfectly easy. The horses race on fixed "tracks," the surfaces of which turn under their feet as they gallop, so they appear to be travelling at top speed without moving at all. It was only a question of putting the tracks facing up and down stage instead of across it. No pains were spared over this scene. There were about 350 supers to form the race crowd and cheer the horses on. It was rehearsed over and over again and it promised a real and novel thrill. Even the principals got excited about it and said they would leave their sacred dressing-rooms and mingle with the mob—they wanted to hear the tremendous applause this novel effect would draw from the excited crowd in front. Everyone was certain of success.

The first night came. The show went splendidly. The fire, the shipwreck and the very undressed girls (according to 1923 standards) plunging into the bathing pool drew loud plaudits. Then came the race. There was a short scene being played downstage before a front cloth whilst the horses were put on the tracks and the crowd assembled. All was ready; the cue came, the lights went on the scene and off thundered the horses, with the racecourse crowd cheering them on in a frenzy of excitement. And then . . . it was over . . . and the stage manager blacked out and everyone stood silent and expectant to hear the volleys of applause from the front which should greet this masterly effort. There was not a sound. Dead silence. And they soon discovered why. The people in front had not seen a thing. Something had gone wrong backstage and a vast black velvet cloth, which should have been raised, had stayed down and, of course, masked the whole scene from the view of the audience. But *Good Luck* triumphed as *The Whip* had done and as *The Garden of Allah* had, in spite of the first-night sandstorm going awry.

Those two popular characters "Potash" and "Perlmutter" visited London again in 1923, at the Garrick Theatre. In a play called *Partners Again*, they played for 100 performances. *Ambush*, another American play at the same theatre, ran for forty-nine performances longer.

The Globe Theatre staged *Aren't We All?* by Frederick Lonsdale, which was really the first of those Lonsdale comedies which were to form quite a theatrical epoch. It ran for 110 nights. The same theatre had a bigger success with Somerset Maugham's *Our Betters*, one of the outstanding plays of the year. It ran, indeed, into 1925, with 548 performances in all. This was Maugham at his very best, with his keen observation of character, his cynicism and satire superbly welded in the right principles of play-writing. It was typical of its period and Maugham shows exactly what the life of the times was like. It was superbly played, as it deserved to be, especially by Constance Collier and Margaret Bannerman. Alfred Drayton, later to become a star in his own right, made a success too.

The Haymarket staged quite a lot of plays in 1923, contrary to its general custom. *Isobel, Edward and Anne* by Gertrude Jennings ran for 100 performances, and a revival of *The Prisoner of Zenda*, with Robert Loraine and Fay Compton, beat it by ten. But *Success* by A. A. Milne failed to fulfil its title, being performed only 39 times. *Plus Fours* by Horace Annesley Vachell, with Aubrey Smith and Peggy O'Neil (who wore the Plus Fours), only lasted for 86; and a revival of *The Importance of Being Earnest* managed to put up a run of 62. Not a good year for the lovely Haymarket.

His Majesty's, the Haymarket's neighbour, had failures with a revival of *The Gay Lord Quex*—George Grossmith in the title role (45 performances), and *Oliver Cromwell* by John Drinkwater scored only 72. William J. Rea played Charles I and Henry Ainley was Cromwell. But success came back there by means of ReandeaN. The play was *Hassan* by James Elroy Flecker, with music by Delius. This was the highspot of the 1923 productions and indeed not only of that year but of many to come. It was a truly beautiful thing, compounded of poetry, music, colour, romance, strong drama and tragedy—an Arabian Night come to life. It was the story of a man with poetry in his soul but not in his appearance—a confectioner who fell in love with beauty and sought his ideal, only to find that in so doing he lost all he had . . . and then started all over again. It was a production such as Sir Herbert Tree might have viewed with pride. It upheld the tradition of his "beautiful theatre." It has been broadcast and revived, but nothing can repeat the rapture of that first production and the memories which it has provided. It did indeed "take the golden road to Samarkand." In this production Basil Dean surpassed all his previous efforts; it had to be seen to be believed. If he had never done anything else, his reputation could have rested on this. It was, like all the ReandeaN productions, perfectly cast. Basil Gill was back there in his stage home, where he had made so many notable successes. He played Raff, the King of the Beggars, and his fine appearance and voice had never shown to better advantage. Esmé Percy, Cathleen Nesbitt, Malcolm Keen, Frank Cochrane, Leon Quartermaine, Edmund Willard and Laura Cowie were others who shone. Henry Ainley played Hassan, his golden voice speaking the poetry of Flecker like a symphony orchestra. Yet, maybe, he was not quite right. You could never disguise the romance of Harry Ainley's appearance, and the romance in Hassan should only be in his soul. His exterior should be devoid of it. One wonders what that part might have been like in the hands of Charles Laughton. But *Hassan* was outstanding. It decorated the theatre of 1923 like a rich jewel. It ran for 281 performances. As a pendant to *Hassan* it is as well to record the doings of ReandeaN in 1923. At the St Martin's they presented *The Great Broxupp* by A. A. Milne, which only ran for 37 performances but gave a chance to two young people, Beatrix Thompson and Richard Bird. *R. U. R.* (Rossum's Universal Robots) came next. It dealt with a subject entirely new then and considered slightly absurd—mechanical men. But it aroused interest and ran for 126 performances. Then came a revival of *The Will* by J. M. Barrie and *The Likes of 'Er* by Charles MacEvoy. In that, Hermione Baddeley made a big success in her first important part. These two plays together ran for 226 performances. Charles MacEvoy was a most tantalizing dramatist who always seemed to be hovering on the verge of great success. At what they called "Playbox Matinées" ReandeaN also presented *Melloney Holtspur* by John Drinkwater, in which Meggie Albanesi gave a vivid and touching performance. At the Queen's, in association with Sir Alfred Butt, they staged a revival of *The Little Minister*, with Owen Nares in the title role; it ran for 125 performances. Basil Dean produced all these plays. He had also produced *The Gay Lord Quex* for Grossmith and Malone.

Matheson Lang came back to the New Theatre and did *The Bad*

Man, which ran for 111 performances. He played a Mexican Bandit.
At the same theatre, *The Lie* by Henry Arthur Jones ran for 187
nights, and there was a revival of *Cymbeline* with Sybil Thorndike as
Imogen.

Gladys Cooper was now installed at the Playhouse as actress-
manageress in association with Frank Curzon. She made a big
success in *Magda* (228 performances) and she also presented a very
different type of play called *Enter Kiki*, by Sydney Blow and C.
Douglas Hoare. This ran for 155 performances and in it with Miss
Cooper was Ivor Novello, steadily making his way towards the front
rank.

At the Prince's, *The Return of Sherlock Homes*, by J. E. Harold-Terry
and Arthur Rose, ran for 130 performances, with Eille Norwood as
the great detective.

There was an American play at the Prince of Wales's called *So
This is London*, with Raymond Hackett in the lead. This transferred
to the Savoy and ran in all for 275 performances. Also at the Prince
of Wales's were *The Co-optimists*, that superior and elect seaside
concert party formed to fight the slump of 1921, although it never
played at the seaside. It was largely the conception of Archie de
Bear. It was a huge success; its Prince of Wales's season in 1923
produced 210 performances. Its members all made a lot of
money.

At the Regent Theatre, in the Euston Road, there was an in-
teresting performance of *The Insect Play*, by the Brothers Capek.
Playing his second part on the professional stage, that of Felix in the
Butterfly Scene, was a young actor named John Gielgud. *Robert E.
Lee* by John Drinkwater, with a first-class cast, ran for 109 per-
formances.

The Royalty had a disappointing year, although a revival of *At
Mrs Bean's* kept it going for 280 performances.

The Shaftesbury Theatre, as regards straight plays, had *The
Rising Generation*, which transferred to the Garrick and was played in
all 280 times. The play was by Wyn Weaver and Laura Leycester.
Great anticipation was aroused by the production of a stage version
of A. S. M. Hutchinson's best-selling novel *If Winter Comes*. The
adaptation was by Macdonald Hastings. With Grace Lane and
Owen Nares in the cast it only reached 53 performances. Playing a
tiny part, that of Coroner's Officer, was Mr Frank Forder, who was
thereby "doubling," for he was also Owen Nares's most faithful valet
and dresser. He was entirely devoted to Nares and had hardly any
life of his own, though sometimes he would refer to a mysterious
"club." Frank Forder identified himself with Nares and always
spoke of "We." "We shall be on the set tomorrow morning," he
would say. Or "We have a dinner party on Sunday. We don't get

much time for anything nowadays." He guarded Nares like a faithful watchdog, he looked after his health and he saw to it that nobody got into the dressing-room whom "We" did not like. He was a very good fellow, and not a bad actor either. I hope he is still alive. He was just over middle height, very speedy in his movements, pale as to hair and complexion and with rather large teeth. But he had plenty of brains and ingenuity and the tact of a diplomat. Now and again he would give the other half of "We" a good talking to and was always listened to with respect. He was in the true line of traditional dressers and was never known to make a mistake.

The St James's did better with *The Green Goddess*, a glorious traditional melodrama written by—of all people—that most distinguished critic, William Archer. He who had so often riddled such plays with criticism now wrote the perfect example himself. With George Arliss in the lead it ran for 407 performances and did the fortune of St James's a power of good. So did *The Outsider*, by Dorothy Brandon, a play on a then rather topical subject, a medical practitioner who was outside the pale of full recognition. Leslie Faber and Isobel Elsom gave splendid performances in that run of 109 nights, which deserved to be longer.

At the Strand Eugene O'Neill's *Anna Christie* ran for 102 performances.

One of the excitements of that year was a play called *The Dancers*, by Hubert Parsons, at Wyndham's. Sir Gerald du Maurier produced it and played in it with a distinguished cast, but what caused all the excitement was a red-headed and beautiful girl from America with a vibrant personality and a most characteristic voice; her name was Tallulah Bankhead and she startled London. She was new and she was "news." Everybody talked about her; gossip writers dogged her. She was the rage. Her entrance into a restaurant was a sensation; not since the era of Mrs Langtry had there been anything like this. She was also a good actress. Her famous greeting "Dah-ling" became a fashion. Everyone wanted to know her, but that was not so easy. Everyone wanted to see her, and that could best be accomplished at Wyndham's Theatre. A lot of young emotional people treated her with the type of mob hysteria now reserved for strangely attired young men with guitars who stand behind microphones and make noises.

To turn to the musical plays of 1923, a start can be made at the Adelphi. The attraction there was *Head Over Heels*, but it only turned its somersault on 113 occasions. W. H. Berry still hung on. This was a production by the commercial management.

The Court had a version of *Omar Khayyam*, adapted by Charles S. M. Raikes with the music of Liza Lehmann and also some of Grieg's, for one recalls an Oriental dancer being sinuous and eastern to the tune of "Anitra's Dance," and somehow making it credible. It scored 86 performances.

The Royal Opera House Covent Garden went in for spectacular revue, called *You'd Be Surprised*, which was described as a jazzaganza. After that nobody need have been surprised at anything. The cast was a real mixture; it contained George Robey, Lydia Lopokova, Leonide Massine, Leon Woizikowsky, Ninette de Valois, Lydia Sokolova and other bearers of big names in ballet, in rather curious juxtaposition to George Robey, a crowd of clever revue players and the Savoy Havana Band. Still, it surprised a good many people and it taught one eminent critic a sharp lesson. As the first performance would not allow him time to write his notice for his paper, he attended a dress rehearsal. He fell foul of the show and especially one sketch, to which he took the greatest possible exception and denounced it in good round terms. But when the first night took place the following evening, that sketch had been withdrawn. He could not alter his notice, which was already printed, and he looked very foolish. Nor could he take credit for having had the sketch withdrawn, for the show was produced on a Saturday night and his notice appeared on the Sunday. He learnt never to write a notice at a dress rehearsal again. *You'd Be Surprised* was transferred to the Alhambra (which provided a better atmosphere for it) and survived for 270 performances. That surprised a lot more people. But it was a tribute to the box office attraction of George Robey.

Daly's staged a revival of *The Merry Widow*, with George Graves in his original part, Carl Brisson excellent as Danilo, and Evelyn Laye as an enchanting Widow. *The Widow* waltzed 222 times. That was followed by a big success, somehow achieved by James White, but he had excellent people round him. It was called *Madame Pompadour*, written by Frederick Lonsdale, with music by Leo Fall. Bertram Wallis gave a splendid performance at Louis XV, Derek Oldham was on top of his form, and Evelyn Laye was Madame Pompadour, glowing, romantic, queenly and beautiful to look upon. This was one of her best performances and stamped her a première leading lady. It ran for 467 performances.

Charlot staged a revue at the Duke of York's called *London Calling* and, despite Violet Melnotte, he had a success. It was written by Ronald Jeans and Noel Coward, who also did most of the music and lyrics. It was the first Noel Coward revue. With him were Ronald Jeans, Philip Braham and Sissle and Blake, but he pervaded the show and his genius for this sort of work was apparent. He played in it, too. Amongst the company were Tubby Edlin, Maisie Gay and Gertrude Lawrence, a leading lady full of that warmth and beauty which were her greatest assets. *London Calling* was really first-class, it abounded with wit, it was fiercely topical and it spared few.

One recalls the burlesque of the Sitwell Family, the male members of which were called "Gob" and "Sago," and a superb piece of burlesque for Maisie Gay as a somewhat overripe and not too agile Britannia singing a patriotic song, which was only bettered by that splendid comedienne's sketch of "Nurse Doodah." Perhaps the most poignant memory is of the grace, beauty and appeal of Gertrude Lawrence singing "Parisienne Pierrot." No wonder *London Calling* ran for 367 performances and Noel Coward was "news."

Albert de Courville and Edgar Wallace had a revue at the Empire called *The Rainbow* which ran for 113 performances.

Robert Evett scored another success at the Gaiety, with José Collins in the lead. This time it was *Catherine*, all about that famous Empress of Russia. The music was selected from that of Tchaikowsky. It was given a costly and magnificent mounting, no expense being spared. The big scene showed the wedding of Catherine to the Tsar, Peter the Great, who was played by Bertram Wallis. The wedding dress worn by José Collins was what would now be called fabulous. It was dazzling. It gleamed and glittered like a stream of molten metal. It was made entirely of sequins and it was said that it took three people to carry it, yet José Collins wore it with ease. She and the Tsar, a most striking couple, joined hands and walked to their thrones while the full orchestra, plus an organ, played "1812" at full blast. That piece of music might not have been an ideal wedding march under ordinary circumstances but in *Catherine* it seemed perfectly right, and most impressive. José Collins was at her best, and that is saying a good deal. It ran for 217 performances.

A revue at the Palace, *The Music Box*, ran for 118 nights, and a musical comedy, entitled *The Cousin from Nowhere*, with Helen Gilliland as leading lady, ran for 105 performances at the Queen's.

There was a musical show at the Shaftesbury, produced there on May 30th and transferred later to the Queen's, which caused some excitement. Its title was *Stop Flirting!* The excitement was caused by something new in the way of dancing by a brother and sister named Adèle and Fred Astaire, whom London saw the first time in this show and took to its heart. It is perhaps worthy of note than on the programmes amongst the list of those described as "Guests" is the name of Marjorie Mars. The Shaftesbury had another success with *Katinka*, with music by Rudolf Friml and with Joe Coyne and Binnie Hale in the cast; it ran for 108 performances.

Charlot was producing at the Vaudeville in 1923 as well as at the Duke of York's. At the Vaudeville he had two shows, both revues. The first was *Rats*. It had Norah Blaney, Gwen Farrar, Alfred Lester, Herbert Mundin and Gertrude Lawrence in the cast, so no wonder it ran for 285 nights. That team of Norah Blaney and Gwen Farrar was to become famous. Norah Blaney, so pretty and accomplished, could sing, play the piano, compose and act as well. Gwen Farrar was an eccentric, odd in appearance, deep-voiced, a really funny comedienne with a turn for doing the unexpected, such as suddenly playing the 'cello with perfect artistry. They were a tower of strength in any show. They were together also in the second Vaudeville revue, *Yes*, with which the public agreed on 118 occasions. Norah Blaney composed some of the music for that.

At what had become the headquarters of Musical Comedy—the Winter Garden—Grossmith and Malone staged *The Beauty Prize*, competed for and won on 214 occasions. George Grossmith and P. G. Wodehouse wrote it and Jerome Kerne composed the music. Leslie Henson supplied the bulk of the comedy and Dorothy Dickson was a certain beauty prize winner anywhere. In the cast appears the name of Winifred Shotter, later to become a leading lady in the Aldwych farces.

Cochran was at home as usual at the London Pavilion and there presented *Dover Street to Dixie*. The journey was made on 108 occasions, and in the show were the amazing Florence Mills and the Plantation Trio, supplying the Dixie atmosphere.

There was in 1923 something very near akin to a tragedy at the Duke of York's. Marie Tempest, the one and only and well beloved, returned from a world tour and opened there with a play unknown to London, but which she had played with success all round the world. It was called *Good Gracious Annabelle*! The house was packed. Everyone wanted to welcome home the Queen of the Stage and to wish her the best of luck, but the show was an utter flop. There was to have been a big party on the stage at curtain fall; trestle tables were laid, heaped with dainties, bottles of champagne stood in ranks ready for congratulations and happy toasts. But so dire and unexpected was the failure that nobody dared go round—not a guest would face the ordeal. It was a very sad affair indeed. However, Marie Tempest revived *The Marriage of Kitty* and all was well.

There was a play at the Criterion called *Advertising April*, in which Sybil Thorndike appeared. It was written by two well known journalists, Harold Horsnell and Herbert Farjeon; the latter was to become a leading writer of excellent revues.

A very striking play came from that excellent little Playhouse in Hampstead, the Embassy, to the Garrick Theatre. It was *Outward Bound*. Written by Sutton Vane, it caused great interest and discussion. As most people know, for it has been so often revived, broadcast and televised, it deals in plain straightforward terms with death and the after-life. It ran for 227 performances at the Garrick on that original production.

Noel Coward had a play of his produced at the Savoy called *The Young Idea*. He played in it himself, with a good cast including

J. L. Sacks, the illiterate
impresario.

Archie de Bear, a foremost
revue producer and great
wit: one of the founders of
the Co-Optimists.

Gus Sohlke, whose dance arrangements captured London.

Julian Wylie, king of revue and pantomime, and supreme technician.

Ronald Ward and Naomi Jacob, the celebrated novelist who is also a first-class actress. It scored 60 performances.

It is interesting nowadays to recall that in 1923 the incomparable Pavlova was still dancing. She did a season at Covent Garden that year.

A new name which must be taken into account is that of Raymond Massey. He had a bit of a fight, as most actors did and that is all to the good. He had been in *Glamour* at the Apollo in 1922, which only ran for 40 performances. In 1923 he was in *At Mrs Bean's* and there he was luckier, for that was a success; and he had been in a Christmas season of *The Rose and the Ring* at Wyndham's. In 1923 he was again at the Comedy in *The Elopement*, which ran for only 14 performances; with him in the cast was another young actor who is now famous on stage screen and television, named Mervyn Johns.

In a play called *Three Birds* at the Criterion was a young man named Leslie Perrins, also destined for success. But *Three Birds* only lasted for 22 shows. He had been at the Kingsway and the Little in 1922 and he had been a Robot in *R.U.R.* He had an early taste of stage failure, too. But he stuck it.

How the theatres fared in 1923 can be shown by a table of the number of plays each presented. Adelphi (3); Aldwych (1); Alhambra (1); Ambassadors (5); Comedy (5); Court (6); Criterion (8); Daly's (2); Duke of York's (6); Drury Lane (3); Empire (2); Gaiety (1); Garrick (5); Globe (4); Haymarket (5); His Majesty's (3); Kingsway (5); London Pavilion (1); Little (1); Lyceum (6); New (5); Palace (1); Playhouse (3); Prince's (2); Prince of Wales's (2); Queen's (1); Regent (4); Royalty (3); Savoy (4); Scala (3); Shaftesbury (4); St James's (5); St Martin's (3); Strand (4); Vaudeville (2); Winter Garden (1); Wyndhams (2). Even those figures are not a complete guide for sometimes certain theatres were closed for longish periods.

Short runs included *Marriage by Instalments* (29), *Trespassers* (7), *The Piccadilly Puritan* (24), all at the Ambassadors; *Peace and Quiet* (22) and *The Elopement* (14) at the Comedy; *Trust Emily* (21), *Three Birds* (20), and *Dulcy* (30) at the Criterion; *Good Gracious Annabelle*! (15) and *Civilian Clothes* (7) at the Duke of York's; *Angelo* (29) at Drury Lane; *Reckless Reggie* (13) at the Globe; *Tancred* (14) at the Kingsway; *Merton of the Movies*, a much heralded play at the Shaftesbury (38); *The Inevitable* (4) at the St James's.

Dancing, motoring, night clubs, radio and the new taste for cabaret—to say nothing of shortage of cash—were all hitting the Theatre.

CHAPTER IX

Vignette of an Actor

WITHOUT doubt, Godfrey Tearle was the outstanding actor of the 1920's. Born of a line of players on both his father's and his mother's side, he was completely of the theatre. He spent his whole life in its service, he was born in it, it possessed him entirely.

His father, Osmund Tearle, was an actor-manager running his own company. He played largely in the smaller cities of the North of England, carrying his art—and he was a superb actor—where it could best illumine and excite the public, in places where the Great Ones did not penetrate. His public loved him and he loved them. He never broke faith with them. He believed that what he was doing enabled him to make the best use of the gifts Providence had bestowed on him. Nothing deterred him from what he considered his duty and although the West End knew little about him his profession knew his value. He would refuse lucrative offers of London engagements which would have brought him money and fame, if their acceptance would have interfered with his own little company and his work. He was as loyal to those who served him as he was to the public which supported him.

There is an outstanding example of this. In 1897, not long after Mr Tree, as he was then, had opened Her Majesty's Theatre, he desired to produce *Othello*, with himself as the Moor. He wanted the best Iago he could obtain, for he was a perfectionist. He wanted, also, an actor capable of such power that the two of them could exchange parts, according to established theatrical custom. Even then, such men were rare, but he bethought himself of Osmund Tearle, whom he considered the very man. So he wrote a most polite letter to Mr Tearle, offering him the part of Iago on most advantageous terms and said that he hoped Mr Tearle would be interested. Mr Tearle was interested, for Her Majesty's had already become the most famous Theatre in Europe, so he wrote back a most courteous and dignified reply, expressing his deep sense of obligation at the honour done him, and saying he would welcome the opportunity of accepting, but raising one small query. "At what period and at what time," he asked, "was the proposed production to take place?" Mr Tree wrote back by return that it was scheduled for April, at Easter time.

Mr Tearle replied at once. He said he deeply regretted that he must decline Mr Tree's most kind and flattering offer, but at that date and time he would be leading his own company . . . at Jarrow! That was what Osmund Tearle was like. And that production of *Othello* did not take place for years, not until 1912, when Laurence Irving played Iago.

Little Godfrey Tearle accompanied his father, mother and their company everywhere. The world for him was confined within the four walls of a theatre (often old, dark, damp and dingy), to theatrical lodgings, and to long slow and cold train jouneys on Sundays, when the talk was entirely "shop." He got the rudiments of education at odd times from private tutors. The importance and dignity of their profession were constantly impressed in his young mind by both his father and mother, who was a Conway. One night, when Osmund was playing at a small theatre in Leeds, he and little Godfrey, aged about six, boarded a tramcar *en route* for the theatre. There was another passenger in that tram, a most distinguished-looking man with an air of detachment, but he greeted Osmund Tearle like a brother and they talked and talked. Osmund presented his son and the gentleman bestowed a most gracious kindly smile on the boy, spoke a few words to him and laid his hand on his head as if in benediction. Then, having reached his destination, he got out, bidding them farewell. "Godfrey," said Tearle senior, "always remember this time and place and all your life remember that gentleman. It is your first meeting with greatness. For he is Henry Irving." And, indeed, Godfrey never forgot.

In 1893, when he was just nine years old and the company was playing at Burnley, his father told him there would be no lessons for him that day. The lad who played the little Duke of York in *Richard III* was ill, and he, Godfrey, was to play it that evening. The boy, who had often seen the play and had a most retentive memory, knew most of the lines already, but his father rehearsed him and he played that night, acquitting himself well. His future was settled, he was now a professional actor. He continued to play quite often until his father decided he must have some decent education and sent him to the Carlisle Grammer School. In 1899 he was back again and played under his father's banner until Osmund died in 1901.

Wanting to see the world, he joined a company which was to tour South Africa, and there between 1902 and 1904 he played over fifty different parts. Then he came home and, being the son of his father, he formed his own company and toured a play called *A Soldier of Fortune*. Afterwards, he joined a repertory company for whom he played Hamlet, Othello, Shylock, Brutus, Romeo, Sir Peter Teazle, Young Marlow and many other parts. Godfrey Tearle learnt his business the hard—and proper—way.

He made his first appearance in London at the King's Theatre, Hammersmith, playing the Earl of Bothwell in a play called *Mary, Queen of Scots* in which the celebrated Mrs Brown Potter—lovely woman but indifferent actress—played Queen Mary. It was not much of a production and not a very good play but I saw it and I remember the tall, handsome and then unknown young actor, his fine voice and his charming smile, when the Queen said to him: "Goes Your Lordship to Scotland?" to which he replied: "Goes Your Majesty?" The Queen flashed back: "You answer my question with another?" and Bothwell replied, his charm and smile lighting the scene; "In the answer to my question lies the answer to yours." That charm, that smile, never left Godfrey Tearle.

In 1907 Oscar Asche engaged him for a small part in his production of *Attila* at His Majesty's, as that theatre was then called, so Godfrey entered the playhouse his father had turned down. He stayed there with Oscar Asche and Lily Brayton playing Sylvius in *As You Like It* (and very handsome he looked) and Ludovico in *Othello*, a play which was in his destiny. Then he toured in *The Hypocrites*. But the eye of Tree was upon him and the son accepted an engagement where his father had reluctantly refused. He played Valentine in Tree's production of *Faust* in 1908. It was then that London first became aware of him.

That was a most magnificent production in every way. The version was by J. Comyns Carr and Stephen Phillips, that poet of the theatre who died so young and so disastrously. It was wonderfully mounted and wonderfully cast. Marie Lohr, a very young girl then, was a most beautiful and appealing Marguerite; Tree always believed in giving Youth a chance. Henry Ainley was Faust, Charles Quartermaine, the Witch, Madge Titheradge, Lisa, Rosina Filippi Martha and Tree was Mephistopheles. I can recall every detail of that play and its impressive mounting; it gave one pride to be humbly connected with it. The opening was typical of His Majesty's. It was "Betwixt Earth and Heaven" where Mephistopheles decided on the ruin of Marguerite. Tree seemed to stand alone in space, which stretched around him, cold, grey, forbidding and illimitable—eternal—without shape, yet having being. I recall that figure making his appeal in that characteristic but compelling voice.

"Mother, still crouching on the bounds of Light
With face of sea and hair of Tempest,
Still huddled in huge and immemorial hate,
Behold thy son and some dark aid extend. . . ."

There came a distant, rumbling roar, like a dam bursting afar off or the thunder of a vast avalanche heard across an Alpine valley . . . and Tree cast up his arms, his face illumined with evil triumph. It was quite unforgettable.

Amongst the grandeur and great names was young Godfrey Tearle. It was there I first got to know him, fifty one years ago. He looked magnificent in his shining armour, moving with grace and speed, kneeling to have his sword blessed before going to the war. Valentine is not a big part but it is a good one for an actor and young Godfrey made it stand right out. I recall his tender farewell to Marguerite, and I can see again his triumphant return as victor, to find his sister betrayed. His rage was as noble as Othello's. He meant to kill Faust and the duel took place, a really spirited fight, with clash of steel, panting breath, hurried footsteps. Then the fatal blow, through the intervention of Mephistopheles, and Valentine's restrained, noble but touching death scene. Godfrey Tearle made a big success.

There is a story of the dress rehearsal of that play showing the tremendous humanity and love of mischief which always possessed Tree, the Chief, as we who served him so proudly delighted to call him. That duel scene was, of course, rehearsed in full armour and costumes, with lighting "as at night." Those who know the story will recall that, whenever Valentine appears to have the advantage of Faust, the invisible Mephistopheles (invisible to all save Faust) parries the thrusts and blows with his own sword. At His Majesty's, whenever that sword of evil touched Valentine's, sparks flew out of both swords like a shower of stars. The swords were, of course, electrified. Godfrey Tearle, as Valentine, aimed a great hack at Faust. The sword of Tree parried it and the sparks flew. Godfrey dropped his sword and, clutching his arm, hopped about the stage in agony. "What's the matter?" queried Tree, in tones of great concern. "I don't know, Chief," said poor Godfrey, "but when your sword struck mine I got a terrible shock." "Nonsense, nonsense!" said the Chief, "I felt nothing. Carry on." So the duel continued with showers of sparks and groans and howls from Godfrey, who somehow managed to cling on to his sword. His fall, when fatally stricken, was most realistic. He lay groaning and clutching his sword arm. Tree gazed at him in apparent sympathy. "Is anything hurting you, Godfrey?" he inquired. "Hurting me, Chief?" said Godfrey. "I think this right arm of mine is paralysed by the electric shocks I got everytime our swords met." "Strange, strange," mused Tree "I don't understand it. My sword sent out more sparks than yours, yet I felt nothing, nothing . . ." and that faraway look came into his eyes which was always there when he perpetrated one of his impish jokes. "No, no, I felt nothing . . . most peculiar . . . unless, of course, it was because I was wearing an insulated glove." He had not told Godfrey to do that; indeed he had stopped the issue of the "prop," just to see what happened. That was typical of Tree. But the glove was there on the first night and Godfrey made his success. Tree was the first to praise him, to mention him indeed, in his curtain speech.

Just as a tail piece to show how the actor-managers did things, the incidental music for that production was composed by Coleridge Taylor, except for one entr'acte in which the music of Berlioz was used.

Tearle stayed with Tree for some time, playing a variety of parts. He appeared as Trip in the famous All-Star production of *The School for Scandal* in 1909. Then he toured again, for Sir George Alexander, and that took him to the wonderful St James's Theatre. Nothing came amiss to him, so far as acting was concerned. He was ready for anything; it made no difference and he played every sort of role. He was in full-blooded melodrama at the Lyceum, in *The Prince and the Beggar Maid;* he toured with Isobel Jay in that Prince of Wales's musical comedy *The Balkan Princess*—playing the part created by Bertram Wallis. Not many people saw him in his full glory when he played Calaf, Prince of Astrakhan, in the ill-fated production of *Turandot* at the St James's. It was one of the most beautiful productions ever done there, yet it failed completely, but Godfrey in a wonderful costume, riding a pony, made a figure which struck all beholders. His voice seemed to forecast the success of the opera to come. He played Captain Hook in *Peter Pan* in 1913, and in the following year came the part which really established him in London—Frank Taylor in Somerset Maugham's *The Land of Promise*.

That play came about because Charles Frohman wanted Maugham to write him a play and Maugham lacked inspiration at the moment. "Go and write a new version of *The Taming of the Shrew*, Frohman suggested, and *The Land of Promise* was the result. No need to describe it; it has been revived, broadcast and televised. Godfrey Tearle played opposite to Irene Vanbrugh, then at the very hight of her power. That act in the lonely shack between the cultured woman and the man who lived a primitive life held and gripped the audience. The battle of wits, the contest between the male denied his conjugal rights and the female who denied him, and his grim determination to beat her (that was where *The Taming of the Shrew* came in) demanded magnificent acting, and got it. This was a very fine play, acted as it deserved. Godfrey Tearle stood in the front rank. All the hard work and labour from his boyhood had come to full blossom. Godfrey Tearle was a real "leading man" (the word "star" was seldom used then). The only blemish on that show were the good looks of Godfrey; women found it difficult to believe that even his warring, unwilling wife could have stood out for so long against such manly beauty, such charm, such strength.

Tearle went on building up a big reputation. He appeared again in Musical Comedy at the Adelphi in 1915, in *Tina* with W. H. Berry and Phyllis Dare. He was quite at home, he had done it before; that was the value of experience. Then he joined the Forces and served until 1919. After that he played Shakespeare with Basil Gill, a remarkable combination of talents, voices and appearances. He visited America with success. Then he scored his big personal triumph in *The Garden of Allah* at Drury Lane, in 1920. He never looked back; he was one of the great figures of the stage. He achieved his own desire to play Othello in London in 1921. On top of that came *The Faithful Heart*, and many more fine pieces of acting.

Godfrey Tearle had every requisite an actor requires. The theatre was in his blood. He had the right height, he was handsome, his figure was magnificent; he had a wonderful smile, great charm and a splendid voice which he knew exactly how to use. He looked and was a man. He was a pastmaster at his job, having acted from childhood. He always said that acting could not be taught but that it could be learnt, and that the only way to learn it was on a stage facing an audience, as he had done. I have already recorded that I agree with him heartily. Godfrey showed his grasp of character when he played James Miggles in *Quinney's* at the Haymarket. He was a splendid and thrilling Henry V, he played all the big Shakespearean roles with the touch of a master. He stood next to Lewis Waller as Brutus and as Henry V too.

There were dignity and breadth in everything he did. He could have been one of the great actors of all time; he could have been the leader of his profession; and he was knighted, very rightly, before he died. But he had one besetting sin: he was a lazy man.

He never feared any part or any comparison. He was always ready to follow another actor; he would take over a part and stand comparison with his forerunner. He did that often, he always held his own, and sometimes triumphed. Sometimes he followed after a length of time, but still faced play goers who remembered the original; he did this in *The Flag Lieutenant*, in *What Every Woman Knows* and, to some degree, in *White Cargo*. Sometimes he would take over a part during the run of a play, as in *The Heiress*. He always brought something of his own which made it a new creation.

But the main trouble was that he seldom sustained his original brilliance for long. He never gave a bad performance, but the electric spark which had thrilled when he first created or took over was apt to dull down. I recall his amazing performance, quite recently, as Antony in *Antony and Cleopatra* at the Piccadilly Theatre, with Edith Evans as Cleopatra. On the first night the audience rose at him; this was the best Antony they had seen. This was what Antony should be. He looked magnificent, he played with genius. Here was the great soldier, ageing a little, softening a little, and falling by his weakness to be the slave of Cleopatra, yet everyone was able to realize why Cleopatra "fell" for him. He showed just the right blurred outline marring the erstwhile greatness of the man. It was remarkable. Ten days later, the bright edge of that performance had gone; he was still probably the best Antony, but the light was subdued, the tremendous attack was blunted. It was as if he was sitting back, a little tired, in a comfortable armchair, wearing his dressing-gown and slippers.

He had risen to fine heights in Emlyn Williams's play *The Light of Heart*. In some ways that was his best performance for many years, perhaps since *The Land of Promise*. He played a man who had been a great actor and still was so, except that drunkenness had so brought him down that he was content to be "Father Christmas" at a Yuletide bazaar. There was to be a revival of *King Lear* and Lears are hard to find. He was remembered. Here was his chance of a comeback, a miracle which would enable him to rub out the past and start again. At rehearsals, he won the admiration of all. He swore off drink and at the Dress Rehearsal he was acclaimed. Before the final test, the first night, he was back on the pinnacle. He had only to seize the chance. . . but, for him, it never came. Temptation came instead . . . he yielded. He never played King Lear. He made his exit another way.

This performance was a thing of great beauty and it is difficult to find words to describe it. Maybe he found an echo of himself in that part; maybe he knew that he had let real and lasting greatness elude him, not from drink—that was never a failing of his—but because of that inherent laziness that would never let him sustain an effort. Maybe it was a physical weakness of which neither he nor his friends knew the cause. But whatever it was, it was there. Godfrey Tearle, for all his success, was himself a tragedy of the stage; his was greatness which never really expanded to its fullest extent. He lacked the neccessary concentration; he liked to take things easily.

When he had been on the stage for sixty years—remember how young he was when starting—he wanted me to write his life story and I was delighted. We were such old friends. I went to see him in some charming apartments he had in Queen Anne Street, just by

Harley Street. I found Godfrey that afternoon sitting in an armchair by the fire. He was wearing a dressing-gown which was so old and disreputable that most people would have thrown it away years ago. He was still in his pyjamas; he had not troubled to dress that day at all. On the hearth was a large pot of coffee from which I poured, at his request. Godfrey did not move. We talked and talked and talked, gathering material for the book, and we had very many laughs over old times. The fire burned low and I rose and replenished it. Then Godfrey slightly bestirred himself. He leant forward, picked up something from beside him and poked the fire, making a blaze. The implement he used caught my eye and when he laid it down I picked it up. It was a very beautiful sword. "Why, what's this, Godfrey?" I asked. "Oh, it's the sword they gave me at Stratford when I played Macbeth. Rather nice, isn't it?" he answered. "And you are using it as a poker?" I said, aghast. "Well," smiled Godfrey, lazily, "it comes in handy. Remember what 'Nym' said in Henry V?" And he quoted: "I dare not fight, but I will wink and hold out mine iron. It is a simple one, but what though? It will toast cheese and it will endure cold as well as another man's sword will; and there's an end of it." He lay back with a lazy laugh, but I was horrified; I sat holding that sword. To me it was precious but Godfrey did not think so. He had played Macbeth and used that sword, so the effort was over. Now for the armchair, the slippers, the fire, the ease . . . and that sword made a handy poker. That was his outlook and all too often his method of life, on and off the stage. He sat back far too much. Yet he wanted to play Othello again and we talked of that, too. I regret he never did so, for the present generation, or some of them, would have seen Othello played, as it should be, by a great actor. But he never had sufficient energy to go on with his life story, or to play Othello again. The tragedy of his death came instead.

All too often he preferred to look on rather than to participate. He even gave the impression, to those who knew him and knew of what he was capable, of sitting back and looking at himself. There was, I think, an inherent sadness in him which made his private life none too happy.

At curtain fall on the first night of *The Light of Heart* he made a speech. He said of Emlyn Williams, and said truly: "Take care of this young man. He is of such value to the theatre." The same might have been said about him: he was precious to the theatre and would have been doubly so in the present period, when there is so much understatement and so little virility in acting. But that was not to be. The real underlying Godfrey Tearle was the figure in his rooms that afternoon, sitting back in his chair, easy, comfortable, in old clothes, not worrying and poking the fire with "Macbeth's" sword. And yet —within him—such greatness.

In the 1920's, with which we deal, he was young and keen and was achieving his real victories. The lamp which he allowed to grow dim—shone very brightly then. Let us remember the fine things he did as an actor and forget the weaknesses of the man. He belongs to the shadows now . . . and probably enjoys it.

CHAPTER X

1924—And not so Gay

T HE outstanding event of 1924 was the British Empire Exhibition at Wembley, advance publicity for which claimed that it would put the Great Exhibition of 1851 (which was held in Hyde Park and which originated the Crystal Palace) completely in the shade. It did not do so and its virtues and shortcomings, as an Exhibition, do not really concern this story, but the effect this much boosted event had upon the theatre in general is of considerable importance. The great question in Theatreland was, whether the Exhibition would be good or bad for the theatre. Were the millions of visitors whom it was claimed this Exhibition would draw to London going to patronize the theatre, or were they simply going to be content with the Exhibition? There were two schools of thought. Everyone agreed that much depended on the weather. The more experienced managers knew that such events as these—Exhibitions, Jubilees, Coronations, etc.—do not help the theatre. In this case it was worse, for Wembley was far away from the West End and visitors to it, on arriving back in town, were so footsore and weary that the vast majority of them did not want to go out again; they just wanted to get their boots and shoes off and go to bed. The people who really made money out of the Exhibition were those who held the concessions for the rickshaws, push-chairs and other methods of transport for taking people around the grounds, and also for the chairs in which to rest. The theatre managers debated amongst themselves and one encounter put the whole affair in a nutshell. It was between those two very odd characters who disliked each other heartily, J. L. Sacks and Edward Laurillard. Both men had one thing in common: they were incapable of speaking readily understood English. They found themselves seated at the same table in the Savoy Grill Room. That was by chance, because there was no room elsewhere, otherwise they would have avoided each other. But they became neighbours of necessity. Laurillard was not speaking to J. L. Sacks, but it soon appeared that Mr Sacks was speaking to Mr Laurillard. And he proceeded to do so at length. He took as his theme the Exhibition and its effect on the theatre. It so happened that he himself had a show at the Empire which was a pretty bad flop. Laurillard had no show on at all, so possessed an open mind.

There were other people at the table besides these two and so Sacks addressed them; not for the world would he have admitted his show as no good, of course.

"All dese peoples coming to London," he said. "Dree millionth of dem. Dats what dey say, dree millionth. Dat is already a lot, eh? Now, de hotels is full, de boarding houses is full—all de places. You von't be able to get a meal, you von't be able to move about. Maybe dey go to the shows (only he pronounced it 'saows), maybe dey don't. Dat aint vot vorries me. Vot vorries me is, vere dey all goin' to sleep?" Laurillard saw his chance. He rose quietly and, gazing at Joe Sacks, said, very clearly and distinctly for him. "At the Empire." And he walked away with dignity, expressionless of face but glowing with inward triumph. Joe Sacks had no reply.

One man of the theatre, however, C. B. Cochran, got involved in the Wembley Exhibition up to the neck. Always a showman, he took the big Stadium and announced a rodeo. The public in those days knew little about rodeos but when they learnt that it had to do with broncho-busting and steers being roped, andgenerally thrown about, the reaction was not too good. There is a quality in the British mind which dislikes cruelty or seeming cruelty to animals and this, to the untutored, seemed very like it. There was a lot of trouble with the Royal Society for the Prevention of Cruelty to Animals and an unfortunate accident at the opening performance led to Mr Cochran and his American partner making an appearance at the Wealdstone Police Court. It all blew over but, so far from Cochran making a fortune as he had anticipated out of this very big show, he may have just covered expenses. It did nobody any good.

What sort of a year did 1924 turn out to be, theatrically speaking? It was curiously uneven. It produced some great successes, a couple of epoch-making plays, and a tremendous number of short runs. Twenty-three straight plays topped the hundred performance mark, and eighteen musical plays did the same. On the face of it, Wembley might have helped a bit and, in the case of the musical shows, it probably did; but the straight plays were successful because they were of better standard than those of the first three years of the decade. There were some pretty bad spots, too.

Gladys Cooper and Frank Curzon, in partnership at the Adelphi, revived *Diplomacy*. Naturally 1924 cannot claim the famous Sardou drama as its own, but that play seldom, if ever, fails, and in this case it had an outstanding cast. That fine actor Dawson Milward played Henry; Owen Nares played Julian; Boris Ranevsky was Orloff; Norman Forbes, Baron Stein; Lady Tree, Lady Fairfax; Robert Mawdesley, Algy Fairfax; Irene Browne, Countess Zicka; and Annie Schletter, The Marquise de Rio Zares. Nares, Norman Forbes, Lady Tree and Annie Schletter had all played the same parts in du Maurier's famous revival in 1913, and so had Gladys Cooper as Dora. *Diplomacy* was a big success. Boris Ranevsky, who played Orloff, was Russian-born and had had considerable stage experience before he came to this country as a refugee. He made good here almost at once by his polished acting and his manners, which were Grand-Ducal. A charming man and a charming actor, he was a founder member of The Arts Theatre Club.

At the Aldwych, when *Tons of Money* had run its course, Tom Walls produced *It Pays to Advertise*, the second of that remarkable series of farces. It was written by Roi Cooper Megrue and Walter Hackett. As it had been produced in America in 1914, Hackett had little chance of delaying the show by his dilatory methods. He was to make up for that later. He did, however, adapt some of the characters slightly for the English version. This play ran for 598 performances, right through the year and into 1925. It was a great favourite with Tom Walls, because the article advertised in the story was "Thirteen Soap, Unlucky for Dirt," and thirteen was his lucky number. It turned up again for him. He himself gave an outstanding performance as an elderly man, and Ralph Lynn was in great form, too. This success put the Walls-Lynn stage partnership on a firm basis. The Aldwych Theatre was taken on a long lease.

The Ambassadors staged, amongst others, a play called *Collusion* by J. E. Harold Terry, who made acknowledgements to Vernon Woodhouse. Another Ambassadors production, *Storm* by C. K. Munro, which afterwards transferred to the Royalty, ran for 116 performances. In it Elissa Landi made her first appearance in London. *Fata Morgana* also succeeded at the Ambassadors. It was an American play, originally produced by the Theatre Guild of New York, and written by Ernest Vadja. It transferred to the Criterion and in all completed 243 performances. In it were Jeanne de Casalis, Reginald Denham (soon to become a leading producer), and a young actress playing her second part on the West End stage, named Flora Robson.

Luck was in at the Ambassadors, for *The Pelican*, by F. Tennyson Jesse and H. M. Harwood, ran for 244 performances; Nicholas Hannen, Elizabeth Pollock and Herbert Marshall (so shortly to become famous on the films) were among those in the cast. But a revival of *A Grain of Mustard Seed* lasted only for 19 nights. Those plays were presented by H. M. Harwood, an experienced dramatist who wrote plays in collaboration with F. Tennyson Jesse, his wife, as well as on his own. He was a Lancashire man, had practised as a doctor and been interested in the cotton trade, but his great love was the theatre. He was lessee of the Ambassadors for several years and maintained a high standard.

The Fake was a success at the Apollo (210 performances). It was by Frederick Lonsdale, with Godfrey Tearle in the lead. And an

American play, by Channing Pollock, ran for 138 performances at that theatre. In an outstanding cast were Henry Ainley, Francis Lister, Helen Haye, Olga Lindo and Morton Selten.

Morten Selten deserves more than a passing mention. He was quite a remarkable actor. Born in 1860, he had made his first appearance in London at the Gaiety in 1881, but had already been on the stage for three years. He toured the world and he played for many years in America, where he attained the front rank of players. He returned to this country in 1919, when I was managing the Owen Nares season at the Queen's. He brought a note in introduction from the author of the play we were casting, Edward Childs Carpenter, and I gave him a part in the play which was *The Cinderella Man*. He was, of course, an immediate success. In Morton Selten, the Victorian Age lived on. His appearance was typical of the period; indeed, he bore a marked resemblance to King Edward VII, although he wore no beard. He had the deportment, the manners, the richness of that rich time; there was about him (metaphorically of course) the atmosphere of champagne, vintage port and the best cigars. One could visualize him on the box of his own four-in-hand. His dress—and he was always perfectly tailored—was also of the period but not ostentatiously so. He clung to the old elegance, the right kind of gloves, the proper ties and exactly the right boots, collars and walking-sticks. He had a rich, mellow voice with a kind of a roll in it which belonged entirely to the days of leisure. His manners were courtly and perfect, but always friendly and genial. He lived in a house in Hampstead which was, as to its interior, the perfect specimen of a Victorian home. His widow, who adored him, as he did her, still lives there and that house, especially the drawing-room, should be preserved for the nation, as the perfect example of a Victorian state apartment. He is indeed, still there, because his ashes in a little vase are in the room. He was a really first-class actor, with a wide range, and his warm and magnetic personality made him very popular. He was just as good on the films as on the stage and many cinemagoers will remember him, especially his uncompromising, unbending Highland Chieftain in *The Ghost Goes West*, who condemned his son not so much for seeming cowardice but for lack of family pride. His performance matched that of Robert Donat, who played the son, and the Ghost which went to America and redeemed the blot on the 'scutcheon.

Olga Lindo was then a young actress who had been in several ReandeaN productions with success and was steadily coming to the front. She had made her first appearance in pantomime at Drury Lane in 1913.

The Comedy Theatre found little or no luck until 1924 had run half its course; then came *The Creaking Chair*, which transferred to the

Little and then to the Vaudeville and accumulated in all 235 performances. This was a thriller by Allan Tupper Wilks, and it really thrilled. Aubrey Smith was in it and so was Tallulah Bankhead, which ensured a big crowd of adoring and half-hysterical young ladies at the stage door, who cried from the gallery on First Nights: "Tallulah, you're wonderful!"

Aubrey Smith was the ideal stage Englishman who had the upright bearing and command of a colonel of the Regular Army and about whom, all the same, there seemed more than a suggestion of white flannels, a blazer and a County Cricket cap. Which was not surprising, because he gained great fame as a cricketer when at Cambridge. He had also captained Sussex and English teams in Australia and South Africa. He had his own style of bowling, coming round the wicket in semicircular fashion instead of taking a straight run, which earned him the title of "Round the Corner Smith." When, very late in life, he went to Hollywood and became a film star at an age when most men were on the shelf, the first thing he did was to form a Cricket XI out of the English actors who were there.

Also in the play was Eric Maturin, who was a real character. He was also a cricketer. A member of the M.C.C., he played mostly for the famous theatrical club, the Thespians. He was an all-round sportsman, shining at golf, squash, riding and tennis, as well as cricket. He was a very keen motorist and went in for speed. He had sporting cars capable of great acceleration and to drive with him was a terrifying experience for nervous people. He could not bear another car to pass him. If one did so, his jaw set, his eyes blazed, down went the accelerator and he overtook the offending car and passed it in triumph often to the public danger, and his own. He was an eccentric. He would undertake all sorts of wagers, to achieve seeming impossible things. Sometimes he won, sometimes not. He had a bet that he would run from London to Brighton in a fixed time, in full evening dress and wearing patent leather pumps. He did not do it. He was found, down and out with exhaustion and fast asleep, on the roadside near Horley.

He was a very good actor in his own line, and nobody could be better in slightly sinister roles. He was a bit spasmodic in his work and given to moments of sudden violence, but he could hold an audience. He was very hard on stage properties, which he treated very roughly indeed, slamming things about and breaking them. I remember in one play he had a telephone on the end of one of those long spring flexes. He liked that and pulled it about to such an extent that he broke it at every performance. Property men did not like him because of the trouble he caused them, but he did not care, and his actions were quite in keeping with the type of part he usually played. He had a most trenchant way of expressing his opinion of a play during rehearsals. If he did not think much of it, he just went to sleep, with no attempt at disguise. Socially his manners were perfect and he detested anything he regarded as "bad form." He so disliked the cast of one play in which he appeared that he spoke to nobody, but brought a spaniel with him to share his dressing-room. He was told that this was against the rules—dogs were not allowed back-stage. He replied that so long as he appeared in that play his dog should come with him, for it was the only gentleman in the theatre. He got his own way.

The Court Theatre, always the home of novelty and striking events, made some more history. Sir Barry Jackson brought his Birmingham Repertory Theatre Company there and staged *Back to Methuselah*. Those who had considered *Heartbreak House* a big mouthful now found that a play could be served to them in courses, like a dinner. This amazing play stunned the playgoers of 1924 and, although at that time it played for only 20 performances and some special matinées afterwards it created much discussion and tremendous interest.

There was a very different production in the same season. This play was a simple, everyday affair, conforming to convention and very much down to earth. It followed *Back to Methuselah* and it was not by Shaw, but by Eden Phillpotts. He was already a veteran novelist and playwright who was—and still is—to Devon what Hardy had been to Dorset, except that his books were as different from Hardy's in texture as this play was from Shaw's. It was called *The Farmer's Wife* and had been played in Birmingham some time before. Produced at the Court, it got a good Press but the business hung fire. Clever and continuous publicity, and that most valuable of all things, word-of-mouth recommendation, soon brought all London to the Court (for 1329 performances), a wonderful record when one realizes that it was a period when very short runs were practically the rule in the West End.

It had no big star names to attract the public but it had young people who were learning their business the right way. To one of them, at least, it brought fame—to Cedric Hardwicke, who is now a knight. He played *Churdles Ash*, a rich Devonshire character, and he captured London. The play was really a portion of a long and excellent Phillpotts novel called "Widecombe Fair," which he lifted out of its context and dramatized. All Londoners wanted to see *The Farmer's Wife* and a great many of them did. If she did not cut off their tails with a carving knife when they ran after her, she certainly took from them a considerable amount of what was in their pockets. Others of that company reached the front rank, too: Colin Keith-Johnson, Eileen Beldon, Scott Sunderland, Amy Veness, Raymond Huntley and Frances Doble.

Laurence Olivier—a beginner in the 1920's—now knighted and leader
of his profession.

Edith Day, the wonderful leading lady of musical plays—and Drury Lane, too.

Dorothy Dickson, delightful and beautiful leading lady of the 1920's.

Cedric Hardwicke was lucky, as well. So many actors, having made such a resounding success in a particular kind of part, are doomed to play nothing else. Churdles Ash was such a part and for some time those who had casting power were obsessed by it when thinking of Hardwicke. But he was, and is, far too good an actor to be so circumscribed, and soon burst out of it, as the world knows. With *The Farmer's Wife* in residence, the Court needed no other tenant in 1924 nor for some time afterwards.

The Criterion, in that year, lived mostly on transfers from other theatres, including *Outward Bound, The Mask and the Face* and *Fata Morgana*. Its own two ventures were rather disastrous—*The Audacious Mr Squires* (15 performances), and *Cartoons*, a revue of which the archcartoonist Tom Webster, then at the height of his success, was part author, and which only managed to run for 42 performances.

For once, the Duke of York's had a successful year, which was entirely due to Archie de Bear, who presented there his best revue, *The Punch Bowl*. This was perfectly mixed—not even Mr Micawber could have done better—and it ran for 565 performances. Alfred Lester was the chief comedian and he also contributed a perfect little etching of an old Punch and Judy man. Later in the run Robert Hale took over, whose son, Sonnie Hale, made his first big success in this same show. Norah Blaney and Gwen Farrar were also in it; one can still hear Norah Blaney singing "All Alone by the Telephone," and the two of them making a duet of "It Ain't Gonna Rain No More." Chili Bourchier, who made a delightful Dog Toby sang "I'll Be Your Chilli-Bom-Bom." *The Punch Bowl* was revue at its best. But then, in his line, Archie de Bear is by way of being a genius and one wonders why he had never been allowed to exploit his talents on Television; he has the requisite gifts for that difficult medium.

In 1924 Basil Dean was almost ubiquitous in the Theatre. He became Joint Managing Director of Drury Lane with Sir Alfred Butt, for after the production of *Good Luck* the man who had been its presiding genius for so many years with such success, who wore the mantle of the great Sir Augustus Harris and made it his own— Arthur Collins—had retired. How he escaped knighthood is a mystery. With him went most of his staff, grown almost grey in the service, and in came the new man.

Basil Dean, with the glory of ReandeaN upon him, his own vast energy and genuine knowledge, seemed the perfect partner for Sir Alfred Butt, who never claimed to be a practical man in stage technique but who was a master of the art of running theatres and knew more about the stage than most of the great ones of today, all the same. Basil Dean went to "The Lane" brimful of ideas. But he was not lucky to the Lane, nor was it to him. Drury Lane is a curious place. Those who know it intimately are sure that it is a conscious entity and that it has likes and dislikes. Those of whom it approves, it will help; those whom it dislikes, it will break. It really does seem to work out that way.

It obviously did not like Basil Dean, for his tenure of office was short. Maybe, too, it was not possible for two men of such strong and contrasted personalities to agree for long. Sir Alfred is the only man ever known to bring business methods to a theatre and make them succeed; but he also knew that the methods he introduced must be suitable to an undertaking which is not a real business and never can be.

With Basil Dean the show came first. What he had to create must not be bounded by finance; it must take the shape he demanded. That was often very costly indeed, for he was, and is, a perfectionist. His first Drury Lane production was *London Life*, a play by Arnold Bennett and Edward Knoblock, which seemed the ideal combination of a man of ideas and an expert craftsman. It had a cast worthy of Drury Lane, a mixture of youth and experience, but *London Life* did not live up to its name. It expired after 26 performances.

Basil Dean fell back on Shakespeare, which had not been seen at the Lane for a long time. He produced *A Midsummer Night's Dream* on Boxing Day, a day long hallowed as the opening of Drury Lane pantomimes. This was a production of great beauty, remembered by all who saw it. Edith Evans and Athene Seyler were Helena and Hermia respectively, Robert Harris was Oberon; Gwen Ffrangcon-Davies was Titania; and Wilfrid Walter was Bottom. It had only a short run. Basil Dean resigned from Drury Lane.

Tiger Cats at the Garrick, with Robert Loraine, Edith Evans and Nicholas Hannen, ran for 122 performances, including a transfer to the Strand.

On 16th January, 1924, a play called *Havoc*, written by Harry Wall, was presented at the Haymarket. This was really the first of the realistic war plays dealing with the horrors of trench warfare. It was not a great play but a scene in a dug-out and the inspired acting of a young man named Richard Bird, now a leading producer, aroused great enthusiasm. It ran for 171 performances. A revival of *The Great Adventure* lasted for 160 nights, but a Galsworthy play *Old English*, despite having Norman McKinnel in the lead, was a long way below Galsworthy at his best.

Out at the Lyric, Hammersmith, a revival of *The Way of the World* did well and put Edith Evans right in the front rank as a mistress of artifical comedy.

But undoubtedly the high spot of the dramatic year happened at the New Theatre on March, 26th. On that night Bernard Shaw's

St Joan was seen for the first time in this country and Sybil Thorndike was recognized as one of our greatest actresses. That first night is now history and the play is familiar to all, but those who witnessed the first performance will never forget it. It was not at all what they had expected. Here was the master-debunker in no debunking mood; for once he seemed sincere. Here was a "Joan of Arc" play entirely different from all others, and with, it seemed, a St Joan who was probably as near the original as could be imagined. Here was a real play, a real drama, a great story, greatly treated. Only in the epilogue did the familiar Shaw assert himself and many of that first night audience thought this part redundant, as many do still. It seems likely that Shaw had intended to debunk the Maid of Orleans, but her inspired simplicity defeated him and he gave us what must be considered his best play—one which will be immortal.

Sybil Thorndike's performance cannot be described in words. It, too, was a case of inspiration. This, indeed, was what one had imagined the Maid to be like. She was the glory and tradition of France, as well as its earth and its peasantry. She heard her immortal voices, yet spoke with the common tongue. That consummate piece of acting is now classic and ranks with the best our stage has ever known. There was a long and distinguished cast, with Raymond Massey in a small part, and Lewis Casson giving a splended performance as "Stogumber." Keneth Kent played the English soldier, and on the programme, against the part of "Dunois' Page" is the name, Master Jack Hawkins. Whatever the theatre of 1924 failed to give us, it gave us *St Joan*.

On May 15th a very successful and long running play was presented at the Playhouse, to be frequently transferred from theatre to theatre; it was called *White Cargo*. In the original cast were Horace Hodges, Franklyn Dyall, Templer Powell, an excellent young actor called Brian Ahearne, and Mary Clare making a big success as Tondeleyo, the very uninhibited native girl. Later in the run C. V. France took over the role of the Doctor from Horace Hodges, and later still he was succeeded by Godfrey Tearle. *White Cargo* was by Leon Gordon and presented by Ida Molesworth. It made a lot of money.

W. A. Darlington, dramatic critic, took his place amongst the few of his calling who have written successful plays. This was an extravaganza—that is the official description—called *Alf's Button*, which ran for 111 performances at the Prince's Theatre and deserved a longer run. It has been revived since. Mr Darlington is a man of charm and humour, and also that rare thing, a dramatic critic who really loves and enjoys the theatre.

There was an important beginning of future greatness at the Prince of Wales's Theatre on June 9th, 1924, with the production of

a play called *The Rat*. It was announced as by "David L'Estrange,"
a nom-de-plume which veiled very thinly two people of the theatre,
Ivor Novello and Constance Collier. The name was made up of
Novello's real first name, David, and Constance Collier's married
name, L'Estrange.

The Rat had been produced on a shoestring at Brighton against the
advice of well-meaning friends. Despite that, it succeeded. It came
to the Prince of Wales's Theatre and was then transferred to the
Garrick; it ran in all for 283 performances. Ivor Novello himself
played the lead in this story of the Paris underworld. Already he had
hosts of admirers, who thronged the stage door to see him leave. He
treated them all with unfailing courtesy and charm, but probably the
strangest tribute he ever received was after the first performance at
the Theatre Royal, Brighton. He edged his way through a host of
excited females who all shouted praise and endearment. One
grabbed hold of him. "Oh, Mr Novello," she gasped, "you was
luverly, luverly, specially when you spat." The success of *The Rat*
started Ivor Novello as a dramatist, for which the theatre could be
thankful.

Right at the end of 1924, on December 16th, a most arresting
play was produced at the Everyman, Hampstead, and came to the
Royalty Theatre. It was written by another young man who was to
became, with Novello, one of the two outstanding personalities and
supports, indeed pillars, of the theatre during the next two decades,
and longer. His name was Noel Coward. In this play he was his own
leading man and the title was *The Vortex*. It was a cry against
the life of the period, an expression of youthful rebellion, but unlike
some which have followed later, it knew what it wanted,
stated it clearly and had proper shape and form. It offended some,
it delighted many. Some considered young Mr Coward as the *enfant
terrible* of the theatre; others, the majority, welcomed him as a very
real and valuable addition to the then very small band of playwrights. They were right. In type *The Vortex* and *The Rat* were miles
apart; the first was a sincere effort to deal with modern life (some
detected a resemblance to *Hamlet* in the scene where Coward, playing
the son, upbraids his mother, played by Lilian Braithwaite); the
second, *The Rat*, was pure romantic drama but excellent theatre.
Both of them were, from such young men, excellent pieces of work
which showed the shape of things to come.

In the year 1924 ReandeaN had only one play which ran for any
length of time at the St Martin's, *In the Next Room* (202 performances).
This had not been produced by Basil Dean, who was busy at Drury
Lane. But he did produce Galsworthy's *The Forest* (58 performances)
and, for matinées, *Gruach*, *The Phoenix*, and *A Magdalen's Husband*, by
Milton Rosmer and Edward Percy. It was while rehearsing for that

play that poor Meggie Albanesi died and a great lamp of the British Theatre went out before it had gained its full lustre. Basil Dean always says that, had she lived to play that part, her performance would have been a revelation to all. Death took someone who could ill be spared, and the footlights flickered indeed.

Dean had also produced *The Way Things Happen*, by Clemence Dane, at the Ambassadors (65 performances), and *The Claimant* (44 performances) and *Pansy's Arabian Night* (by Walter Hackett, 25 performances) at the Queen's. The footlights had flickered for him and for ReandeaN, too. From the St Martin's to the Queen's went a play called *The Conquering Hero*, by Alan Monkhouse, which dealt with the aftermath of war and deserved a far longer run that the 60 performances it attained.

The Savoy had an unlucky year, relieved only by *The Sport of Kings* by Ian Hay, in which that graceful actor-sportsman, Basil Foster appeared, and which ran for 319 performances.

Wyndham's was not particularly lucky, either. A. A. Milne came to the rescue with *To Have the Honour*, which, with Gerald du Maurier and Madge Titheradge in the leads, reached the respectable total of 207.

The plays produced at each theatre (including transfers) were, in number: Adelphi (3); Aldwych (1); Ambassadors (7); Apollo (3); Comedy (9); Court (2); Criterion (5); Drury Lane (2); Empire (1); Gaiety (2); Garrick (7); Haymarket (4); His Majesty's (3); Kingsway (3); Little (6); London Hippodrome (1); Lyceum (4); Lyric (1); Lyric, Hammersmith (3); New (3); Oxford (4); Palace (1); Palladium (2); Playhouse (2); Prince's (3); Prince of Wales's (3); Queen's (8); Regent (2); Royalty (6); St James's (3); St Martin's (4, and some special matinées known as *The Playbox*); Savoy (8); Scala (3); Shaftesbury (3); Strand (6); Vaudeville (4); Winter Garden (2); Wyndham's (4).

An outstanding event of 1924 was the opening of a new theatre, the Fortune. This was the beginning of quite a crop, planned and arranged during the war boom. Nowadays there is constant news of theatres closing down; in 1924 they were opening. The Fortune is still there, in Russell Street, opposite the Stage Door of Drury Lane. It occupied the site of an old tavern called "The Harp" where Edmund Kean used to revel. Up to the end of its existence they would show you a dent in the wall said to have been caused by Kean hurling a pint pot at a drinking companion, and evidently missing him. The Fortune was built by a gentleman named Cowan, who delighted to call himself Lesser Columbus. It is a small intimate playhouse and, in accordance with the trend when it was built, it specialized in expensive seats to the almost total exclusion of the cheaper ones. It is believed that its exterior is a replica of the original

Fortune Theatre, built in 1599 by Edward Alleyn in Golden Lane. E.C., near the Cripplegate Institute.

The present Fortune opened on 8th November, 1924, with *Sinners*, presented by Ida Molesworth and Templer Powell, who had been so lucky with *White Cargo*. That luck did not hold at the Fortune which failed to live up to its name, the play lasting for only 26 performances. *When Knights Were Bold* was revived for the Christmas attraction.

In addition to the short run of *Sinners*, other brief stage existences were *The Fairy Tale* (Apollo, 28); *Far Above Rubies* (Comedy, Alfred Sutro, 43); *This Marriage* (Comedy, 20); *The Other Mr Gibbs* (Garrick, 18 performances. In the cast of that was Winifred Nathan, scion of an old theatrical family and, in the ordinary way, a regular first-nighter and very charming lady); *The Royal Visitor* (His Majesty's, 9); *The Very Idea* (Kingsway, 9); *Kate* (Kingsway, 30, a ballad opera. In the cast was Mavis Bennett, destined to be the first star singer on radio); *Morals* (Little, 16); *Falling Leaves* (Little, 15); *Under His Protection* (Lyceum, a Western by Andrew Emm—A. Melville—42); *Her Market Price* (Lyceum, 54); *The Hour and the Man* (New, 36); *The First Kiss* (Oxford, 43); *Conchita* (Queen's, 9); *Come In* (Queen's, 28); *The Show Off* (Queen's, 40); *Polly Preferred* (Royalty, 32); *Bachelor Husbands* (Royalty, 32); *Lord of Creation* (Savoy, 40); *Blinkers* (H. A. Vachell, Savoy, 11); *The Magic Crystal* (Scala, 14); *The Perfect Fit* (Shaftesbury, 20); *The Daredevil* (Strand, 16); *The Flame* (Wyndham's, 22). Others have been noted elsewhere.

The footlights were flickering considerably. Nowadays, if a play comes off after three months, it makes news. Nobody took any notice of the flops in 1924 but one or two deserve a few words—for instance, *Conchita* at the Queen's. It was written by Edward Knoblock, who had many successes and was a most skilful play-doctor, too. Heading a very good cast were Lyn Harding, a splendid actor, and Tallulah Bankhead, by then the darling of the "gods" and fashionable society. It ran for 9 nights, but such was the uproar that it nearly finished on its first evening. Tallulah's fans were distraught and in tears, and would have wreaked violence on the malcontents if they could have got at them. But it was a very bad play.

In the cast of Galsworthy's short-running *Old English*, there is a notable name on the programme, bracketed with another as "Two Clerks." That name is Godfrey Winn, who has since earned fame in another sphere. His associate Clerk was Cecil Trouncer. And Somerset Maugham had what for him was a failure. His play, *The Camel's Back*, at the Playhouse survived for only 76 performances.

There was a see-saw of fortunes amongst the musical plays, too. *The Three Graces* at the Empire, despite a score by Franz Lehar, only achieved 121 performances.

José Collins played lead in *Our Nell* at the Gaiety. It had been a play about Peg Woffington but it was altered to Nell Gwynn. The music was by H. Fraser-Simson and Ivor Novello, the book by Louis N. Parker and Reginald Arkell. José Collins wore a red wig and Arthur Wontner played Charles II. Despite a first-class cast and a special solo dance by the famous Espinosa, it ran for only 140 performances. Then Robert Evett and José Collins left the Gaiety, to which they had brought three years of prosperity. They were followed by a play from America, called *Poppy*, which it was announced would bring back the old glamour of the theatre. It did not do that, but it ran for 188 nights; the cast included Anne Croft, Reginald Sharland and W. H. Berry, who had left the Adelphi at last.

Patricia, a charming show at His Majesty's, with music by Geoffrey Gwyther, and Dorothy Dickson as leading lady, reached the century and deserved more.

Revue was popular. *Yoicks* at the Kingsway scored 271; and at the Little, *The Second Little Revue* ran for 174 nights. *Leap Year*, produced by Julian Wylie at the London Hippodrome, ran for 471 nights with George Robey, Betty Chester, Laddie Cliff and Vera Pearce.

The Merry Widow at the Lyceum, with Carl Brisson and Evelyn Laye, played 223 performances.

A really outstanding musical comedy was *The Street Singer* at the Lyric, with a good story by Frederick Lonsdale, music by H. Fraser-Simson, with some additions by Ivy St Helier, which ran for 360 performances. In it were Phyllis Dare and Harry Welchman, at their best.

There was a curious musical production, or play with music, at the Lyric, Hammersmith, called *Midsummer Madness*, and in it was Marie Tempest, who had been, years before, a Queen of Musical Comedy at Daly's. It scored 128, and a revival of *The Duenna* at the same theatre ran for 141 nights.

The Co-optimists, now a London institution, were at the Palace for 207 performances. De Courville produced *The Whirl of the World* with a star-studded cast at the London Palladium, including two remarkable dancers, Nattova and Myrio, and a man who had little to do then, but whose turn came later, he being Tommy Handley.

Charlot's Revue at the Prince of Wales's was perhaps the most brilliant musical show of the year. Nearly everyone of eminence was concerned with this book and the music, and there was a cast to match, including Phyllis Monkman, Maisie Gay, Morris Harvey, Peter Haddon, Henry Kendall, and a coming radio star named Leonard Henry. The result was 518 performances.

The audience did not respond to the invitation in the title of *Come In* at the Queen's, although the cast included Lee White and Clay Smith. It was only played 28 times. Then Elsie Janis came back

there, with an entertainment she called *Elsie Janis at Home*. And
Mother was at home, too. They received their friends 74 times.
In the company was a double act at the piano making their début
here, Layton and Johnson.

Toni at the Shaftesbury did better; it played 248 times, with Jack
Buchanan in the lead. A revival of *Stop Flirting* at the Globe reached
194. Gilbert and Sullivan operas, at the Prince's, played 250 times.
Puppets at the Vaudeville, with music by Ivor Novello, and with
Binnie Hale and Stanley Lupino in the cast scored 254. *Odd
Spot* at the same theatre reached 106, but *The Looking Glass* at the
Little, although done by Albert de Courville and Edgar Wallace,
only managed to reach 56.

The Winter Garden fell back on a revival of *Tonight's the Night*,
Grossmith and Laurillard's old success at the Gaiety. "G.G." was in
it, and Leslie Henson repeated the part which had first brought him
fame in London. Heather Thatcher, Sylvia Hawkes and Winifred
Shotter were also in the company. It ran for 139 performances. It was
followed by *Primrose*, with music by George Gershwin, and although
Leslie Henson was in this too, being the resident Winter Garden
comedian, it did not come up to expectations, although it ran for
255 performances. In 1922 *The Cabaret Girl* had run for 462 nights—
the downward slide was getting steeper all round.

It did not look as if the Wembley Exhibition had helped much.

CHAPTER XI

The See-Saw of 1925

ROYAL DEMISE, the official title of death amongst Royalty, always affects the theatre, and did so more in the old days than now, but such an event still cast deep gloom in the 1920's. The year 1925 felt the effect of the death of the much beloved Queen Alexandra, which occurred on November 20th. It came as a shock to the nation, for her illness was very short. She captured all hearts when she first arrived here to marry the Prince of Wales, (King Edward VII). Lord Tennyson, the Poet Laureate, always did a fine job on such occasions and he hit the right nail on the head when he welcomed her as "Sea-King's Daughter from over the Sea." That caught the popular imagination, and that is how they always thought of her. She was a very lovely woman and her character matched her looks. She set fashions; her style of hairdressing led to the "Alexandra Fringe" and later, when as the result of an illness she limped a little, ultra-smart and fashionable people adopted a limp, too. She was as respected as she was loved, and there was never the slightest breath of reproach against her. The great success of Rose Day was because she sponsored it. Until age and disability prevented her, she always drove through London on that June day and everybody bought a rose; London seemed enveloped in a mist of delicate pink. She was a very great lady and her passing snapped a link with the Victorian Age.

Her popularity was such that during her lifetime she completely overshadowed Queen Mary; the people of this land did not then realize the greatness of that wonderful woman, though they were to do so later. When they both attended a public function, Queen Alexandra got the most applause. I recall them both attending a Charity Matinée at the Palace Theatre, when the cheers were much greater for Queen Alexandra than the perfunctory applause for Queen Mary. Shortly after, Queen Mary got the full-throated cheers herself, and was as well beloved as ever Queen Alexandra had been; more so, in fact. She was more accessible. The Sea King's Daughter went to the theatre but she was never the devoted upholder of the drama that Queen Mary showed herself to be. Queen Alexandra had a disability which grew upon her and in her later years was almost stone deaf, but nobody would have realized it, for she always knew who everyone was, and was gracious and kindly. She never heard much of what was taking place on the stage. That matinée at the Palace already referred to afforded an example of her deafness. There was a bit of bother during the interval because she said she had lost a little bottle which she wanted. The box was searched, the route to it scrutinized and every inquiry made; the Royal Room was turned upside down. Seated in her chair surrounded with cushions, Her Majesty looked on with a beaming, encouraging smile. The searchers attached to her suite exchanged audible comments as to what she could have done with it, but she did not hear a word. One of them formed a decision and took the bull by the horns. He asked her to rise. When she understood what he was saying, she did so, and there was the bottle tucked away among the cushions. She was delighted to get it back and lavish in her thanks. She explained that she had a little cough and in the bottle was the means of relieving it. One immediately accepted the Royal explanation.

That matinée was indeed Royal, for those attending it included Queen Alexandra, Queen Mary, the Queen of Norway, Prince Olaf of Norway (then a small boy in a sailor suit), the Princess Royal (Duchess of Fife) and her two daughters. The Princess Royal arrived very early indeed. I received her and prepared to escort her to the Box. "Don't do that," she said. "I know my way. You wait for the others. I came early so as to get the best seat. I'll just go up and take it." And she did. Next to Queen Mary, that Princess Royal (Duchess of Fife), was the greatest friend and supporter of the theatre, and she ran Queen Mary very close. She went to every show, or at least to those which ran long enough to enable her to do so. She always occupied the Royal Box and in attendance was Mr Walter Grant, representative of the firm of Ashton and Mitchell, who looked after the job of getting the tickets for Royalty. She would come in her car, driven by her chauffeur Armstrong, who was well known to every theatre manager. Every manager and almost all the players knew Her Royal Highness, too. She always wanted members of the cast presented to her; she knew all about them and one always felt she was a personal friend. Her memory was prodigious. She forgot nobody and if they suffered from a complaint she always remembered to ask about it. In the early 1920's I was suffering badly from rheumatism, a result of the 1914-1918 war, and she suffered from it, too. We would have long talks about it and, if either of us discovered anything which gave relief, we would exchange the remedy. She always liked to have, in advance, a programme of the show she was to visit and would study it carefully. When she saw the play, the programme was impressed on her memory and she never had to consult a copy during the performance. If she liked a play, she would come several

times; she would send her staff, at her own expense, and often buy
£40 or £50 worth of tickets to send to her friends. Her interest had a
real and practical side. If she was very struck by a play, she would ask
for a script of it to read, and always send it back most meticulously,
with some notes about it and a letter of thanks signed by herself and
sometimes entirely in her own very legible handwriting. She wanted
very much to come to a first night on one occasion and asked me if
she should do so. She said she had heard that the presence of
Royalty on such occasions sometimes had a disturbing effect on the
audience, but she did so want to come. Of course, I told her she
would be very, very welcome, (although actually we would have
preferred her to stay away, for she was right as to the effect on
audiences, especially in those days). But, because of what I said, she
came and enjoyed herself. Unfortunately the play—it was *It's All
Wrong* at the Queen's—was not a winner. She was, like all the
Royal Family, the most thoughtful and considerate of people. When
I was in charge of the Alexandra Palace, she consented to come and
open a big outdoor Fête. Naturally I received her and just as
naturally, the function being outdoors, it was raining hard. I had a
large carriage umbrella ready for her shelter. "No, no, Mr Pope,"
she said. "Thank you very much but I won't trouble about that. I
think umbrellas look so dumpy. I'll just go round with you as I am."
And she did, so we both got soaked. But she spent over £100 at the
stalls, all the same. There was nothing imposing or regal in her
appearance but that did not matter; she did things in the Royal way,
and everybody in the theatre adored her.

As regards the happenings in the theatre of 1925, they are a little
difficult to set forth. There were a great number of productions, a
large number of failures and many very short runs. The best way is
to deal first with the good plays, or those which succeeded, which is
not by any means one and the same thing. Only a few plays scored
over 100 performances but a few had very long runs. As was customary in the 1920's, the musical plays shone brightest, for it was the
year of *No, No, Nanette* and *Rose Marie*.

Gladys Cooper and Frank Curzon revived Pinero's *Iris* at the
Adelphi, with Henry Ainley also associated in the management. He
and Gladys Cooper played the leads. In a distinguished cast, however, one member failed. He was replaced at very short notice by
that rising young actor-manager-dramatist-composer, Ivor Novello,
who made a big success. *Iris* ran for 152 performances. A musical
play flopped there, called *Love's Prisoner*, which only reached 28
nights, despite having Harry Welchman and Helen Gilliland.
Success came, however, with *The Green Hat* by Michael Arlen, the
approved chronicler of the Smart Set and Mayfair. This had a
brilliant cast, including Tallulah Bankhead; her understudy in that

show, also playing "A Maid", was Beatrix Lehmann. Tallulah's fans
had no shocks on that first night and, although Hannen Swaffer
made a violent attack on the play in the *Daily Express*, it ran for 128
performances. It was followed by *Betty In Mayfair*, a musical version
of *The Lilies of the Field* by John Hastings Turner with music by H.
Fraser-Simson. This scored 182. That summer, at the Aldwych, the
phenomenal success of *It Pays to Advertise* had almost run its course.
Tom Walls had arranged for its successor, of which he had great
hopes. Walter Hackett had come to him and told him the story. It
embraced all the Aldwych cast and it seemed ideal. It was a variant
of *Romeo and Juliet* in modern style, and it started while the characters were at school! Tom was the school captain, immensely
popular and magnificent at games, but no good academically.
Ralph Lynn was the studious boy, hopeless at games but winning all
the prizes. There was antipathy between the two. Then we were to
see them later in life—Tom as a very successful business man, Ralph
the brilliant scholar finding no outlet for his talent except as an
interpreter attached to Cook's Tours. Of course, one had a daughter
and the other a son, and those two young people fell in love, despite
the hostility of the parents, and the Romeo and Juliet motif took
charge in a farcical manner—or so Hackett said. In the first act
which actually showed them all at school, the illusion would have
been created by extra large scenery and "props" to dwarf the performers—it sounded fine to a producer like Tom Walls—and the
spectacle of "Bunny" Hare as a schoolboy being bullied was en-
trancing. The play was commissioned, the cast all put under contract, a provincial date booked for a try-out, but the script did not
materialize. Tom pressed Hackett, who sent him ten pages of the
first act, that being the traditional amount with him. He was
harassed and pressed and constantly invented excuses until Tom
began to suspect the real truth. The position was most serious, big
financial considerations were involved and nothing could be done;
all they had was the first ten pages of the play. Finally he commanded
that the most elusive Hackett should appear before him. Hackett
came to see Tom one night in his Aldwych dressing-room, in the
second interval. Tom, keeping his temper, told the big American
the position and said he must know, then and there, where the second
act took place. Hackett roared with laughter at what he said would
take place therein; he split his sides but he uttered no word which
gave the slightest clue. He muttered something, in response to an
enraged outburst by Tom Walls, about a villa in the South of
France. Tom knew the worst. He rose to his feet in majestic rage.
This man could not finish his play, had no idea beyond the original
germ. "Hackett," he roared," you're a bluff! You don't know anything about it. Get out of here and at once, before I throw you out!"

And the bison-like American removed himself with speed as Tom advanced upon him. He could move pretty quickly on occasions, especially if physical violence threatened. Tom sank back in his chair. He did not know what to do. Ruin stared him in the face—all those responsibilities and no play anywhere! His call came and he played the last act without really knowing what he was doing. The company saw something was the matter and wondered if Tom was "tight."

When the curtain fell, those of us directly interested were sent for to Tom's dressing-room, where we were told the situation. Nobody could find a solution; this seemed like the end. We were sitting silent, pondering, thinking, when the telephone rang. Wall's dresser answered it and, turning to Tom, said in his quiet voice: "It's for you, sir." Tom motioned him away. "It's Mr Leslie Faber, sir," said the dresser. "I think it may be important." Tom took the phone. Leslie Faber, that fine actor, said: "Oh, Tom, I don't suppose you want a play, do you? All your plans will be made. In fact, I heard so, but I have just read a farce which seems right up your street and I was wondering, if I sent it along, whether you could find time to read it with a view to the future." "Where's the script now?" gasped Tom. "I've got it here with me at the Club," replied Faber. "Put it in a taxi and send it down to me at once, to the Aldwych stage door, old chap, will you?" said Tom. Leslie Faber, a bit surprised, did so. We sat waiting, hardly speaking, as the minutes ticked by. Then the script arrived and was rushed up. We sat up half the night reading it.

First thing the next morning, Tom Walls telephoned to the author to come down to the Aldwych, sign a contract and collect a cheque on account of fees. He was going to produce this farce at once. The author expressed great pleasure but said he didn't think he could come down. Tom was insistent, and the author still excused himself. Then Tom got cross and seemed almost to jump down the telephone after the author, who said, with great reluctance, that he would come down. We all sat and waited again. In due course a man was shown in, muffled up in overcoat and scarves, and with a cap pulled down over his eyes. It was the author. He signed his contract and took his cheque without removing any of his heavy covering. "Now," said Tom, "why couldn't you come down at once without all that argument?" "Well," said the author, "it was a bit difficult. It still is. You see, I've got whooping cough." And he filled the room with his whoops. He was Ben Travers; that play was *The Cuckoo In The Nest* and it began that long series of Ben Travers farces which were such an important part of the Aldwych success. It was produced on July, 25th 1925, and it ran for 376 performances; and it was also filmed. Thus is theatre history made.

Incidentally Walter Hackett never did finish his play. He had a second chance later, when he wanted money desperately, but he never got beyond those first ten pages. He could not solve his plot. As a crime reporter in New York he had solved many mysteries for the police, but his own plots beat him.

The Apollo Theatre had a very good revue, called *By the Way*. It transferred later to the Shaftesbury and ran altogether for 341 performances. The music was by a young composer who had already had some separate numbers in London revues and had done excellent work in touring revues. He is now our leading composer of light music, Vivian Ellis. Cicely Courtneidge and Jack Hulbert were in *By the Way*. Another Apollo revue, called *Tricks*, which had the Trix Sisters in the cast and for which Helen Trix did a lot of the music, did not have a long run. The Ambassadors had one or two outstanding events. *Hay Fever*, by Noel Coward, which transferred to the Criterion and ran for 337 performances, had Marie Tempest and Graham Browne in the lead. There was very great interest in *The Emperor Jones*, by Eugene O'Neill. This gave London its first sight of Paul Robeson as an actor. He had played previously at Blackpool but had not been seen in Town. Now, as Brutus Jones, he made a very deep impression, although the play only ran for 43 performances. The Ambassadors also staged a revival of H. Granville Barker's *The Madras House*, which scored 100 performances. At the Comedy, much was expected of an American play called *Tarnish*, starring Grace Edwin, but it only reached 55 nights. At the same theatre, *Lavender Ladies* was a success. There were exquisite performances in it by Louise Hampton and Mary Jerrold. Louise Hampton was a real star who never looked the least bit like one. There was no theatrical flourish about her. She dressed quietly and might have passed as a hard-working suburban housewife. She could be seen any morning around Charing Cross Road, doing her shopping with a string bag or basket laden with purchases. There was nothing to mark her out, unless you looked into the face and eyes and saw the great intelligence therein. She was one of the best and most sensitive of English actresses. Mary Jerrold, also, was a very lovely actress indeed, with a warmth and sympathy all her own.

The Comedy had a success with *9.45* and in the cast was a young man named Walter Hudd, who had also had experience with ReandeaN and is now a front ranker.

Mixed Doubles, a farcical comedy by Frank Stayton, ran for 102 performances at the Criterion, with a cast headed by Aubrey Smith and Yvonne Arnaud. Also in it was an actor named Ian Fleming, so often seen on television nowadays.

The big man of finance, James White, tried his hand again at Daly's. A revival of *The Dollar Princess* ran a short while, and then he launched *Cleopatra*, which he firmly believed would eclipse *Madame Pompadour*. But this time the Serpent of Old Nile was not so seductive, despite the music of Oscar Straus, and the fair beauty of Evelyn Laye, who could in that respect challenge the duskier charms of the original. It only lasted for 110 nights.

The most dramatic and outstanding event, musically, of 1925 was the adoption by Sir Alfred Butt of big musical plays at Drury Lane. He had to encounter opposition and criticism from many sources. A lot of people professed to see the degradation of Old Drury by the performance of musical comedy there. They did not know that musical plays had been part, and a very considerable part, of the attractions there ever since that playhouse opened in 1663. But Sir Alfred is a man who knows his own mind and thrives on opposition. He has a knack of winning his battles and he won this one. So, on March 20th, 1925, he presented *Rose Marie*, from America. The phenomenal success of that play is now history. It ran for 851 performances, establishing a record which was not lowered until *Oklahoma*, also from America, beat it. London went mad about *Rose Marie*, The first night was a triumph; the fine male voice Chorus of the Mounties was acclaimed, but the great excitement was the Totem Dance. The poor girls who danced it thought they would never be able to stop; on and on went the applause and on and on they danced until they fell down with exhaustion. One of them was named Marjorie Robertson, who is now Anna Neagle, the first Lady of our cinema screen.

In the lead, that wonderful artiste, Edith Day, was at her very best, and that is saying a good deal. So was Derek Oldham, and their singing of the now so well known Friml and Stothart melodies was beautiful. Little Billy Merson, from the Music Halls and revues, as Hard-Boiled Herman shattered the tradition that so often Drury Lane was death to comedians. It may not have been a very good part, but he made it seem so. And *Rose Marie* brought to Drury Lane Oscar Hammerstein II, who had that theatre in his destiny. With Otto Harbach, he had written the libretto. Despite bad conditions all round, and the poor run of luck which Drury Lane had been experiencing, *Rose Marie* proved that a good show always triumphs.

There was an element of drama around this production, centred on the box office. "The Libraries" or "The Trade," as the ticket-selling agencies are known in theatreland, had been invited to see a dress rehearsal at which there was no audience. They decided they did not like the play and, when they interviewed Sir Alfred Butt on the matter, they refused to "do a deal." They just would not buy any seats in advance. They intimated to Sir Alfred that he had a flop. He thought otherwise. So did Oscar Hammerstein. He was leaving for New York the following day and he offered to bet "The Trade" that when he returned, a year hence, *Rose Marie* would still be running. They turned down the bet as they turned down the "deal." They were adamant. So was Sir Alfred. He told them that, as they would not take a chance, they would have no seats reserved for them, no facilities, no commission on sales and that, if they wanted seats for the show, they would have to buy them from the box office for net cash. Nor could they issue their own tickets; those of the theatre must be used. They were horrified but Butt would not budge. That continued right through that long and prosperous run. The Libraries lost thousands in commission and booking fees. The theatre made much by not having to pay commission. The gentlemen of "The Trade" learnt a lesson.

A musical play not from America ran for 94 performances at the Empire. It was a musical version of the celebrated farce *The New Clown*. It was called *Boodle* and Jack Buchanan, June and Elsie Randolph were in it. *Boodle* was followed by The Bard—yes, Shakespeare was played at the Empire, in the person of King Henry VIII. That terrific historical figure hardly ever fails on our stage. This was a Sybil Thorndike production. She had played Greek Tragedy at the Holborn Empire; now she played Shakespeare at the Empire, even if the Empire had become a Theatre. Associated with her in the venture were her husband and Bronson Albery, now Sir Bronson, of the New, Wyndham's and Criterion Theatres.

Sybil Thorndike gave an inspired performance as Katherine of Aragon. She had a wonderful cast and the programme makes most interesting reading, for under the heading of "Bishops, Lords, Officers, Guards, Scribes" etc—to which nobody at the time paid much attention—are two names which now leap to the eye: Laurence Olivier and Carol Reed (the latter the leading film director in the country, the former the leading actor knight). *Henry VIII* ran for 116 performances, too.

Luck, which had been fitful at the the Gaiety, returned with the production of *Katja the Dancer*, a musical play which transferred to Daly's and ran in all for 505 performances. Lilian Davies and Ivy Tresmand were in the cast. But the Gaiety's next venture was not so good. It was *The Good Old Days*, written by Oscar Asche, with music by Percy Fletcher. The burly, not to say fat, Asche also played lead, and produced the play. He had cobblestones laid in the stage to add a touch of realism. They did not get much wear and tear, for the horses' hooves and the coachwheels only ran over them for 37 times. They were an awful nusiance to remove. *The Good Old Days* had a good cast, but nobody liked it.

J. L. Sacks the fantastic, came unstuck at the Gaiety, too, with a play called *The Blue Kitten*, despite Bobbie Howes, W. H. Berry, Roy Royston and Ethel Levey.

Owen Nares and Marie Ault in *The Little Minister*, a Basil Dean
Production at Queen's Theatre.

Leslie Faber, an outstanding actor of the 1920's.

Lyne Harding as "Dr. Grimesby Rylott" in *The Speckled Band*, one of the favourite parts of this great actor.

The Garrick saw a revival of *Old Heidelberg*, with Ivor Novello
giving an excellent performance in the part created by Sir George
Alexander; and the same theatre had a success with *Rain*, although
that play transferred to the St Martin's. This was a dramatized
version of Somerset Maugham's story *Miss Thompson*. Basil Dean
gave it an excellent production and Olga Lindo made an outstanding
success as Sadie Thompson. Also at the Garrick was a stage version
of Thomas Hardy's classic, *Tess of the D'Urbervilles*. This came to
town from a converted cinema in Barnes, which was used as a
theatre by a most extraordinary character named Philip Ridgeway.
He was a weird, eccentric but very likeable man, who just missed
being a genius. He did incredible things in the theatre in the 1920's.
A Londoner born, he read for the Bar at the Inner Temple but
became an actor. At one time he dabbled in the cotton trade, too,
when playing in Manchester. He decided to become a producing
manager. His first effort was a revival of *Jane Clegg* at the Grand,
Croydon, in 1923. One of the things missing in Ridgeway's otherwise often brilliant make-up was originality. In his theatrical
career he dealt almost entirely in revivals. He was indeed the
resurrectionist of the theatre. He hated being alone and he would sit
in my office for hours, pondering on what long-buried play he could
disinter to rattle its bones again behind the footlights. Whilst pondering he would constantly strike matches to light his pipe—which
never kept alight—and throw the burnt matches on the floor all
around him until he sat in a sort of fairy ring of expended flame.
Then an idea would strike him. He would shout the name of a play
and hurry away.

He was always hungry for publicity. He loved seeing his name in
print and would go to great lengths to achieve this. He put out a
story once that he was going to form a brotherhood to free Russia
from the Bolsheviks and would lead the crusade on a white horse.
Nothing came of it but it made a good story. He had another idea of
running a theatre, admission to all parts of which would be one
shilling—"The Shilling Theatre." He did actually get that going,
though it did not succeed, but he worked minor miracles.

He took the little cinema theatre over at Barnes with a negligible
capital. He drew all London which was interested in the theatre out
to Barnes to see what went on. Sometimes he played in the open air on
Barnes Common, but it was in the little tucked-away theatre that he
did remarkable work. Of course, it was a question of revivals. He
proclaimed Chekov to be the greatest of dramatists and he presented
his plays. He made a vogue of them. He had the immense good
fortune to persuade Komisarjevsky to produce them. "Kommis," as
his friends called him, was really a genius of the theatre. To work
under him was an education to a young player; he could devise

productions out of almost nothing and make them look remarkable
by his artistry and his supreme ability in lighting. Given a few
second-hand flats, an old backcloth, some paint and a moderate
lighting set, he would give you Beauty. It cost almost nothing at all,
nor did he ever want a big fee for himself. His reward was achievement and in that he was rich. His production of *The Three Sisters* at
Barnes was memorable, and about £20 would have covered the cost.

Under Ridgeway's management at Barnes were produced *Tess of
the D'Urbervilles*; *Ivanoff*; *Uncle Vanya*; *The Three Sisters*; *The Mayor of
Casterbridge*; *The Cherry Orchard*; *The Government Inspector*, and many
other plays. Ridgeway engaged many promising young actors just
starting their careers. Making his first appearance on the professional stage at Barnes in 1926 was a young man fresh from winning
the Gold Medal at the Royal Academy of Dramatic Art, whose
salary was about £2 a week and whose name was Charles Laughton.
That was the sort of thing Ridgeway did. He spread himself over
Tess of the D'Urbervilles. He went down to Dorchester and managed
to see Thomas Hardy, O.M., himself, then almost a recluse and
hard to get at. 'But Ridgeway would have got by St Peter. He
discussed a production of *Tess* with Hardy and turned on all his
charm, of which he had plenty. He and Hardy became friends, but
Hardy would not come to London to approve the play, so Ridgeway
offered to bring it to Dorchester and, if the great novelist would allow
it, to play it in the drawing-room of Max Gate, his home. He got
permission, with one proviso. There must be no publicity over this;
no Press man must set foot over the threshold. That Ridgeway
promised to observe but he explained that certain paragraphs must
appear in the papers to inform the public about the impending production in Town. That Hardy readily understood. So Ridgeway took
his company down to Max Gate, with Gwen Ffrangcon-Davies as
"Tess." And with the company went most of the theatrical columnists and gossip-writers of the Press. Ridgeway explained to them that
as newspaper men they could not enter the Holy of Holies but that
they could "walk on" as "supers" to make the necessary crowd. He
had made no promise about "extras," and that is what they did.
Hardy was delighted with all he saw. Gwen Ffrangcon-Davies sat at
his feet and listened to all he had to say about his "Tess." He praised
Ion Swinley, Austin Trevor, Drusilla Wills and the rest. He gave
the whole thing his blessing. He never knew about the Press "extras."
There was vast publicity, but Ridgeway, like Vincent Crummles,
could not imagine how these things got into the papers. Transferred
to the Garrick on 2nd November, *Tess* ran for 50 performances and
Gwen Ffrangcon-Davies scored a well deserved success.

Philip Ridgeway became quite a figure in the theatre all through
the 1920's. Violet Melnotte called him her Napoleon. He immediately

declared she was his Cleopatra, though where the connection arose was not clear. But Melnotte never got the better of him. He was often assailed by enemies but he did not care. He was the complete optimist; he took many blows with a smile and just pressed on, like the theatre of which he was part. He was also an opportunist and showed it by breaking into broadcasting when that became very popular. Basically he was a lazy, indolent, easy-going man, yet he was always up to something. He was lavish of ideas but lacked the creative ability to carry them out. He had an immense sense of humour and was a good companion. However much his luck was out, he never despaired. When trouble surrounded him, he never swore—and his profession can be very vocal in that respect. All he would say was: "Oh . . . pickles!" It was his nearest approach to profanity.

Noel Coward, now in the front rank of dramatists, had a success at the Globe called *Fallen Angels*, with Tallulah Bankhead, Edna Best and Austin Trevor in the cast. It ran for 158 performances and shone amongst the large number of most indifferent plays of that year like a jewel.

There was an exciting event at the Haymarket. That great American actor John Barrymore came there to play "Hamlet" and he was magnificent. One thing upset him, however. That was the tinkle, rustle and clinking caused by the service of the matinée teas, which are never completed before the interval is over. He had not met this before. He stood it for a bit and then lost his temper. He came right down to the footlights and, glaring at the audience, said scornfully: "Tea . . . tea. . . tea!" The audience looked at him in astonishment. Of course they were having their tea. It is what they had come to the theatre for. They bore him no ill-will, however, he was an American; how was he to know that the basic reason for playgoing in this country is to be able to eat and drink? He had to accept the inevitable. His Ophelia was Fay Compton, the best of our time.

The Haymarket had a big success with *The Man With A Load of Mischief*, by Ashley Dukes, which ran for 261 performances. Fay Compton was in it, for she was then the Haymarket's resident leading lady.

The Birmingham Repertory Company did some good work at the Kingsway with *Caesar and Cleopatra*, *The New Morality*, *The Old Adam* (by Cecily Hamilton), but what caused most interest was their production of *Hamlet* in modern dress. Colin Keith-Johnson came out of *The Farmer's Wife* to play Hamlet, did it very well, and went back to his Devonshire surroundings again. *Hamlet* ran for 86 performances in modern attire—longer than Barrymore had lasted at the Haymarket.

Ridgeway brought his production of *The Seagull* from Barnes to the Little for 56 performances.

Julian Wylie produced a revue called *Better Days* at the Hippodrome. It was in many ways his best production there but perhaps, for that house, it was a bit too—shall we say?—artistic. It only ran for 135 performances and it ended the sequence of Wylie shows. The theatre can be hard. One failure wipes out many successes. In came a musical comedy from America which got a warm welcome. It was *Mercenary Mary* with Peggy O'Neil. All London sang and whistled "Tie a String Around Your Finger" and *Mercenary Mary* ran for 446 nights.

Cochran did two revues at the London Pavilion in 1935, one was *On With the Dance*, with book and lyrics by Noel Coward, who shared the music with Phillip Braham, a composer always in demand. (Cochran had just been made bankrupt but you could not keep him down.) This was a most elaborate show and the first in which "Mr Cochran's Young Ladies" were billed to appear. There were two ballets by Massine, Alice Delysia was leading lady, Ernest Thesiger and Douglas Byng had a wonderful duet as two old ladies, and Coward's song "Poor Little Rich Girl" was very popular. It ran for 229 performances. The other was *Still Dancing*, which ran for 113 nights.

"The London Revue" at the Lyceum, devised by Norman Lee, only ran for 77 performances but had good things in it, notably an Australian actor named John Kirby, who made a big success as a taximan, and Pearl White, a star of the silent films, in which she appeared in a weekly serial entitled *The Exploits of Elaine*, which ran for what seemed to be ages.

Matheson Lang had a season at the New, reviving *Carnival*, and then staging *The Tyrant*. In both those plays were two young men then playing small parts, Donald Wolfit and Alec Clunes. Both are famous today and Wolfit is Sir Donald, one of the best deserved stage knighthoods for years. At the New was also *No 17*, a thriller by J. Jefferson Farjeon, which transferred to the Duke of York's and ran for 210 performances. The playgoers of the 1920's loved thrillers, especially those dealing with mysterious Chinamen, secret panels which opened suddenly, and ghastly shrieks which rang forth in the dark. If crime does not pay in the workaday world, it nearly always shows a dividend in the theatre.

Reginald Denham produced *The Moon and Sixpence* at the New, too, a stage version of Maugham's story by Edith Ellis. It did not quite make the grade, even though Henry Ainley and Grace Lane played the leads. Yet it was a much better play than the American mystery thriller called *The Gorilla*, which ran for 134 performances at the Oxford.

There was a landmark in musical play history at the Palace, where the firm of Clayton and Waller, both experienced men of the theatre, produced *No, No, Nanette*. Produced on March 11th, it ran for 665 performances. The music is always popular and was composed by Vincent Youmans. Everybody knows "Tea for Two" and many of the other songs. Binnie Hale, George Grossmith, Joseph Coyne and Vera Pearce led the cast. *No, No, Nanette* did what *The Belle of New York* had done years before; it speeded up the rather leisurely methods in vogue. It is one of the classic Musicals, as they are now called. It was a highlight of 1925.

Albert de Courville produced a good revue at the Palladium called *Sky High*, which ran for 309 performances and which was followed by *The Folies Bergère Revue*, staged by Tom Arnold. To make it really French there was a genuinely funny cockney comic in the lead, Ernie Lotinga. Robert Chisholm, the tall handsome Australian with the operatic voice, sang *Le Rêve Passe* as a Napoleonic Soldier, and brought down the house nightly.

An operetta by Franz Lehar, called *Frasquita*, with José Collins in the lead, failed at the Prince's Theatre. An unsuitable book had something to do with it. It was only played 36 times.

The Dancing Mothers played at both the Queen's and St. James's, with Gertrude Elliott and Godfrey Tearle, and was quite a success. A. E. Matthews gave a wonderful performance in *Beggar On Horseback*, a play before its time. *Lightnin'*, an American play, was a success at the Shaftesbury. At the St James's, *Grounds for Divorce* scored 118 performances with Madge Titheradge, Lawrence Grossmith and Owen Nares. There also was a revival of *The Wild Duck*, in which that remarkable actress Sybil Arundale played, to whom Ibsen, musical comedy, music hall and pantomine all came alike.

But the big St James's success was the Lonsdale comedy *The Last of Mrs Cheyney*, produced there on September 2nd, and staying there for 514 performances. Sir Gerald du Maurier produced it and played in it. This was a fine play with a magnificent cast and was in the best tradition of the British theatre in every way. It added a much needed touch of lustre to 1925, indeed the whole decade. It will be observed that du Maurier had left Wyndham's, where he had been so long.

The ReandeaN management at the St Martin's was on its last legs. It was breaking up, but still the record was good. There was *Spring Cleaning* by Frederick Lonsdale (262 performances); *The Show* by John Galsworthy (37 performances); *Rain*, transferred from the Garrick, *Easy Money* by Brandon Fleming and Sydney Carroll (37 performances); and a revival of *The Silver Box* (15 performances). Dean produced *Spring Cleaning*, *Rain* and *The Show*. Then he went to America.

Another big success began its career at the St. Martin's. A young impresario named Harry I. Cohen had a play but lacked finance. He took the unusual course of advertising for a backer in the papers and he found one. He produced his play but it was not a success. He was standing watching it disconsolately one night from the back of an almost empty dress circle, when a friend told him of a play on tour which he had seen and which he believed was a winner. Cohen got details and went to see the show. He had not much money left but there might be a chance of a second try. He saw the play, he secured it, and brought it to the St Martin's. It succeeded there and it went from theatre to theatre and made a fortune. It was *The Ghost Train.* It was written by Arnold Ridley, who had been a schoolmaster. This paid him slightly better.

Sun Up at the Vaudeville (234 performances) had Lucille La Verne as its star. Another play at the same theatre, which had an unlucky year, was notable for one thing only: that celebrated critic James Agate was part-author. It was called *Blessed Are the Rich.* It enriched nobody, quite the reverse. It was only played 12 times.

The Winter Garden kept its flag of success flying with *Tell Me More* (music by George Gershwin) with a score of 263. It had now almost a stock company led by Leslie Henson, and a definite policy which showed good results.

The music of Franz Lehar showed slightly better results at the Shaftesbury than it had done at the Prince's and Empire recently, for *Clo-Clo* ran for 95 performances. That included a transfer to the Adelphi.

There were so many plays on and then off again that it is not possible to cope with them in short space. Some short runs were *Anyhouse* (20) and *Growing Pains* (14), both at the Ambassadors; at the Comedy *The Gentleman in Waiting* 20 performances, *The Crooked Friday* (29), and *The Ring O'Bells* (13); the Duke of York's had *De Luxe Annie* (7), and *Nicolette*, a musical play (12); the Fortune, *L.S.D.* (19), *Yetta Powlowski* (10); the Garrick, *Courting* (24), and *Cristalinda* (12); the Little, *Persevering Pat* (27), *Adam and Eva* (16), and *Gloriana* (17). (In that appeared John Gielgud. who had also understudied there in *The Vortex.*) *Just a King* at the Lyric ran for 14 performances. At the Oxford there were a revival of *Kismet* (21), a Pirandello Season, (16) and *Carry On Sergeant*, a Bruce Bairnsfather revue (35). At the Playhouse *The Prisoner of War* and *The Desire for Change* both ran for 24 performances. At the Queen's there were *Salomy Jane* (12) and *The Man from Hong Kong* (24). But the Savoy had a winner in *The Unfair Sex* (226). The St James's had some unfortunate ventures like *The Meddlers* (6) and *The Guardsman* (17). Short runs at the Strand were *The Sea Urchins* (37), *The Signal* (16), and *Ordeal* (22). *Sometimes* at the Vaudeville only stayed there for

28 shows. At Wyndham's *The Man With a Heart* by Sutro and with du Maurier in the cast (25), *Little Miss Bluebeard* (13) and *The Round Table* (21).

The theatre was, by and large, having a bad time. Broadcasting was making deep inroads. A bad habit, too, had crept in, that of giving short weight. Plays were advertised to start at 8.30, actually began at 8.45, had two very long intervals and would be over by 10.45. That was a bad and shortsighted policy. But where there were experienced management and a standard of production, there was still success. Not a lot, but enough to keep the footlights from going right out.

CHAPTER XII

1926—and Nearly a Blackout

AS the decade of the Doubtful Twenties moved towards the Fateful Thirties things did not improve in the theatre. That institution was to suffer a blow which sent it reeling but from which, with its amazing elasticity and its ability to absorb punishment, it came back to fight on. But it bore the scars for some time afterwards. The year 1926 saw more short runs in the theatre than any year preceding it, or since, except when the opening of the Second World War shut it down altogether. But it recovered even from that. It was very ill-equipped to take such punishment as it received in 1926, but its tenacity brought it through.

The blow which struck the theatre was that which struck the whole country—the General Strike. That attempted to paralyse everything and nearly succeeded. It was the greatest Labour upheaval of our time—of any time. It had been brewing for a lengthy period and it was precipitated by a lockout and strike in the coal-mining industry on April 30th. The coal miners had been simmering with dissatisfaction for years. Now they were backed by the entire Labour forces of the land. It was not so much a battle between Capital and Labour as between Labour, as represented by the Trade Unions, and the rest of the population. It did not last very long—from May 3rd to 12th, but it was sharp and bitter. Transport closed down, nothing could be moved, people were stranded unless they had private cars and petrol—and no more petrol could be distributed. Food, fuel, everything was brought to a standstill. It could have been a ruinous deadlock. The Government took action but the people, who did not believe in this sort of strike, took action more quickly. Work went on under the most extraordinary conditions. Newspapers came out in miniature editions and were distributed somehow. Necessities were moved, too, and that great quality of improvisation, for which the British are so renowned, went into top gear. Milk supplies got through. People got to work and to business by divers means. Everybody helped others and the great majority were dead against the strikers. I got down to the West End one day by the only means of transport which offered—I rode down on a hearse, fortunately with no passenger inside. I was a Sergeant in the Special Constabulary, and every night, with a specially picked

squad, I guarded a vital railway bridge and tunnel. Men flocked to
join the Specials and help to maintain order. Buses ran with volun-
teer drivers and conductors; the windows of the vehicles were
protected by wire netting against the stones and bricks hurled at
them by the strikers. I was a welcome passenger on any bus, in my
uniform, and would sit by the driver with my baton ready. The
Government were urged to use the troops but at first refrained from
doing so. Many blamed it for that. But the voluntary spirit was in
full swing. Amateurs took over signal boxes and drove trains. Early
every morning one went North from King's Cross, driven and stoked
by Oxford undergraduates, and we used to cheer them as they
entered our tunnel. The radio sent out the news and was of the
greatest service. *The British Gazette*, a tiny paper edited by Winston
Churchill, got itself printed and distributed. The T.U.C. ran a rival
to it, called *The British Worker*. Business and professional men became
railway porters or milkmen, and did all sorts of jobs. Undergraduates
from both Universities drove steam trains and ran the Tubes as
well. For a time there was almost a carnival spirit abroad. Hyde
Park was the great distributing centre for London's food and milk.
Everyone who had a car used it for some national purpose. As the
strike proceeded and police could not be spared troops were called
in to escort lorries bearing food, each being labelled for identification
and they were respected as Red Cross Ambulances in war. There
were occasional fights and disorders, but it says much for the good
sense of the British people that there was so little general violence.
At length food convoys rumbled through the streets, guarded by
armed soldiers in full battle dress, with bayonets fixed. Armoured
cars began to patrol, too, for tempers were running high. But on
May 12th, the strike collapsed. Men began to drift back to work and
soon the trickle became a flood. The Great Strike was over.

It was a tremendous victory for the ordinary citizens of this land,
whose voluntary efforts had won this battle. The strikers realized
that the great bulk of the nation was against them. That was the
deciding factor. It cost the country many millions of pounds—and
it hit the theatre very hard indeed.

Managers did their best to carry on under these unprecedented
conditions. Some succeeded, others found it impossible. There were
no audiences save for a sprinkling of foreigners and other visitors
stranded in London. Those with the longest purse managed to
tide over, but it was a dreadful time for the theatrical profession. All
contracts and agreements were suspended. It was bad enough as it
was; had it lasted longer, many would have been completely ruined.
It caused repercussions throughout the whole year. It was a terrible
year in every way and yet, amongst the damped smouldering of
the theatrical bonfire, some embers managed to glow and soon

burst forth into flames again. But, apart from the enforced closure in 1939, this was the theatre's darkest hour.

Somehow, 38 plays managed to run for a hundred performances or more. They did not in any way balance those which fell by the roadside but, in view of the conditions, it was remarkable. It goes to show that a good play takes a lot of killing. There were roughly 173 plays produced in London that year, so the proportion of casualties can be reckoned. One good sign was that a number of straight plays achieved good runs; the drama was fighting back amidst the welter of light musical entertainment.

There was a musical play called *Aloma* at the Adelphi, a version of a successful drama produced at the Lyric in 1919 called *The Bird of Paradise*. It dealt with Hawaii and came from America. It ran for 138 performances. *Merely Molly* at the same theatre was not so lucky. Written by John Hastings Turner, with music by Herman Finck and Joseph Mayer, it only lasted for 85 shows, despite Godfrey Tearle, Morton Selten, Helen Haye and Evelyn Laye in the cast. This also included a comedian who has since become famous, named Max Wall.

The Aldwych showed what actor-managerial conditions and a settled policy could do. It staged its second Ben Travers farce, *Rookery Nook*, and it scored 409 performances. The company was now almost the stock company which remained for years, led by Tom Walls and Ralph Lynn, with Tom still playing old men. People had now begun to go to the Aldwych as a habit. They knew the fare offered and knew that it would be good.

John Galsworthy's *Escape* was staged at the Ambassadors and had a run of 243 performances. An American play called *Is Zat So?* at the Apollo was also a success. In it was James Gleason, who was also part author and a film star. And among a fine cast was George Curzon, the son of that splendid actress Ellis Jeffreys. He had served in the Royal Navy, leaving with the rank of Lieutenant-Commander, before he went on the stage. He played small parts in several unsuccessful productions and understudied Owen Nares in the Adelphi revival of *Diplomacy*, his first taste of success. While searching for work, he heard of a play in which there was a part of a naval officer. He thought that might suit him, but the management turned him down, saying that he was not the right type at all. If he did not get the job, at least he got a good laugh.

He was at the Apollo again in 1926 in a play called *The First Year*, with quite a good part in the run of 180 performances. That changed his luck. In this play, there was also an American actor named Ernest Truex, small in size but large in talent, with a personality in which wistfulness mixed with charm. He had been seen in London before in *The Fall Guy* and, although the play failed, he made a success. He did so well in *The First Year* that he decided to stay here. He fell in love with England and England liked him. As time went on, this first-class actor became Anglicized to a quite surprising extent.

Marie Tempest had a success at the Criterion with *The Cat's Cradle*, written by Aimée and Philip Stuart, whose gentle comedies had quite a vogue. This one ran for 148 performances.

Basil Dean had left ReandeaN and now operated on his own as Basil Dean Productions Ltd. He produced a play by Noel Coward —and a good play, too—called *Easy Virtue*, which had the American actress, Jane Cowl, as its star. She left before the end of the run and her part was taken over by her understudy, Grizelda Hervey, who also played it on tour and made a name for herself. Dean also produced another Coward play, *The Queen Was in the Parlour*, at the St Martin's and then transferred it to the Duke of York's. It ran for 136 performances. In this play the young genius, Coward, who was so representative of the times in which he was living, stepped back into that well-loved land of Ruritania, and did it very well, too. Madge Titheradge played the lead.

In December, 1926, the Duke of York's had a pretty bad flop. This was *Liliom* by the distinguished Hungarian dramatist, Ferenc Molnar, whose plays have nearly always been unlucky in this country. This particular adaptation was by Osmond Shillingford and Anthony Ellis. A previous version had been done at the Kingsway in 1920 under the title of *The Daisy*. *Liliom* was presented by the amazing Philip Ridgeway; it was near enough to a revival to suit him and he was always attracted to anything at all out-of-the-way, Well, *Liliom* certainly was that. He offered the leading part to Ivor Novello, who liked it. Ivor always took his job very seriously and he wanted to work under Komisarjevsky, who was producing *Liliom*. Ridgeway had not much capital and Ivor offered to go fifty-fifty with him in the venture; there was not the slightest objection to that. A first-class cast was got together, with Fay Compton as leading lady. There were two young beginners in it too, Marjorie Mars and Charles Laughton (his name has already been mentioned in connection with the Barnes Theatre). When Ivor saw the salary list he thought that Charles Laughton should have a little more money. Ridgeway replied that this young actor had only recently left the Royal Academy of Dramatic Art, that he was getting a fine chance, and that salaries should be based not only on apparent ability but on experience as well. Fay Compton upheld this view, so Ivor gave way.

Liliom opened at the Duke of York's on December 23rd and had a very bad first night. A novel effect introduced into the scene which portrayed the entrance to Heaven went wrong and nearly choked the audience. They did not take kindly to this whimsical ante-room anyway, in which an angel was polishing up the stars. It did not grip: such things are very difficult to put over. Despite some brilliant acting by Fay Compton and a very good performance from Ivor Novello, the play got a bad Press. Business was terrible, so the management gave away complimentary seats by the handful, and members of the profession, ringing up to ask if they could see the show, were told to come to the box office where seats would be at their disposal. Nurses from hospitals were invited, also, to come to the box office.

Violet Melnotte was dead against all this. Used as she was to "flops" in her theatre, she did not take kindly to being involved in one herself and in this venture she was not receiving a rent but a share of the takings. Her share was negligible. One night, when only a few pounds in cash had been taken, and there was a crowd of "guests" in the vestibule, she suddenly gave orders that the box-office was to be closed! It was about half an hour before the curtain was due to go up. The box-office manager and her own house-manager pleaded with her but in vain. Her "Napoleon," Philip Ridgeway, tried his very considerable powers of persuasion. He pointed out that some very important people had been invited. How could they get their seats if the box-office was closed? They would be deeply insulted. "I don't care," stormed "Madame." "I won't have this crowd of awful people with no soles and heels to their boots trampling over my carpets and ruining them. Close the box-office at once!" The box-office manager dared not disobey. That meant the sack. So the box-office was closed. Guests arrived, found they could not get their seats and were equally infuriated. They protested, they argued, they hammered on the box-office window—all to no avail. Madame stood there like a thundercloud, with lightning flashing from her heavily blued eyes. It was a dreadful evening for everyone.

Liliom only achieved a few performances. Everybody lost money, including Violet Melnotte, the custodian of carpets. Strangely enough, this play was a great success years later at Drury Lane, but not under the name of *Liliom*. It was turned into a "musical" by Rodgers and Hammerstein called *Carousel*. It just goes to show.

The best that the Garrick could do in 1926 was *None But The Brave*, a sort of melodramatic farce which managed to get a run of 106 performances; it transferred to the Royalty. The Globe did not fare much better; it had nine shows in the twelve months but some of them managed a short stay—*All the King's Horses*, with Allan Aynesworth, Irene Vanbrugh and Jill Esmond-Moore in the cast, which trans-ferred to the Playhouse to run for 113 performances in all; and *Ask Beccles*, which got to 150 nights. There was also a revival of

Trelawny of the Wells, with Margaret Bannerman as Rose.

This Woman Business at the Haymarket, by Benn W. Levy, with Fay Compton, Frank Cellier, Leon Quartermaine, and Clifford Mollison in the cast, ran for 187 performances, a promising début for Mr Levy, who has since become one of our skilled and thoughtful dramatists. And the luck of the Haymarket was well in when it presented a play, *Yellow Sands*, by Adelaide and Eden Phillpotts (the veteran Mr Phillpotts of *The Farmer's Wife*). It ran for 610 performances, and is popular with Repertory Companies and on television today. In this Cedric Hardwicke gave another study of a bucolic old gentleman, tinged with salt this time. In the cast also were Frank Vosper—his tragic end unthought of—and a young actor named Ralph Richardson, who had only made one previous appearance in London—at the Scala Theatre for the Greek Play Society—and who now played Frank Varwell. *Yellow Sands* was what might be called a "twice-nightly" play, for both Hardwicke and Richardson have reached knightly rank.

The Best People, an American play by Avery Hopwood and David Cray, ran for 309 nights at the Lyric, and another American play there, written entirely by Avery Hopwood, scored 180. It was *The Gold Diggers* and in it was Tallulah Bankhead.

Prince Fazil, with Henry Ainley, Madge Titheradge and Godfrey Winn in the cast, ran for 109 performances at the New, but that theatre's great success in 1926 was a fine, outstanding play by Margaret Kennedy and Basil Dean, *The Constant Nymph*. Edna Best, as Tessa, scored a triumph and put herself right into the front rank. It was a lovely performance; all the wistful tragedy of the unfortunate girl shone with clarity. Noel Coward played Lewis Dodd and was outstanding, too, on exactly the right note. Dean gave the show a cast worthy of it and amongst the names were Keneth Kent, who gave an excellent study of Birnbaum, and a young actor called Cecil Parker, with repertory and Abbey Theatre experience, but making his first appearance in the West End. Basil Dean put all he knew into this play. Always a hard taskmaster, he polished and polished until the company nearly went mad; he was meticulous about the smallest details. He knew he had a diamond and was determined to make it shine. He did so. It ran for 587 performances and was the most discussed play of the year.

There was a sensational "flop" at the Prince of Wales's, a play called *Ashes* by Countess Cathcart. After a terrible first night, it only ran for five performances.

Sybil Thorndike did a notable revival of *Macbeth* at the Prince's, with herself (as Lady Macbeth), Henry Ainley (as Macbeth), Lewis Casson, Basil Gill, and Master Jack Hawkins (as Fleance). Bad luck dogged this splendid production.

At the same theatre, transferred from the Queen's, was *Downhill*, by that composite playwright David L'Estrange, who had been so successful with *The Rat* and who was, of course, a nom-de-plume for Constance Collier and Ivor Novello. Ivor played in it himself and in the cast was D. A. Clarke-Smith, a good actor who died very recently in 1959. It ran for 93 performances.

The Queen's had a big success with *And So To Bed* by J. B. Fagan, a real man of the theatre. This was, of course, the now well known comedy about Samuel Pepys, a character superbly played by Edmund Gwenn with Yvonne Arnaud as Mrs Pepys. It ran for 331 nights.

Seymour Hicks and Robert Courtneidge joined hands at the Savoy. They revived *The Truth About the Russian Ballet* and *Sleeping Partners*, by Sacha Guitry. In that, the amazing Seymour Hicks repeated that masterly performance previously seen at the St Martin's during the First World War. His very long scene without one spoken word, yet with the audience understanding his every thought, was one of the outstanding performances ever given on the British stage. Lovely Ellaline Terriss (his wife and now Lady Hicks) and Edmund Gwenn were with him.

At the St. Martin's the career of ReandeaN was ending, but it did so with glory and closed the best chapter of stage history between the two wars. The last productions were *Scotch Mist* by Patrick Hastings (an eminent King's Counsel, as they were then, and eventually Sir Patrick), with Godfrey Tearle and Tallulah Bankhead, (114 performances); *They Knew What They Wanted* an American play by Sidney Howard, (110 performances) with that fine actor Sam Livesey and Tallulah Bankhead; and *The Queen Was in the Parlour*, which transferred to the Duke of York's. All those were produced by Basil Dean. At the St Martin's was also a charming and clever play called *Berkeley Square* by John L. Baldestone, which ran for 181 performances and was a highlight of 1926.

The St Martin's came under the management of Reandco—the Co being E.P. Clift, who had been ReandeaN's general manager.

An American play at the Strand, by Anita Loos and John Emerson, called *The Whole Town's Talking*, kept them talking for 119 performances. Then came to that theatre one of the best and slickest crime plays seen on the stage. It was the best kind of American crook play, with speed, grip and probability. It laid bare the gangster racket and was eventually transferred to the Adelphi, running in all for 252 performances. It was called *Broadway* and had an all-American cast. Some of the players remained here, becoming popular by their work and for their own sakes, too. Notable among them was Ben Weldon, whose study of the nightclub waiter made you feel tired to see him and your feet to ache in sympathy with his; also Bernard J. Nedell as the sinister chief crook, a masterly study of quiet but relentless villainy; Olive Blakeney (Mrs Nedell) as the grumbling, grousing and quarrelsome show girl; and Hartley Power, who played the impassive, imperturbable detective, with his catchword "Hello, Steve." (He stayed here for keeps, became one of our best leading men and served as a Special Constable in the Second World War.)

At Wyndham's, Ivor Novello staged a costume play about the Borgias, called *The Firebrand*. He looked most handsome in the period costumes and gave a very good performance. With him was Constance Collier. This ran for 79 performances and would have done better in less troubled times.

Edgar Wallace stepped into the front rank as playwright at Wyndham's with *The Ringer*. It was his first success and it owed a tremendous amount to the "carpentering" done to it and its production by Sir Gerald du Maurier, so much so that Wallace insisted on giving him half his royalties. When the undoubted genius du Maurier had done with it, *The Ringer* was a very good crime play indeed. Edgar Wallace always wrote at top speed, seldom stopped to think and took many things for granted, believing that his audiences would do the same. That was part of his vast egotism. But du Maurier knew better. The play was splendidly cast, with Dorothy Dickson as the heroine, stepping out of musical comedy into drama with complete efficiency, Leslie Banks, Nigel Bruce, Leslie Faber and especially Gordon Harker, as the scared and frightened Cockney burglar. Despite the strike, *The Ringer* rang the bell 410 times. Edgar Wallace was established.

Some mention has already been made of the musical plays of 1926. There were some good ones, but many failures, and some which paid the penalty of running into the General Strike.

At the Lyric, Hammersmith, Nigel Playfair produced *Riverside Nights* by himself and A. P. (now Sir Alan) Herbert, a wholly delightful concoction on a subject dear to Herbert's heart, with music by Frederick Austin and Alfred Reynolds. There was never much money behind that Lyric venture and the General Strike was a bad blow. They thought it a good idea to take the play to the Ambassadors in the heart of London, to make it easier for playgoers, and then they took it back again to its Hammersmith home. It ran for 229 nights. It was the first of the operettas by Sir Alan and it deserved success. In the cast were Marie Dainton, a well known actress and mimic who had played lead in that famous musical comedy, *A Chinese Honeymoon*, and a young actor then at the beginning of his career—to become famous on stage later and especially on radio as an old watchman sitting by his fire bucket—Richard Goolden.

The Palladium, where things were done on a vast scale, presented *Palladium Pleasures*, a revue which ran for 309 performances and the music for which was by Vivian Ellis. He did some remarkable work in it, including a ballet which was danced by Anton Dolin and a very elaborate scene entitled "Mothers of the World" with Toots Pounds as the Virgin Mary—at the Palladium! In this revue was one of the funniest sketches ever written, (the work of that real professional, Lauri Wylie) called "Unnecessary Remarks", in which everyone said the most obvious thing, with the most hilarious and perfectly natural consequences. Billy Merson left Hard-Boiled Herman in *Rose Marie* to play in this revue, under a previously made contract. There were also Lorna and Toots Pounds, John Kirby, Leslie Stuart and George Clarke.

George Clarke was a splendid light comedian who never really got his full meed of fame. He played the sort of silly-ass parts in which G. P. Huntley had specialized—well-dressed gentlemen with the best of intentions but the slackest of brains. It was a type which was practically dead when George Clarke played it, for the First World War had accounted for most of those well-bred but apparently rather stupid men. The provinces loved it but the West End looked rather askance. Clarke, a most charming fellow on and off the stage, a first-class athlete and a most amazing wood carver, was not only a fine actor but a most expert dancer and a master of mime. In *Palladium Pleasures* his terrible troubles caused by a phone call box and armfuls of parcels were quite wonderful. He also specialized in having trouble with motor cars on the stage—real ones not property ones—and his seemingly reckless but really expert driving caused as much laughter as thrills. He had as a partner a mature young lady named Tiny Mite, who looked about six or seven but was a whole lot more. An Inspector of the Society for the Prevention of Cruelty to Children, who came upon her enjoying a whisky and soda in the Palm Court at the Palladium, nearly had heart failure.

Billy Merson in *Palladium Pleasures* was the real red-nosed vintage Merson so popular on the Music Halls. He did a good impression of Sir Harry Lauder, amongst other things, and made a "Lauder" speech to the audience, exhorting them to save their bawbees, adding amidst applause that he had done so himself. Later, one was not so sure.

A song was sung in that show which was the first to be "stunted" and publicized in advance and which succeeded. It was called "Valencia" and was sung by Lorna and Toots Pounds, who, whilst singing, threw bunches of violets to the audience. But the big hit in that show was something quite different. The curtain swept up and disclosed not a vast spectacular scene filled with girls in glittering costumes weaving and dancing in elaborate routine whilst the

Gladys Cooper, actress-manager of the 1920's who gave that period distinction.

Yvonne Arnaud, whose gurgle and squeak enchanted millions.

Tom Walls and Winifred Shotter at the Aldwych Theatre, the home of great farces.

orchestra played fortissimo, but a simple backcloth before which sat a quiet, elderly, silver-haired man gazing pensively at a grand piano. The audience stared and wondered. Then he began to play very softly, so softly that the audience had to strain their ears to listen. But his music grew louder and that audience began to move its head in rhythm with the tunes and to pat its feet in time. They let the melody take possession of them; as the melodies grew more familiar, they grew louder. Unable to resist the magic, the audience started to sing the songs they knew so well, and a great wave of enthusiasm swept across the theatre, for the man at the piano was Leslie Stuart, playing his own compositions which have become folk songs of our race. Unmoved by the cheering, he played on and on—"The Little Octoroon;" "Little Dolly Daydream;" "I May Be Crazy," and "The Lily of Laguna" and others—and the singing and applause grew and grew into a tumult. Suddenly he stopped, silence fell, and the stage darkened. He struck some chords, loud and commanding; the orchestra joined in; the lights went up; that backcloth behind him rose and there was the realization of the tune he played, "The Soldiers of the Queen"—Guards Band and all. It was a veritable triumph and a come-back for that ageing genius, who had been experiencing a very bad time. His melodies were as lovely as ever. There were tears in all eyes, in Leslie Stuart's as well. He had again won a victory, but it was to be his last.

The Empire had a big success with *Lady Be Good*, starring Adèle and Fred Astaire (326 performances).

That magical place, the Gaiety, had lost its magic. It varied between indifferent and quite bad musical plays. *Riki-Tiki* ran for only 18 performances. Philip Ridgeway staged—revived, of course —Gogol's *The Government Inspector*, with Charles Laughton in the cast (imagine Gogol at the Gaiety) A short season was played by Sacha Guitry and Yvonne Printemps. *Love Adrift* went adrift after 45 shows, and a revue called *By the Way* ran for the same time. Then the rot was stopped by *Lido Lady*, with music by a young American composer called Richard Rodgers and with Jack Hulbert, Cecily Courtneidge and Phyllis Dare in the cast. It ran for 259 performances and brought back laughter to the Gaiety.

At His Majesty's there was a musical play based on a romantic comedy previously seen at the St. James's, called *Old Heidelburg*. Its new name was *The Student Prince*, with music by Sigmund Romberg, and it ran for 96 nights. So *Wildflower* was transferred there from the Shaftesbury; the music was by Vincent Youmans and the inevitable Oscar Hammerstein and Otto Harbach wrote the book. This ran for 114 performances. *The Co-optimists* had a successful season at what is affectionately called "H.M.T."

The London Hippodrome presented *Sunny* with book, of course, by Hammerstein and Harbach—from whom there seemed to be no escape—and music by Jerome Kern. Binnie Hale, Elsie Randolph and Jack Buchanan led a good cast. It was a big success and ran for 363 nights.

Charlot's Show of 1926 did not follow the success of previous similar productions. It only last 87 performances at the Prince of Wales's. Yet it had Jessie Matthews, Herbert Mundin, Anton Dolin, Sunday Wilshin—one of the beauties of the period—and Harold Warrender in the cast (he became famous on screen and stage).

Queen High, suitably enough at the Queen's Theatre, ran for 198 shows, with Sonnie Hale, A. W. Baskcomb, Hermione Baddeley and Joe Coyne in it.

At the Vaudeville Archie de Bear hit the target with *R.S.V.P.*, with Robert Hale, Mimi Crawford (who later became Countess of Suffolk) and Cyril Ritchard in the company. Norman O'Neill did the music and there were additional scenes by a young man named Greatrex Newman, whose *Fol de Rols* are now so popular. The public responded to the invitation on 295 occasions. *Vaudeville Vanities*, which followed, was not so successful, but to show the shape of things to come there were additional tunes by two young men destined to become radio stars, Kenneth and George Western.

Kid Boots kept the flag of musical comedy flying at the Winter Garden. It came from America and gave Leslie Henson a wonderful chance for comedy, of which he took full advantage. After a run of 172 performances it was followed by *Tip Toes*, with Dorothy Dickson back as leading lady.

Cochran staged *The Cochran Revue*, 1926 at the London Pavilion. He engaged Spinelly, the French star, for this and had tremendous trouble. She was for ever walking in and walking out again. Despite the strike outside and the constant strikes of Spinelly inside, thanks to a good cast it reached 148 performances.

Then, also at the Pavilion, he presented *Black Birds*. This was an entirely all-Coloured Show, in itself something of a novelty and, of course, from America. It was devised and produced by a dynamic personality named Lew Leslie. He was the only white man in the outfit. The coloured folk adored him. He was at once their master and their friend. His word was law and he got the most remarkable results out of the artists. Such attack, such speed, such complete team work and so much talent packed into one show had seldom been witnessed. It was not the first all-Coloured show London had seen; that had been a musical comedy called *In Dahomey* at the Shaftesbury in 1903. *Black Birds* swept to success. Its star was Florence Mills, who sang like a nightingale, danced like quicksilver, and had a personality which compelled. She and *Black Birds* were

the talk of the town and ran for 279 performances. It is also worthy
of note that 1926 was the year in which the Charleston became
popular. There was a most interesting theatrical event at the
Shaftesbury Theatre on November 17th. A comedian from the
Music Halls ventured into West End management—ventured? no,
dashed—as a star of musical comedy. He was Billy Merson, who has
crossed these pages before. This very small man with the rather sad
face and wistful dark eyes had made a big reputation as a red-nosed
comic with an occasional dash of burlesque pathos. He had run
away from home to clown in a circus. He had gone on the Halls
with a partner—they were Keith and Merson. They had a hard
struggle. They knew what it was to be stranded in a town without
the fare to the next "date." Once Billy Merson had raised that fare
by means of a top hat which he possessed and used in the act.
Wearing that topper and a most respectable expression, he called at
houses saying that he was a piano tuner. Would they like their
piano tuned? Nearly every house had a piano then. He knew nothing
whatever about it, but his smile, his earnest manner, his pleasant
voice and, above all, the top hat, inspired confidence. He "tuned"
a whole lot of pianos, and raised the necessary fare. What happened
afterwards was no concern of his. But it is likely that the importance
of that top hat which had got him out of his trouble and its effect
upon the people he interviewed did something to him psychologic-
ally, as will be seen.

Billy Merson had every requisite for a low comedian—a curious
figure, a mobile face, large expressive eyes, a touch of pathos which
he could use well, and also a good singing voice. But he had not one
vestige of romance, one touch of polish or charm, or any of the good
looks such as the hero of any musical play requires. He was a good
eccentric dancer, he had a wonderful sense of timing, he was very
strong and his clowning had taught him acrobatic tricks. He was a
good actor and had done very well in revue sketches; above all, he
had starred in *Rose Marie* at Drury Lane itself. That had rather
turned his head. He had received over £400 a week. He believed that
now he also had a sufficent following from music hall and theatre-
goers to venture into management on his own account. That is the
most dangerous step any actor can take, but it did not scare Billy.
He was the supreme egotist; his self-confidence was astounding and
he had yes-men all round him.

He acquired, from Daly's Theatre, a musical play by Oscar
Straus which had toured but never come to town. He proceeded to
destroy it completely and have another written in its place. He
retained some of the Straus music and got Vivian Ellis to write the
rest. Graham John wrote the book. There were endless discussions
in the Merson dressing-room, in his little flat in Holborn and at his

Thames Ditton home. At all those places he entertained lavishly.

He wanted a manager. Now I was at that time in charge of publicity at the Palladium, where he was playing. I knew him well. I had helped him a lot when he was at the Palace in *Hullo America*. He asked me to help him again. I took on the job because I liked him. I did not know the snag then. We got together a fine cast and we got the Shaftesbury Theatre. We got the prettiest chorus London had seen since the great days of the Gaiety. As yet the show had no name. Billy offered a £5 prize for the best title and a chorus girl won it with the suggestion "My Son John," which had a slight application. He had a large number of lucrative music hall contracts. Such was his confidence that he bought himself out of them for a large sum. He was sure he could not fail, and the show went into rehearsal. Then the snag appeared. Billy Merson had got bitten with a West End complex. True, he was going to play a comedy part, but he was not going to be the eccentric little red-wigged and red-nosed comic everyone loved. Bless you, no! He was going to be the only real rival to Jack Buchanan. That was how he was going to play it, dressed as smartly as Jack himself, the best dressed man on the stage. The difference between the tall, slim grace of Jack Buchanan and his own short-legged dwarfishness did not occur to him. I talked to him seriously, but with tact. I was brushed aside. I tried plain speaking and was ignored. The stars of the show, Anne Croft, Reginald Sharland, Vera Pearce, and Betty Chester all had a go. It had no effect. Billy Merson was going to have his own way. He went to the best tailors and got suits which would have been wonderful on anyone else but which on him looked a little sad. He told everyone what to do, even David Miller, who produced. The only person who completely disregarded him was Eddie Dolly, brother of the Dolly Sisters and a wonderful dance producer, who did not listen to him but kept on and, by dint of shouting at the girls and bullying them, calling them fatheads and, in moments of stress, jumping on his own hat, he produced routines and ensembles which were exhilarating and thrilling. But not even the shoemaker and scenic artists escaped the instructions which Billy Merson poured on them. The trouble was that you could not dislike the little man; there was something so nice about him. But I saw disaster approaching. Something must be done to save Billy from himself.

Now the second act took place on the Lido, which had just become popular. Billy ordered a couple of most elaborate costumes for himself, entirely out of keeping with the part. I saw my chance; at all costs I must make Billy into the comic again, if only for a little while. I thought that, when he found how successful he was in that, he would drop all the other nonsense and be just Billy Merson. He was now so busy doing everyone else's job that he neglected to see

about his second costume, a gorgeous military affair, entirely unsuitable for everything. I had carefully suppressed the order. When
he wanted to try it on, it had not arrived, and we kept up that
pretence until the last moment,indeed right up to the dress rehearsal.
Then, of course, there were tragedy and chaos. I took charge. This
was what I had been waiting for. I hustled the panicky Billy into
the largest pair of Lido pyjamas we had got, so large that they hung
down over his hands by a good twelve inches and were equally long
in the leg. I shoved a dab of carmine on his nose, forced him into
his old red wig, clapped a fez on his head—and sent him on. There
was a roar of welcome from the invited dress-rehearsal audience
at the sight of this familiar figure. Even the cast laughed, and Billy
joined in the quartette "I Like the Polka Best" like the real clown
he was. It was a riot. He decided to "keep it in." But, in the next act,
he was back again in "faultless evening dress." Nothing could be
done. It opened at the Shaftesbury, as stated, on November 17th.
If it had all been like that spot in the second act, it would have been
a huge success. That went with a roar of cheers. Everyone from
stars to chorus worked splendidly. But the pivot of the whole thing
was wrong—because Billy was not himself. When a play is so un-
balanced, it either fails, or is very lucky if it just gets by. And that is
what *My Son John* did. It got a good enough Press, a small library
deal, but what the public wanted to see, the comic little Billy
Merson, was not there. I set my teeth and decided on publicity. I
happen to know a good deal about that. With the devoted help of
my many friends in Fleet Street, Billy Merson and *My Son John*
became news. We stunted everything. When Billy was unwell and
had an X Ray which disclosed the presence of a needle in his posterior
"Billy Merson Gets the Needle" was on the front page. The Lido
Pyjamas became famous, and we broke all records for the theatre
on Boxing Day. I had him clowning in the ring of Bertram Mills's
Circus—everything. We ran for 255 performances, which shows what
publicity can do. Billy Merson lived in a dream. He visualized his
next show. He wanted to play *Richard III*. He said he "saw himself
in the part." I would find him lurking about muttering "Is this a
dagger which I see before me, The handle towards my hand."
When I told him that was *Macbeth*, he said it did not matter—it
was all the same thing, Shakespeare, you know. But there was no
next play under Billy's management. He lost a big action brought
against him by an agent concerning his engagement in *Rose Marie*
and it cost him dear. He had not got the wealth of which he boasted;
extravagance had reigned. I was frequently hard put to it to find
the cash for the weekly "treasury" and often Billy had to go without. Apart from a friend who invested £1,000, he was his own backer.
At the end he went back to the Palladium which he said was his

spiritual home. No more management for him. But it shows how slight is the line between success and failure. Had he been content to be himself, he would have succeeded. He and I were firm friends up to his death, and he died the same incurable little optimist, still weaving plans for the future, which were never to be fulfilled. But that was typical "Theatre" of the 1920's.

CHAPTER XIII

Really West End

IT is often the custom in the theatrical profession to describe something or somebody as "West End." It means that the gloss and polish are there, the assurance and sophistication, the ease and lack of self-consciousness of the town-dweller as against the little gaucheries of the provincial. Those who are so described naturally take it for granted, but those to whom such a label is not affixed cannot understand it at all. They know it in their hearts, or most of them do, but will never admit it. Yet many artists who have greater talent than those labelled "West End" never get that desired distinction. This "West End" atmosphere is not easy to acquire. It is usually inherent and it may express itself through people who were not always part of London, but it is unmistakable when seen.

If ever there was a man on our stage to whom that title really and truly belonged, it was Jack Buchanan. He was entirely "West End." Yet he was not a Londoner; indeed, it is seldom Londoners who become "West End." He was born in Scotland and he loved his native land, but there is no doubt at all that he was, in every way, the living presentiment of what "West End" meant.

In that, he was the legitimate successor to George Grossmith. That wonderful man, son of Grossmith the Savoyard, was the pillar of the Gaiety for years. Indeed, he was in himself the male embodiment of the spirit of that enchanting place. He was tall, slim, not particularly good-looking, but with distinction, ease and elegance, a real knowledge of the theatre and a leader of male fashion. He was the idol of the ladies and the envy of the men, like the character named Archie, of whom he once sang. And Jack Buchanan was his more modern counterpart.

Buchanan first appeared on the stage in 1912. He made his way upwards with a steady climb, on tour in musical comedy, in town in Revue, and, whatever he did, no matter how small the part, he was always noticed. There was a personality, an individuality, which got over to the audience. He came into real prominence between 1917 and 1920 in Charlot's revues. He was talked about, he looked "interesting"; actually he looked delicate, and in those days he did indeed have very bad health, which was the reason why he was not in the Forces. But he fought his own battle against that ill health and he won. By 1921 he was a big favourite. *A to Z* perhaps put the crown on his head. Greatly daring, he went into management in 1922. He did not make Billy Merson's mistake. He was Jack Buchanan and Jack Buchanan he remained. That was what the public wanted and it was really no trouble at all for him to give it to them.

The girls were wild about him; men admired him, too, and envied him his tailor and the immaculate ease with which he wore his clothes. But it was not clothes which made him famous, nor was it any "gimmick;" it was talent and personality.

He went to America, and there became as great a favourite as he was at home. New York, which considered itself highly sophisticated, had something to learn from this elegant young man with perfect manners, poise and complete self-control, who let his individuality have its head but never overdid anything. He was accepted as the real type of English gentleman (that he was a Scot did not matter). This indeed was Mayfair. This was the incarnation of the West End and in him there seemed concentrated the centuries of breeding and culture which they knew the British possessed. Jack did not mind that, nor did it turn his head. For all his immense success and popularity, he never put on side, he had no airs and graces. He was just Jack Buchanan. He was a very good actor; he knew exactly how to produce himself and that easy, almost indolent manner was not just chance. It was carefully pointed and lit from within; it was "lined in" with the care of an artistic make-up, with the "highlights" in exactly the right places. It was really glossy without ostentation; it was so sleek and, if you like, streamlined, that it made the perfect whole.

He was not good-looking in the approved idea—there was no perfect profile, no striking features, but it was a face which had the greatest possible attraction. It was individual; you could not forget it. Perhaps it looked best when he smiled that slow but charming smile from under the brim of a silk hat. And he knew how to use his eyes, indeed, every feature.

He was always completely at his ease, a great asset, for he always put an audience completely at theirs. He had wonderful control over them. There was always a ripple of genuine pleasure in the applause which greeted him, which gave it a value lacking in the "receptions" accorded to many others. There was friendliness in it, and genuine pleasure to see him; he and those "in front" were in perfect accord.

He had not really got a good singing voice, but he knew exactly how to use it. His diction was perfect. There was a slight huskiness which was as much a part of him as his walk, a curious walk which might not have seemed graceful in anyone else, but it was the walk of a dancer. There he would be, in his perfect clothes, looking as if he had been poured into them, holding an audience in the hollow of his hand, playing with them, seeming to chat with them individually, making each of them feel that he was singing or talking directly to them. They would listen enraptured. Then he would suddenly slip into a dance. Those dances of his were as characteristic as everything else about him. They were not showy or acrobatic, they were just Jack Buchanan, leisurely, effortless, and exactly right. Nobody else could do the same sort of thing. And they were essentially West End. He never missed a single point in his songs, yet he never seemed to make an effort. They, too, were good form, they were West End. He was a real master of timing. He had great gifts of comedy, he knew how to get laughs; he could clown upon occasion, and his clowning was of the best quality and West End, too. The real secret was his immense charm. He was quite conscious of it and knew exactly how to control it, to keep it in small focus or turn it right on. But it was always there.

He was also a very good actor indeed in straight comedy, and an excellent producer. He did everything there was to do in a theatre and did it well. He was acclaimed equally in London and New York. He was a star of the stage, films and radio. When television arrived, he became a star of that, too, without the slightest effort. It is a cruel medium to face, especially for a man of the age he had then reached; it reveals every line, every wrinkle, every blemish and sign of age. But the charm of Jack Buchanan rubbed that all out.

He took—he even built—theatres and ran them. He was a good judge of a play and of talent. He made a few mistakes. He was one of the most popular men in his profession, a real pal and a mixer with men, and adored by the girls. Yet for the greater part of his life he was a bachelor and, when he did marry, he was supremely happy. It gilded his last few years. He was a good man of business and reputed to be very rich. It is probable that for a portion of his life he was so. Yet at the end there was no fortune; perhaps the West End to which he belonged took it from him. He was a kind and generous man—though he did not give indiscriminately but wisely and well—a fine staunch friend always ready to help a deserving case and to go out of his way to do a good turn.

He could take the stage and hold his own with the greatest stars on both sides of the Atlantic, and more than hold his own. His perfection of manner, individuality, his mastery of his job and his charm could not be beaten down. I recall the opening of the Stage

Door Canteen in the Second World War. The premises that had once been Lyons' Popular Café in Piccadilly had been turned into a club for the forces of all the allied nations. Its opening night was a sensation. It was jammed beyond capacity. I expected the balcony to collapse at any moment. The Rt. Hon. Sir Anthony Eden, who came to declare it open, had to fight his way through a vast excited crowd. Yet, although this was the theatre's own gesture to the Forces, not a great number of stars put in an appearance. Dorothy Dickson and Beatrice Lillie were there; both had worked themselves to the bone over its foundation and that night they nearly worked themselves to death. Then Jack Buchanan arrived. His mere presence seemed to have a tranquillizing effect on the noisy, milling crowd. He went on the little stage, he told stories, he sang and he danced. They cheered and cheered again. He told them what to do to make things easy—to keep the doorways clear, those in front sit down so that all could see. They obeyed at once. Then something else happened. Another great star arrived in the person of Bing Crosby. The audience went mad. Bing was as good as Jack in his own way. He, too, sang to them, yarned to them, cracked jokes; he signed autographs, he was pushed about as Jack had been and enjoyed it, just as Jack did. Then the two of them went on the stage together and for half an hour they wisecracked at each other, right "off the cuff" and totally unrehearsed—a performance which anywhere else would have cost many pounds. Here were two really great artists working together, each supreme in his own line, each perfectly confident of himself, giving and taking gags, never trying to crab each other, an example of professionalism at its very best. It will live in the memory of all who saw it. Bing Crosby had to go on to another appointment, but he had spent a couple of hours there, and we had to get him out over the roof and down the fire escape. Jack Buchanan stayed on and kept the ball rolling, tirelessly, without seeming effort, and always with charm and good temper. Those boys and girls from all over the globe were in the very heart of the West End with him, and saw its living essence in him, too. None of them will forget it.

The only time he was a bit scared was when he undertook to follow Ivor Novello in *King's Rhapsody*. Ivor was dead and if the show, in the height of its success, was to continue, somebody very special must step into the breach. Before he went away on his last holiday to Jamaica, Ivor had asked Jack, for whom he had the greatest admiration, if he would play the part until he returned. At that moment it had not been possible. But now, when the call came, knowing it would be Ivor's wish, he agreed. They were old friends and their admiration for each other was mutual. Jack Buchanan was scared. He knew what it meant. He was following a popular idol, as individual in his way as Jack was in his, and following him in a part which he had played best of all. So he had a consultation with me, a friend of both parties; we discussed the line of procedure and agreement was reached. Jack knew he would be challenging comparison and in this case, Ivor being Ivor, he was not so sure. But as the talk between us proceeded he grew more at ease. He would, of course, play it in his own way, but the end must be a bit different. Ivor came out of the darkness of the great cathedral in which he had been hiding to see his little son crowned in his stead. His beloved wife, knowing him to be there, dropped a white rose as she followed her son down the aisle. In silence and solitude, Ivor, all in black, picked up that rose, gazed at it, kissed it and knelt before the High Altar. That was essentially Ivor and it electrified the audience, but it was not Jack Buchanan by any manner of means. He found his way, however in our talk. And so, he came out of the shadows, silently and sadly, he picked up the rose and gazed at it. He did not kiss it, he did not kneel at the altar; he bowed deeply before it and, with the rose in his hand, disappeared into the cloistered gloom from which he had emerged. It was dead right, and it was Jack Buchanan.

He always said that the first night on which he played that part was his most agonizing experience. There were so many people in the audience who had seen Ivor, not once but many times. The company around him had played with Ivor, many of them for years. But he did it perfectly; there was not a twitch or a quiver. He was master of himself and his audience—doing the hardest job his profession could put upon him.

In the 1920's Jack Buchanan was one of the pillars of that musical stage which really kept the footlights burning in that awkward period. And when he died, so recently, the nation mourned him. People who had never met him felt that they had lost a friend. So, indeed, they had. A light had gone out, a breach been made which could not be filled. He who had given joy now occasioned sadness at his exit.

There was a large crowd at the Memorial Service at St. Columba's, the chief Scottish Church in his beloved West End. Its simple, dignified, white austerity was very different to the top hats, white ties and mink in which he had moved for so many years. Yet one felt that this place was basically the true Jack Buchanan, too—something real, strong, genuine and deeply rooted in its own soil and the hearts of his people. A piper played a lament and his friends took their leave of somebody whom they had loved.

Something had gone out of life, out of the theatre, and out of the West End itself, when Jack Buchanan, who had suffered pain bravely and without complaint, went to his rest in the manner of his own race, and yet in the heart of the West End. He left no successor as the personification of the West End he represented, for that West End had passed, too. When Jack Buchanan held the stage the footlights never flickered.

CHAPTER XIV

Ups and Downs of 1927

IN 1927 there were eleven productions in the West End of London which did not reach 20 performances, and thirty which did not reach the very modest total of 50. Those figures were exclusive of revivals and "seasonal" plays. The footlights had gone very dim, yet here and there in the topsy-turvy world of the theatre, some still shone brightly. Outside the theatre the world was in a state of flux.

Jerome Klapka Jerome, novelist and playwright, died. He had begun as a City clerk and then became a schoolmaster. His *Idle Thoughts of an Idle Fellow* and the classic *Three Men in a Boat* showed him to be a very great humourist. He wrote many successful plays, the best being *The Passing of the Third Floor Back,* in which Sir Johnstone Forbes-Robertson was so memorable. Arthur Bourchier, one of the last of the actor-managers of the old School, passed on, too. For years he had controlled the Garrick Theatre and later, right up to his death, he ran the Strand. Never a great actor, he still had considerable drawing power, and shone in the portrayal of strong-willed and rather ruthless men. He staged *Treasure Island* and was a very fine Long John Silver. He did good Shakespearean work and his best performance was as King Henry VIII in Tree's wonderful production at His Majesty's. Bourchier was the best bluff King Hal in living memory. He died of pneumonia in Johannesburg, a city which, in the same manner has taken toil of other excellent actors since.

The theatre had its own triumph in the world of sport. Frank Curzon, one of the best and most popular theatre managers and a great sportsman, won the Derby with "Call Boy," even the name being "of the theatre." Curzon had had many stage winners but none gave him more pride than this. It was the first time the theatre had ever won a Derby, but it was to do so again. Curzon, who was very ill at the time, nevertheless went down to Epsom and led in his horse, with Elliott "up."

The climate did not help the theatre much during the month of December, a bad theatrical month until the Christmas holidays begin. For December 19th, 1927, was the coldest day for 32 years and on December 21st there was a silver thaw which caused 3,000 street accidents.

Another theatre magnate left this world in 1927, one of the new school of industrialists and financiers. This was James White, the fabulous millionaire. He had got control of Daly's but he never understood the theatre. Things began to go wrong for him and the theatre had helped in his downfall. In the office where once the great George Edwardes had sat, James White played cards all night long, surrounded by his boon companions. Drinks flowed like the tide and amazing things happened. But the end was near and White knew it. He had made up his mind what to do. One day he gave a sealed parcel to the stage door keeper at Daly's. "Now, listen carefully," he said, "you lock this up and let nobody see it. Don't tell anyone you have got it. Don't give it to anyone but me—when I ask for it. And when I *do* ask for it, argue with me, will you? Ask me if I am certain I want it. Don't be afraid, have a row with me if you like, but make quite certain that I really do want it. Understand?" The stage doorman said that he did, and locked the parcel away. It remained in its drawer for some time and the man himself had almost forgotten it. Then, on the evening of June 26th, James White suddenly demanded that parcel. The stage doorman remembered his instructions. He argued with the man from Rochdale, but White was quite determined. "Give it here," he said, "I know what I'm doing." The stage doorman passed it over and James White went out of that stage door. He never re-entered; he went out for good, for on the following morning the world heard that he was dead by his own hand, and thousands were ruined by his fall. In that parcel was the means of his death.

Some figures have already been given of the failures in the theatre but there are also some successes to chronicle. The Adelphi, however, had a bad year until December came. Then that amazing couple, Jack Hulbert and Cicely Courtneidge, staged a revue called *Clowns in Clover*. It was a big success, running for 508 performances. Paul Murray was then associated with Jack Hulbert and Cecily Courtneidge. A delightful Irishman, he did much good work in the theatre. Heading the cast were Jack and Cecily and June. For a short while, Elsie Janis, the great American star, joined the show. I represented "Mother" and Elsie in Europe and they took this engagement dead against my advice. "Mother" insisted. For once I failed to shake her. It was the only time Elsie ever flopped—really flopped personally—in this country. Even her impersonations, usually so brilliant, did not "get over" because she imitated American artists whom London had never seen. Yet so wonderful was she as a mimic that Gaby Deslys fled the theatre when Elsie imitated her on the stage. She used no special make-up for this;

she used to put a row of hairpins on the stage before her, twist up her hair, shove in a pin—and she was the very person she purported to be. *Clowns in Clover* was the last occasion on which Elsie appeared in this country. "Mother" was desperately ill at the time, and shortly afterwards that curious amalgamation was over. But for years friends received Christmas cards whereon "Elsie and Mother" sent their wishes. While Elsie was at the Adelphi I used to sit for an hour or so with "Mother," who was in bed in that familiar suite at the Carlton Hotel. I was there one night when Elsie returned with a curious letter from the Adelphi management which she could not understand. It was her "notice." She had never had that before.

Success continued at the Aldwych, where the actor-managerial and policy system reigned under Tom Walls. In 1927 the play was *Thark* by Ben Travers. It ran for 401 performances.

Those Aldwych first nights were something to remember. The audience gathered like a happy family, laughing and joking as they took their seats. It became necessary for each member of the company, all established favourites, to speak lines "off stage" before making their entrance. The sound of their voices brought tremendous applause. Had they waited until they got on stage, their receptions would have seriously held up the action. Tom Walls, who always produced or directed, as the phrase now has it, was always so busy about this that on first nights, despite a week's try-out, usually at Southsea, he was never certain of his lines. When he "dried up," he made no secret of it. "Now then, Bobbie, what's the line?" he would shout to Bobbie Dunn, the stage manager, who would give it to him, loud and clear. Tom would then resume, with a broad wink at the audience which always brought laughter and cheers. At the end, everybody took "calls" and when Ben Travers, the author, took his, Tom would always try to trip him up, but Ben, one of the nicest of men, got wily and evaded him. It was all part of the fun and the Aldwych farce tradition. Whatever was happening elsewhere the Aldwych footlights burnt brightly.

The Ambassadors had a big success with *The Fanatics*, produced there on March, 15th. It transferred to the Queen's and then went back to the Ambassadors to finish a run of 311 performances. Written by Miles Malleson, it was one of the outstanding plays of the year. And *A Spot on the Sun*, by J. Hastings Turner, with Marie Tempest, W. Graham Browne, Frank Cellier and Lady Tree, from whom the tempestuous Miss Tempest got no change, were in the cast. It kept the theatre busy for 126 nights.

A play which had been a colossal success in America, where it ran for years, came to the Apollo Theatre. It was *Abie's Irish Rose*. It did not repeat its American success but with that excellent actor, Joseph Greenwald, in the lead, it put up 128 performances.

Despite the doubtful times, new theatres were being built; they had been conceived and put in hand during the boom years. The Fortune had already opened, and in 1927 another did so, the Carlton in the Haymarket. The first presentation there was *Lady Luck*, a musical play by Firth Shephard, destined for fame, with additional scenes by Greatrex Newman and music by L. Hart and Richard Rodgers. Leslie Henson, Cyril Ritchard and Madge Elliott were in the lead. This gave the new playhouse a fine start with 324 performances, but that luck did not last. The Carlton is now a cinema.

As if to counteract this addition to theatrical ranks, 1927 saw the end of the Empire in Leicester Square, originally a theatre and then a world-famous music hall, but reverting to theatre status again towards the end of the First World War. The last attraction was *Lady Be Good*. There were sentimental scenes on the last night, many of the audience carrying away relics and fittings as momentoes. It was, indeed, the end of an epoch. The world of the Empire had changed and, although it was not yet realized, the British Empire was changing, too. But the bars had a wonderful night, because so many middle-aged and elderly gentlemen wanted to have their last drink in the "dear old Empire."

Pavlova was still delighting London in 1927; she did a short season at the Royal Opera House, Covent Garden.

The Marquise, a very good play by Noel Coward, ran for 129 performances at the Criterion, with Marie Tempest, W. Graham Browne, Robert Harris, Godfrey Winn and Frank Cellier in the cast. At the same theatre *The Happy Husband* just topped the century by nine performances. A splendid cast included Madge Titheradge, Lawrence Grossmith, Charles Laughton, Mabel Sealby and A. E. Matthews. Ruth Draper was at the Criterion for a season, too. She was now an established London favourite, having been first seen at the Aeolian Hall in 1920 and playing a short season at the Garrick in 1926. She appeared there again in 1927 before going to the Criterion. Another Criterion play was *Quest* by Ralph Stock (143 nights).

Daly's, which saw the end of James White, staged *The Blue Mazurka*. Although the music was by Franz Lehar, it only lasted for 139 performances. *Peggy-Anne*, with music by Richard Rodgers, and Dorothy Dickson in the lead, played for five less. During 1927, Daly's experienced one of its worst nights. This was provided by a play by Noel Coward, entitled *Sirocco*. It was to have gone to the Duke of York's. I had taken over that place as manager, for Violet Melnotte, and I did not believe in this play. I had read it, I thought it would fail and, by a bit of manœuvring, I managed to evade it and it went to Daly's instead. I went to the first night to see if my

Lily Elsie, the original Merry Widow who returned to the stage in the 1920's.

Margaret Bannerman, leading lady alike in musical and straight plays.

George Robey, the Prime Minister of Mirth who became a Shakespearian Actor in the 1920's.

MR. BILLY MERSON.

Billy Merson, comedian ruined by a top-hat complex.

judgment was right, and stood quietly at the back of the Upper Circle.

Now Noel Coward had struck an unlucky patch; they come to everyone in the profession and those who are really of the theatre fight through them grimly and survive to succeed. Noel Coward did that. Basil Dean, who was producing *Sirocco*, was having a bad patch, too. He had produced a play by Noel Coward at the Duke of York's called *Home Chat*, which was a failure and had to some extent put me off *Sirocco* (and details will be told later). It was a thousand pities that both author and producer of *Sirocco* were out of luck at the same time. *Sirocco* had a fine cast, with Ivor Novello and lovely Frances Doble in the leading parts. Coward was already a considerable figure in the theatre; Ivor was still on his way up, but he was box office draw even then.

It is difficult to know exactly what went wrong on that first night. It was not a good play by any means, but it hardly deserved the reception which it got. It was one of those curious things which happen from time to time in the theatre. There was a strange brooding atmosphere as the audience gathered. From the very start, even before the curtain rose, there seemed unrest in the pit and gallery, but the hostile reception was not pre-arranged. There had been no wicked plot. It just happened because audience, actors, playwright and play were never in accord with each other. The audience was a brilliant one and the author sat in the front of his box reading telegrams of good wishes. There was a sort of deathly calm when the curtain rose instead of the excited murmur and then hush of interest, That play never "got them" for a minute. A love scene between Frances Doble and Ivor Novello drew rather derisive laughter, which was not surprising because they had to roll about on the stage together in a kind of romp. From then on, the play had gone. The storm, so long gathering, began to break and, when the final curtain fell, there was pandemonium. It was as if the old uninhibited days of eighteenth-century playgoing had returned: it was like "The Chinese Festival" at Drury Lane or Kean's reception after the Cox divorce case. Its violence was not of the twittering twenties but of the more virile days of old. Coward faced that audience with a smile. He has plenty of pluck and never runs away from a hostile demonstration. It might have been better, though, if he had not appeared on this occasion. His friends in front did their best, but were drowned by howls of disapproval. Dean, who always kept away from the theatre on first nights until the very end, arrived at curtain fall and at first took the noise to be cheering. Frances Doble was pushed on to say a few words of thanks. With tears streaming down her face she stammered out that it was the happiest night of her life, and there were yells of derision! Nobody was spared. The audience not only fought the play, they fought each other. Beside me at the back of the Upper Circle a Cowardite and anti-Cowardite resorted to fisticuffs, and lookers-on formed a ring in which they could fight it out. It was a dreadful night for all concerned.

Coward had a contract with Cochran to provide a revue. Because of *Sirocco* he sent Cochran a telegram to tear that contract up, but the old and experienced man of the theatre told him not to worry, and was right. Somehow *Sirocco* survived for 28 performances.

Until I took over the management of the Duke of York's for Violette Melnotte, five plays had been staged there between January and June. One play only ran for 20 performances and a revue faded out after 40. Now, I was not afraid of "Madame," as most of my predecessors had been (their name was legion). On taking over, I arranged to bring in a "shocker" from the Little Theatre, where it was doing moderate business. I reckoned it would do better on a main thoroughfare. That shocker was *Dracula*. "Madame" did not altogether approve, but I had luck and persuaded her. I got that show in so that her share was fifty per cent of the box-office takings. I told Madame all about the horrors of the play and shook her steely nerves. On the first night, she did not go into her box as usual but waited a bit. Then she took a peep through the little spyhole she had near her office. She saw nothing; the auditorium was black as the nethermost pit and suddenly across the darkness came a terrible unearthly scream as of a soul in torment, which seemed to cut across the blackness like a flash of lightning. It was enough for "Madame." She lost her nerve, she had a cab called, and was driven away to the Piccadilly Hotel. The next morning she was off to her beloved Metropole at Brighton. She never entered her theatre while *Dracula* was running. I was glad of that, because she had a rule that no seats must be sold at a cut price. I had a big demand for seats at 5/9d and, when the Upper Circle was full, I "jobbed" the back stalls at that price and took a whole lot of money. The "returns" delighted "Madame" and she never found out how they were attained. I let forth much publicity, too, and the Press Agent, the excellent H. C. G. Stevens, co-operated nobly. As soon as the audience entered, they saw a trained nurse in full uniform and wearing a row of medals. On asking what she was doing there, they were told she looked after the "faints." It was autosuggestion and it worked; nobody ever went away, but there were faints at every performance. Nobody ever blamed the play; it was always something which they had had for dinner. Only one man was frank. He was in the gallery and he fled so fast that he fell right downstairs and injured his head badly. An ambulance was called, but he admitted it was all his own fault. He said he was allergic to blood and he just could not explain why he had come to see this Vampire play. That fine actor, Raymond Huntley, now in the front rank, was Count Dracula and at the Duke of York's Sam Livesey played Van Helsing. It did very good business and then transferred to the Prince of Wales's, where it ran on. Then came a musical version of *The Beloved Vagabond*, for which that gifted composer Dudley Glass supplied the score. Frederick Ranalow played Paragot, Lilian Davies was Joanna, and Mabel Russell returned to the stage to play Blanquette. Leslie French was Asticot. There was a slight *contretemps* on the first night which shows how small a thing can upset the rhythm of a play. When somebody asked the villain of the play where Paragot was, his reply came clearly! "He has gone to the dogs." This presumably dramatic line was hailed with a great roar of laughter, which surprised all the players. Dog-racing had just become popular, but that was not what the villain had meant! Dog-racing became a menace to the theatre. *The Beloved Vagabond*, without being a smash hit, had to move out to make room for a play for which "Madame" had already contracted and it went to the New. It ran in all for 107 performances. Its backers believed that they had a great success, especially when the gallery began to queue for the first night on the evening before. But those people had come to welcome back Mabel Russell.

The play which ousted *The Beloved Vagabond* was the before-mentioned *Home Chat* by Noel Coward. It was produced by Basil Dean. There was nothing the matter with the cast, which included Marda Vanne, George Relph, Nina Boucicault (back in the theatre where she had created "Peter Pan"), Henrietta Watson, Madge Titheradge, Arthur Margetson, Tom Woods and George Curzon. But there was nothing in the play. It was just a piece of chat and the slender story was rather incredible. Noel Coward announced that he had written it in three weeks, which left a loop-hole for the critics of which they were not slow to take advantage. In plain, unvarnished words, it "got the bird." Yet I managed to get a "guarantee" out of the ticket agencies whilst the boos still rang in their ears. For once, there was an unauthorized person at that very secret conclave. It was Philip Page, the distinguished critic. He had remonstrated with some of the malcontents who were booing; words ran high and they threatened him with personal violence. I intervened, whisked him into my office and dispersed the blood-thirsty seekers for vengeance who nevertheless prowled about outside for some time. So "Peter" Page, as we called him, saw how a deal was done. The show and the deal expired on the same evening, the 38th performance, but the Libraries lost no money. They just got out. They had gambled on the name of Madge Titheradge and had been right to a copper.

That reception had made me determined that I did not want *Sirocco* and I managed to get rid of it, as stated, for I wanted something else. Despite bad business, there was a shortage of theatres at that moment; there nearly always is as Christmas draws near, the season at which every manager hopes to reap a golden harvest and so very seldom does. I knew that William Gaunt had to find a theatre for a production he had on the road, which for contractual reasons had to be produced in Town on or before a certain date. I got a report about that play from the provinces, a good one, I liked the name of the author, P. G. Wodehouse, and I liked the cast. I got Mr Gaunt, the great man from Yorkshire—or, at any rate, his general manager—into a corner. They had to come to me. I let them the theatre at £450 a week, an outrageous price for the Duke of York's as it was then, and by far the highest rental Violet Melnotte had ever received. I was "taken over" as manager in the contract according to custom, and I gave myself a rise for the run of the play. So everybody was pleased, even "Madame." She actually gave me a Christmas present—one solitary pearl dress stud. Fashion, and my dress shirts, called for three.

That play, *Good Morning, Bill*, was a success. Its star was Ernest Truex and with him were Vera Lennox, Lawrence Grossmith, Dorothy Minto and Frank Cellier. It ran for 146 performances. London took Truex to its heart. This nice little man was sometimes subject to fits of depression. When they afflicted him, he would go down to the United Services Museum in Whitehall and gaze upon the uniforms and relics of Field Marshal Lord Wolseley "Now, Ernest," he would say to himself, "look at what he did. He made things 'all Sir Garnet.' And he was even smaller than you are."

At the Fortune there was a very good Lonsdale play, *On Approval*, produced by Tom Walls, who had taken over this small theatre. There were only four characters, played by Valerie Taylor, Ellis Jeffreys, Edmond Breon and Ronald Squire (who gave one of his usual polished performances). This was, all round, one of the best acted plays in town. It ran for 469 performances and at the end, although it had played to capacity nearly all the time, the profit was something like 11/-. The Fortune did not hold enough money for such plays and casts.

The poor old Gaiety was in almost total eclipse. Its only production lasted for a mere 38 performances and was called *The Girl From Cooks*. However much the public might have followed "the Man from Cooks," there in the old days they did not "Follow the Girl" in 1927. This was a J. L. Sacks venture. Joe was having a sticky time, too. *Peter Pan* went in for Christmas.

The Garrick lived mostly on transfers and Ruth Draper. The Globe had one success, *Potiphar's Wife*, a sensational story like a newspaper serial, but it caught on. The author was a journalist, Edgar C. Middleton, who did Theatre Notes for the *Westminster Gazette*, which had been revived as a daily paper. Paul Cavanagh, Henry Oscar, Martita Hunt, Jeanne de Casalis and a young actress named Adrianne Allen made successes. It eventually transferred to the Savoy, running in all 142 performances.

Drury Lane followed up *Rose Marie* with *The Desert Song*, with music by Romberg, and book and lyrics by Oscar Hammerstein, in whose destiny Drury Lane lay so certainly. If the success of this big spectacular musical play did not equal that of *Rose Marie*, it did well enough with 432 performances. Its exciting story (rather improbable but who cared?), with its romantic settings in Morocco with the Riff warriors galloping over the hills, and the ideal pair of lovers, Edith Day and Harry Welchman (she, wonderful as Margot Bonvalet, and he, all that could be desired as Pierre Birabeau, alias "The Red Shadow") made this a play which delighted the women. The duet "Mine Alone" caused heart flutterings, and when the Red Shadow carried his Margot out into the moonlit desert, well, romance held full sway. The male voices in "Riding for the Riffs" were a delight. Comedy was in the safe hands of Gene Gerrard and Clarice Hardwicke. There was no argument about a library deal for this play; it was done before production.

Luck had deserted His Majesty's. *The Wicked Earl*, despite Cyril Maude in the cast, ran for only 30 performances. There was a most extraordinary revue staged under fantastic conditions and backed by a very rich young man about town, who was not quite so rich afterwards. It had a curious first night. It was called *White Birds* and it seemed to have no ending. It went on and on and on. Many of the audience left in despair of ever seeing the conclusion. It had almost everything and everybody in it, except shape, make and timing. José Collins, Maurice Chevalier, Maisie Gay, Anton Dolin, Gwen Farrar, Billy Milton, George Gee, all struggled in vain. It was not an entertainment but a feat of endurance. Lew Leslie, of *Black Birds*, produced it, but he had not the same control over the "White Birds" as he possessed over the Black variety. They most certainly did not flock together. Cut to ribbons, it staggered on for eighty performances with immense losses. But *Oh, Kay*, with music by George Gershwin, and Gertrude Lawrence in the lead, played for 214 nights.

One of the most charming plays of the year was *Marigold*, presented at the Kingsway. It was a delightful and delicate love story of the days of the young Queen Victoria—not the Queen's love story, of course, but she was a pivotal character. You never saw the Queen and the final curtain fall on an audience tiptoe with excitement, just before her entrance. The Kingsway was looked

upon as being unlucky but *Marigold* changed all that by running
for 649 performances. Hubert Harben, Angela Baddeley, Norman
Page and Jean Cadell were in the cast.

The London Hippodrome had a smashing success with *Hit the
Deck*, with music by Vincent Youmans. A big, outstanding hit was
registered by a comedian named Sydney Howard. This chubby,
simple-minded man from Yorkshire—from Newton, near Yeadon,
a typical woollen town and "reet Yorks"—rose to the top at one
bound. He had had plenty of experience and now came the chance.
He took it in both of those marvellous hands of his which seemed
to be always getting in his way—which seemed so awkward but
were so immensely expressive. Indeed, they obeyed Casca's command in *Julius Caesar*. "Speak, hands, for me." His homely bearing
and manner, his simplicity and his general good nature endeared
him to all. He went right to the top and to film stardom as well. He
was exactly the same off the stage as on. When success compelled
him to make something of a show, he lived in a smart hotel, out
of which he would sneak guiltily and be found having "a coop of
tea and a boon" at a little shop round the corner. He was much
happier there. He would come to my little informal club at the
Duke of York's—the Poison Parlour, where everybody in Fleet
Street and nearly everybody who mattered in London could be
found—and sit very quietly in a corner, listening to the conversation. He said it was "coolture." He got his big chance because
another comedian fell ill, but Robert Sydney Howard, with his
heart of gold and his talent, deserved every moment of his fame and
good fortune. There is a plaque to his memory in his native town
and he would have been very proud of that.

In 1927, Cochran presented *One Dam Thing After Another* at the
London Pavilion, another link in the necklet of really West End
revues which he wove there with such sophistication. The music
was by Richard Rodgers; he and Hammerstein were already writing
their names on the London Theatre in the 1920's. In the cast of *One
Dam Thing After Another* were Sonnie Hale, Mimi Crawford, and Jessie
Matthews. This young lady had started in the chorus and had
understudied Gertrude Lawrence in *Charlot's Revue* in 1924. She
went to America with that and, when playing for Gertrude Lawrence,
she attracted attention. She was in the *Charlot Revue* of 1926 and
from that Cochran engaged her for the London Pavilion. There
were brilliance and a queer kind of magic in her; she had great
ability and power of attraction. In this revue she sang "My Heart
Stood Still." Her big eyes, her almost childish appeal, and her
sincerity were such that the hearts of the audience stilled with hers.
She was a big star after *One Dam Thing After Another*.

In that revue Sonnie Hale impersonated Hannen Swaffer, the

most dreaded of all critics. He wanted to get it all absolutely right, so he summoned up courage to ask Swaffer's help. Swaffer not only helped him but actually lent him clothes. On the first night Sonnie looked and behaved so much like Swaffer that it seemed as if the trenchant scribe had left his favourite pitch at the back of the circle and invaded the stage, as indeed he would have done with the slightest encouragement. For Swaffer always loved publicity, to be talked and written about, to be stared at, to be the centre of controversy. Now to be imitated in one of Cochran's revues— Cochran with whom he was either at daggers drawn or on the most friendly terms—filled him with delight. He was very pleased. He said to me: "He l-l-looked exactly like me—in those d-d-dirty clothes, that awful hat and cigarette ash all over him. Disgraceful —but—just l-like me." I had seen it too, but that did not stop Swaffer describing it. *One Dam Thing After Another* ran for 237 performances.

Edgar Wallace got a winner at the Lyceum called *The Terror* (246), in which were a young man named Carol Reed (now our leading film director), Mary Glynne and Dennis Neilson-Terry (son of Fred Terry and Julia Neilson). But he had a failure at the Savoy with *Double Dan*, nine nights only.

The Garden of Eden had a good run (232) at the Lyric, with Eva Moore, Eric Maturin and Tallulah Bankhead. And good work was done with revivals at the Lyric, Hammersmith, notably of *The Beau's Stratagem* and an amusing production called *When Crummles Played*, with Wilfred Shine as the provincial manager "of Roscian Renown," Miriam Lewes as "Mrs Crummles" and Herminone Baddeley as The Phenomenon. It played 115 times.

The New Theatre found a success in *The Wrecker*.

The Palace Theatre brought in a musical play from America, some of the music of which was written by Rodgers and Hart. It was a big success called *The Girl Friend*. This must not be confused with the recent record-breaking musical *The Boy Friend*. But *The Girl Friend* did pretty well for the 1920's, scoring 421 performances. It had that delightful dancer and artiste, Louise Browne, making her London début and scoring an immediate success. And also a brilliant little comedienne named Emma Haig.

The Apache ran for 164 performances at the London Pavilion, with Dorothy Ward and Shaun Glenville (tried favourites) and also Carl Brisson.

Somerset Maugham's *The Letter* was a success at the Playhouse. Gladys Cooper gave a splendid performance and it was played 328 times.

The irrepressible Philip Ridgeway abandoned for the nonce his resurrectionist tradition and embarked upon a new musical comedy

production at the Prince of Wales's Theatre. This was *The Blue
Train*, written by Reginald Arkell and Dion Titheradge. with
music by Robert Stolz. Ridgeway persuaded Lily Elsie to play
the lead and in a good company he had Arthur Margetson, Cecily
Debenham and Bobby Howes. Lily Elsie was as lovely and gracious
as ever, like a Spring morning. But Ridgeway knew when that show
opened that his expenses exceeded anything it was possible for him
to take even if the show played to capacity at every performance.
Yet, somehow, it ran for 125 nights, which was typical of Ridgeway
and the theatre of the 1920's.

Crime played for 125 performances at the Queen's. *The Crooked
Billet* scored 172 at the Royalty.

At the St James's, where Gilbert Miller was making a splendid
fight to preserve the distinction of that famous theatre, there was
Interference, with Gerald du Maurier, Herbert Marshall, Herbert
Waring, Frank Lawton and Hilda Moore. It had a long run (412)
and richly deserved it.

The White Chateau at the St Martin's was a most interesting
play by that imaginative author Reginald Berkeley. It only ran
for 36 performances but it deserved to do much better. It was
before its time.

The High Road at the Shaftesbury was Lonsdale at his best. It
had a cast worthy of it: Mary Jerrold, Gertrude Kingston, Fred
Kerr, Allan Aynesworth, Ian Hunter, Cecily Byrne, and Alfred
Drayton (who made a big personal success). In the first week of
the run Fred Kerr, who played Lord Trench, fell ill. The stage
manager, C. Barnard Moore, took the part over at a moment's
notice and played it splendidly. *The High Road* ran for 237 performances.

A revue, *Blue Skies*, was a success at the Vaudeville, and an
outstanding success was *The Vagabond King* at the Winter Garden.
This was a musical version of the St James's romantic play *If I
Were King*. The music was by Friml. Winnie Melville and Derek
Oldham were Katherine de Vaucelles and Francois Villon respect-
ivly, and that fine actor, H. A. Saintsbury, was a magnificent Louis
XI. But perhaps the best thing in the show was the performance of
Norah Blaney as the tragic Huguette du Hamel. The music is
popular today. "Only A Rose" and "The Vagabonds' Chorus" are
practically classics. King George and Queen Mary went to see
The Vagabond King on August 8th and the management had to
contrive a Royal Room adjoining the Royal Box, for such a thing
had been omitted when the theatre was reconstructed. But all was
well.

Running on into 1927 at the Palace was a play which had been
produced the previous year, called *Princess Charming*, a Clayton and

Waller production—Evelyn Laye had taken over the lead during the long run.

Seymour Hicks adapted a farce from the French and called it *Mr What's His Name*. It was produced at Wyndham's on April 25th and ran until July 23rd (104 times) with Hicks himself in the lead.

There were highlights as well as blackouts in 1927, but very little stability. American musical plays were steadily replacing those of home-made variety. Hannen Swaffer inveighed against this. As critic of the *Daily Express*, his power was great and his personality greater. He was an outstanding figure in the world of illusion—and, maybe, part of it himself.

CHAPTER XV

Critics, Newsmen and—Hannen Swaffer

ALL through the 1920's the theatre was "news;" that is to say, it got considerable space in the Press. Nowadays that space is absorbed by television, radio, gramophone records and films, and the theatre hardly gets a mention. In the 'twenties the theatrical Press Agents rose to their full power and there was a very close liaison between Fleet Street and the playhouse.

Some of the critics changed during that decade, some from one paper to another, and, of course, new people appeared. W. A. Darlington was still critic for the *Daily Telegraph* and is so today— a man who really enjoys going to the theatre and a critic who deals out justice, although sometimes he tempers it with mercy. *The Times* was represented most augustly by Charles Morgan, who brought the dignity of that important newspaper with him into the auditorium along with his own distinction, and his evening cloak which singled him out from his colleagues. E. A. Baughan, quiet, kindly and knowledgeable, represented what is now the *News Chronicle*. Ivor Brown attended for the *Manchester Guardian*, and moved to the *Observer*. There was Bernard Buckham, who was not only dramatic critic of the *Daily Mirror* but also editor of its Gossip Page. He was large, burly, genial, avuncular and very popular, and there was a forensic air about him, too. And also on the *Daily News* (now *News Chronicle*) was a very charming man and good journalist, who sometimes acted as dramatic critic and who was in charge of all the theatrical news, named Alan Borthwick.

Two outstanding figures were Philip Page and Alan Parsons, who was to succeed Page as dramatic critic for the *Daily Mail*.

Philip Page, always called "Peter" because it was not his name, was dark, handsome and extremely accomplished. The product of public school and Oxford, he was a first-class musician, an expert pianist and organist, a good composer and a man who could conduct an orchestra with skill. He did so at Drury Lane when that famous film *Intolerance* was shown there. He was a great wit. He wrote the shortest notice known in the history of our dramatic criticism. The play was called *Oh, Yes*! Philip Page simply wrote *Oh, No*! There was really no more to be said. He was a very good critic; if he did not like you, he was always most polite, but that politeness had the point of a poniard. He is now in retirement.

Alan Parson was a most lovable fellow who had never quite grown up. He was irresponsible, especially in money matters, with which he could never cope at all. He was Eton and Oxford, very proud of both, and was really very erudite. He loved the theatre and was never so happy as when in one. He had been a Civil Servant but he did not like that. He found the constantly recurring Minutes a great trial. There was one which pursued him and to which he knew not the answer. The chance of escape came when he was offered the job as critic on the *Daily Sketch*. He jumped at it, and the last thing he did when leaving the Ministry was to burn that terrifying minute in his office fire. No more was ever heard of it; perhaps he had found the right answer.

He had married Viola Tree, daughter of Sir Herbert Tree. In many ways she was even more vague than he was, especially in financial matters. They were perpetually in straits but always overcame them. Viola, who was a most delightful person, had a good deal of her father's magic about her. She was amazingly democratic and would travel third class on Continental railways, a matter of extreme discomfort then, but she never worried. Once when entering France from Italy, the Customs officials wanted her to pay duty on a large bunch of bananas which she was carrying. She refused. There was one of those long, impassioned scenes which so often occurred in those days with Continental officials. Viola refused to give way. She walked back to the other end of the station, which was on Italian soil, ate every one of those bananas and then walked back to the French side and asked what they proposed to do about it now? She could, on occasions, be an amazing good actress, and at other times very bad—another inheritance from her great father. But to know her was to love her.

Alan Parsons was an amazingly handsome man, dark, wavy-haired, extremely distinguished and tall; he was most picturesque. He looked like a prince of the Italian Renaissance stepped from the canvas of an Old Master. He was a good critic, but fidgety. He would never sit in his seat. He roamed about the back of the Dress or Upper Circle, and from there wrote his notice. His great tribulation, when he was on the *Daily Mail*, was that his copy had to be in to catch the early editions which went to press before the play had finished. He always had to be told the plot and the ending by somebody who knew—very often myself, for we were bosom friends—and he would try and get it into his head while scribbling his notice on a bit of paper held against the wall at the back of the Circle. He would groan while labouring at this and very often bash his head against firebuckets. Readers of the London edition, of course, got a full and considered notice, but that for the provinces was a bit scrappy, through no fault of his. Plays did not begin before 8 o'clock in those days. He was a most popular man and his great joy was to be in my unofficial club "The Poison Parlour." This met at the Duke of York's Theatre and afterwards at the Whitehall Theatre. There everybody who was anybody in Fleet Street or the theatre could be found most evenings. Indeed, visiting celebrities were brought to it to be introduced to this quite unique gathering; otherwise their knowledge of London was incomplete. Actors, dramatists, managers, producers, Fleet Street in every rank, artists, poets, jockeys, sportsmen, pugilists, policemen, detectives, novelists, doctors, clergymen, business men, Members of Parliament, even Cabinet Ministers—not to omit crooks and criminals on occasions—came to the Poison Parlour. Its Chairman was Hannen Swaffer. I must write its full history some day. It was an outstanding feature of the theatre of the 1920's and 1930's.

Other critics and newsmen were A. Macgregor, of the *Evening News*, a good critic who only spoke to an actor once in his life and that was Malcolm Keen; S. R. Littlewood of the *Morning Post* (afterwards Editor of *The Stage*), learned in theatre lore and a great connoisseur of sponge cakes; Harris Deans, Maurice Willson-Disher, Hubert Griffith (critic for some time of the *Evening Standard* and also a dramatist—his nickname was "Tippy"); George Munro (who did notices for what was then Allied Newspapers; later he became a crime reporter and said he hardly noticed the difference); Jesse Heitner (now the distinguished Editor of *The Sphere* and *Eve*); John Young (then on the *Evening News*, now Night News Editor of the *Daily Express* and one of the best journalists who ever walked Fleet Street); a nice, gentle fellow named Dudeney (who was critic for the *Daily Sketch* and had a fondness for the word "fragrant" which frequently found its way into his notices—often aptly); Gordon Beccles (whose full name was Beccles-Wilson, very tall and very tough); and Ewart Hodgson (who took over the theatrical news on the *Star* when that splendid journalist and man of knowledge, H. Cozens-Hardy, gave it up). "Cozens," as he was called, would talk to himself, and write his "story" on scraps of paper as he walked along the street, but he knew everybody worth knowing, and everything about everything worth knowing, too.

Amongst the critics on first nights was a very scholarly-looking man, pale of face and benevolently dignified, who always wore a black skull-cap. He had an episcopal air and might have been a bishop. He did not mix much and some of his colleagues did not know who he was or what journal he represented. When they discovered that he was critic for the *News of the World*, it always came as a bit of a shock. He had been a first-class writer of lyrics for musical comedies and his name was Frank Clement. Later in the period came Jesse Collings, who caused a minor sensation by writing his notices in verse, and good verse, too. He was an amazing, much travelled man, and a very good fellow. He still lives, I am glad to say.

Rossiter Sheppard did "notices" for the *People* then and is still on that paper. In the 1920's he had not grown that beard which gives him a Grand-Ducal appearance and over which, and the moustache which accompanies it, his eyes still twinkle and smile —a man who knows his job. There was Reginald Simpson of the *Sunday Chronicle*, who became a successful playwright and also editor of that paper. There were many more but one man deserves special mention, J. G. Bergel of the *Evening News*. Jack Bergel was very dark and wore glasses which flashed whenever he moved his head. He had a great sense of humour, he was always on the verge of a joke—a rather academic joke as a rule because he was of Balliol—and he always had his mouth wide open. His knowledge was encyclopaedic. He wrote not only on the theatre, but on skating, ski-ing, aeronautics, Bridge, Chess, Morris Dancing and scores of other subjects. It is probable that he covered Tennis, too—he most certainly played it—he was a kind of journalistic Admirable Crichton. Any new subject coming into the news was immediately handed to Jack Bergel and it was found that he knew all about it. Had he been alive today, he would have been the expert on nuclear matters and space travel. He took everything in his stride. Many journalists have written learnedly on matters about which they knew nothing, but Bergel actually knew. He could absorb knowledge as a sponge does water. As a critic he was baffling to managers who did not know his methods. They would perhaps glance at him during the show, for a good notice in the *Evening News* was always wanted. There he was, gazing at the stage, with his mouth wide open and with the closest attention. Sometimes he would laugh heartily and, if it was that kind of play, the manager would be overjoyed, but he was likely to find a bad notice the next day. For Bergel went by contrasts: if he laughed, it was because he was bored and was laughing at something conjured up in his own mind; if, however, he sat silent and solemn, the observant knew that he liked the play. He was a very gallant young man. He became a Transatlantic Air Pilot during the Second World War and between flights would often call in to see me at Drury Lane. But he lost his life, and those who knew him mourn him sincerely.

There were, of course, the twin giants of Sunday journalism, James Agate and St John Ervine and there was J. C. Trewin, another man of theatrical knowledge. There was—and is—George Bishop, now of the *Daily Telegraph*, but then of the *Observer*, and later the last editor of that very famous theatrical journal, *The Era*. William Pollock (Bill to his friends) was theatre correspondent of the *Daily Mail*. He also wrote about cricket, which he loved. Other men who were critics were James Wentworth Day (a great authority on nature matters, as well), Tom Driberg (now an eminent political figure); and Salusbury (a man who looked exactly what a Guards officer should be, but who was and is an Australian and a first class journalist). And there was A. E. Wilson of the *Star* (first-class).

As regards the "columnists," apart from Ewart Hodgson of the *Star*, there were two of considerable importance. Hodgson had a great sense of humour, a most infectious, deep, gurgling laugh and a habit of regarding all first nights as battles. "What, have hostilities broken out again?" he would say, when reminded that the curtain had risen. The other important couple were Norman Hillson, who was "Argonaut" of the *Evening Standard*, and the one and only Eric Barker, "The Stroller" of the *Evening News*. Hillson, who is still most active, was at times quite astounding. He would do things which struck the beholder dumb, and which at times also so affected his Editors. He would write things which were as vivid as flame. He was a most baffling personality, always surprising you with something new, but he knew how to get "news" and he got it. Stone walls did not a prison make, nor iron bars a cage, if "Argonaut" was after a story. He would storm such things and emerge with the scalp in his hand. He had a manner which reduced nervous or shy people to the depth of inferiority complex, yet his manners were beyond reproach. He believed in the best. I remember that Fleet Street was going to honour me by giving me a Leg of Mutton Supper. Hillson took charge. There was no leg-of-mutton supper; what emerged was a banquet, and a good one, too. He had a most vivid imagination which enabled him to see through doors, and concrete walls. He was always on the brink of founding a newspaper but somehow it never materialized, which was a pity because a journal with Norman Hillson "in the chair" would have provided the liveliest reading. His kindness of heart would have got him out of bed at 3 a.m. on a snowy morning to do a good turn. He writes very good books. But he could be quite terrifying to the person who tried to withhold the story he wanted.

Eric Barker, "The Stroller," now in honourable retirement, was probably one of the greatest newshawks Fleet Street ever possessed, not only on theatrical subjects but on all matters. Sherlock Holmes was a flat-footed policeman to Eric, when he was on the trail. Nothing could be hidden from him; the Sahara did not contain enough dust to throw into his eyes. Not only was he most acute personally, and possessed of tremendous knowledge of people and their contacts, but he built up an immense organization of his own. He had all sorts and conditions of people who "tipped him off." They included dealers in real estate, solicitors' and barristers' clerks, eminent legal figures, registrars of births, marriages and deaths, cloak-room attendants, barbers, odd men who sold newspapers and would come sidling up to whisper in his ear, barmaids, doctors, leading ladies and gentlemen, and chorus girls.

He covered every field where news was to be found. He would tell you himself—he was most meticulous in speech and manners—that "he did not only write on theatrical matters, but obtained great scoops for his newspaper." Once when a witness in a lawsuit and on oath, he so informed the judge, and nobody spoke more truly. His scoops were as innumerable as they were varied. It was not possible for a celebrity, or anyone whom he considered to be a celebrity, to do anything without Eric Barker knowing all about it. Those who thought they were going to have a nice, quiet, secret wedding at an outlying Register office, suddehly read of their intentions on the front page of the *Evening News*. A fat property-deal going through with business secrecy was disclosed to the public in the same way. In the theatre it was hardly possible to sneeze without Eric Barker knowing all about it.

He performed miracles in the way of news-gathering. His joy was to get a "Contents Bill" devoted to one of his stories, and he had a large collection of those which told the world of his scoops. He would buy an *Evening News*, read it in the street, gloat for a few seconds and then rush off to show his friends what he had accomplished. His mind worked like lightning. He did not have to storm the fort, as did others; he always knew of the postern gate which was open and through which he went to emerge with his scoop. When out on a story he allowed no obstacles to stand in his way, nothing could deter him from his end. And if he thought that story worth while, seldom, if ever, was he beaten. Whilst in pursuit of it he would speak little, but his eyes seemed to revolve in their sockets. It is hard to express this, but that is what they seemed to do. His friends, on beholding this phenomenon would steer clear of him. You must not balk a faultless bloodhound of its prey. He performed other marvels. Once he sent a beautiful girl as a candidate for the chorus, to George Edwardes at the Gaiety. He did not send her in the usual way, but as a parcel, addressed and labelled. She was delivered at the stage door of the Gaiety by a Post Office Official as a parcel. She got the job, too, and deserved it. Eric had an eye for beauty.

Although he was so quick in getting his story, he was by no means so expeditious in delivering it, either in writing or by telephone. He was so meticulous that it took him quite a long time. It must all be perfectly correct, every detail accounted for, nothing omitted. When he telephoned a friend, the person so honoured knew that he was in for a long sitting. Eric would have nothing taken for granted. It must all be set forth. He knew all about it, everybody else must know, too. He was one of the best known and best liked figures about town, but it did not do to run into him if you were in a hurry.

At times he would grow wrathful and had quite a turn for denunciation. He denounced that little club of mine when it first formed itself, for that was what it did. He did not know much about it but he did not approve. He said it was nothing but "a Poison Parlour." The members hailed this and adopted it as the name, with acclamation. He was most annoyed, but in the end he became a member, too, and found there was no poison there. He was a notable figure at first nights, in full evening dress with a gardenia in his button hole; he was never without that, in or out of evening dress. To first nights he usually escorted a very beautiful girl— not the same one but she to whom, for that occasion, he had awarded the Golden Apple.

He was educated at Dulwich and was a great believer in the Public School tradition and in Good Form. Things must be done the right way—the polite way—and he carried this out in his paragraphs, which never descended to the easy familiarity of Christian names. He expected the same politeness towards himself. If a friend of his was ill or in hospital, Eric would be tireless in inquiries and would call in person. He expected that in return, too. He had a bad accident which kept him in hospital a long time. He kept a list of his callers, and when he got out he made it pretty hot for those who called themselves his friends but had not come to see him.

With all his eccentricities, he helped many people, especially young beginners in their profession. He would go out of his way and give himself immense trouble to do a good turn to somebody he liked. Those whom he did not like were in no doubt about it. Eric Barker, "The Stroller," had a heart of gold and still has, although today he strolls but little. He is remembered with gratitude and affection. And, as a contrast to his work, he writes very good verse. He was one of the greatest newsmen of the theatre, especially during the 1920's and after.

There remains the (symbolically speaking) massive figure of the man who towered like Everest over the journalistic and critical side of the theatre in the 1920's—the spare, strange, gaunt form of Frederick Hannen Swaffer. Swaffer ("Swaff" to his friends) was the greatest journalist of his day and it has been a long day. For years before he became a regular dramatic critic he had dominated

Macbeth at the Court Theatre in modern dress. Macbeth (Eric
Maturin) with the daggers, after the murder of the King, and Lady
Macbeth (Mary Merrill).

Jessie Matthews, great
star of revue.

Fay Compton, great Eng-
lish actress whose "Mary
Rose" shone in the 1920's.

journalism, when there were giants in Fleet Street, too. He had
raised circulations, put falling papers back on the map and shown
his amazing instinct for news in many ways. He had been reporter,
Art Editor and Editor-in-Chief. He had held almost every post in
Fleet Street. He had served under Lord Northcliffe and he held
"The Chief" and his memory in the highest respect. He does so
today. He, too, got innumerable scoops; he was always jumps
ahead of his rivals. It was he who started Eric Barker in journalism.
Among other things he invented the Gossip Writer and the Gossip
Column, which afterwards he would deride. But he is like that,
a master of the volte face; you never knew where to have
him.

Sometimes people would court him to enlist his support in a
venture. That happened once when he became a dramatic critic.
He was campaigning against the influx of American plays. Some
men, who had an English musical comedy, laid their plans before
him and sang the praises of the show. He boosted it in his columns.
They got into financial difficulties and they borrowed money off
him. The production came along and they chuckled. Whatever the
other critics might say, they had got Hannen Swaffer. Had they?
All the notices were bad but Swaffer's was the worst of the lot. He
thought it was bad when he saw it and he said so, for he always tells
the truth. That was and is his speciality.

He would espouse seemingly lost causes and win victories for them.
He would lead campaigns. He was feared by everyone in the
theatrical profession and hated by many, but he fought for the cause
of Actors' Equity and had much to do with its establishment. He
was really a very good influence in the theatre, for he made the
actors and actresses afraid of what he might say of them and that
kept them on their toes. Such a thing does good, not harm. There
is nobody today with that kind of power.

Whatever he may think himself, Swaffer was not a great dramatic
critic from the academic point of view, judged by the standards of
Clement Scott, William Archer or A. B. Walkley. But in some ways
he was better, for the reason given above. Also, he always knew
what was going on behind the scenes. He instilled wholesome fear
and destroyed false quantities and fake. If you were sincere, you
had nothing of which to be afraid. He was your friend. But if he
thought there was carelessness, bad workmanship, slipshod methods
or second-rate quality, then the whip cracked. His "notices" of
plays were always more in the form of news stories than studied
criticism. He went right to the heart of things like a surgeon's
knife. The first question asked about a new play was "What did
Swaffer say about it?" and it was to his notice in the *Daily Express*
that public, management and players turned first. That was what

mattered. He judged from his own high standard of endeavour. Many people came under the lash of his pen. Certain managements barred him from their theatres. He was in no way abashed. He told the public about it and gave his own reasons. The management had no opportunity of answering back. The barring never lasted for long. He would win.

He was always quarrelling and always making friends. With him, a quarrel lasted just as long as he felt aggrieved. Then it was over. Sometimes his adversaries did not feel the same way, but they would find that, although they were not speaking to Hannen Swaffer, he was speaking to them, and would do so without any inhibition. So what was the use? The feud died. One aggrieved actress slapped his face in public in the Savoy Grill, his daily haunt. She was the one who suffered. Swaff made it into wonderful publicity for himself and that year his Christmas cards showed him having his face slapped and wishing his friends "A Merry Xmas and a Slappy New Year."

No journalist ever exercised such power over the theatre as did Swaffer in the 1920's and the 1930's. He made the theatre "news" —hot news—because when he wrote about it, hosts of people who admired him, but who were not previously very interested in the theatre, read what he had to say and had their interest in the theatre stimulated thereby. Swaffer was afraid of nobody. He won his greatest victory over himself. And he conquered, too, almost entirely, a terrible stutter which had stood in his way when he was a young man. He became a brilliant, forceful and fluent public speaker. The announcement of his name filled the hall for any meeting.

When it came to news, he always got it first. He never went to look for it, it came to him. Normally a paper will not use a story which has appeared in another journal first. But the other theatre correspondents had to waive that rule, otherwise they would have had nothing about which to write. It became the unwritten law that Swaffer had the story first. In the mornings, he sat in his study, in the top flat overlooking the Nurse Cavell statue in Trafalgar Square, where those who had news brought it to him. They would find him in his pyjamas, with a dressing-gown slung on, often unshaven and presenting to the uninitiated eye a rather frightening figure, with his unbrushed hair standing almost on end. He would allow them to state their case and they had to do it quickly, for he had no patience and loved to talk himself. Then, when they had told him, he would tell them. That usually took some time. But it was amazing to see who came up those flights of stone steps, men and women with names famous all over the world. He treated them all alike. His table was littered with papers, books, documents and periodicals in the bravest disarray. He sat, quite unperturbed, playing Patience with a pack of very dirty old cards. I knew him very well for years and was always in attendance when he wrote his articles for the *Daily* and the *Sunday Express*. Swaff knew me and trusted me. I was able to help him, out of my own intimate knowledge of the theatre. That association lasted for years and the friendship exists today, although our paths have drifted apart, which began when Swaff deserted the theatre for politics. Except for callers, the only other person present was Swaff's faithful secretary for long years, Kate Goodson, whom he always addressed as "Miss" to her face and called "old Kate" behind her back. But Mrs Swaffer, a gentle and gracious lady would come in to see me, and Rose, that wonderful maid who is still there, would bring coffee.

I thought it was about time that Swaff had a new pack of cards, for those he used were shocking. So, on his fiftieth birthday, over 30 years ago now, I bought a large silver cigarette box, and put a new pack of cards in it. I had an inscription engraved on the box stating the event it celebrated and adding "To the Man who has Inspired me Most." That box is still there. I was quite sincere in those words. It was Swaff's standard of quality, his devotion to his work, his hatred of bunk and his fearless fights which inspired me, not his political views (of which he talked so much) or the flamboyant eccentricities which had become part of him, or even some of his methods.

I went to the small but very select dinner party he gave on that occasion a most unusual event for him to entertain in such a manner. The company consisted of Mr and Mrs Swaffer, the Duchess of Hamilton, Miss Lind-Af-Hageby and Miss Estelle Stead—and myself. It was not a gay party; the talk was mostly about the cruelty practised in the slaughter yards of Chicago and the iniquity of infecting mice with cancer for research. On that occasion Swaffer did very little talking. That was unusual, for mostly he did it all; nobody else had a chance. Words flowed from him like Niagara. One eminent man who tried to interrupt him was told curtly: "You shut up!" and he did. Nowadays Swaff is extremely deaf. Probably this does not worry him very much because he very seldom listened—or appeared to listen—to anyone but himself.

One of his qualifications for dramatic criticism was his immense success in dramatizing himself. All the world knew that gaunt frame, that unmistakable face with its expressionless mask, that shabby black hat and equally disreputable clothes covered in cigarette and cigar ash, the famous collar and stock tie. He loved to be stared at. He felt it was his due. At first nights he never occupied his stall, he stood at the back of the stalls and circle with Alan Parsons (whom he liked very much) and often I completed the trio. He never appeared to notice anything, but he did not miss a detail.

He had no outside hobbies, no interests beyond his devotion to spiritualism. Probably his happiest nights were those he spent in my "Poison Parlour," where he talked and talked and talked and others sat and listened, but hardly spoke a word. For years he scarcely missed a night. If there was a first performance at another theatre, he would pop in first and come back later. Yet first nights, new plays and what the critics thought of them—and many used that room—were never discussed in "The Poison Parlour." There was so much else to talk about—into the small hours.

Very few people knew or even saw the real Hannen Swaffer underneath the façade he presented to the public, There is, beneath that terrific selfconfidence, that apparent complete reliance on the first person singular, that seeming arrogance, a very gentle soul, often with a very simple mind, rather a shy man in many ways who has a kindly nature and who has done extremely generous things of which nothing was ever said. Of all the men who wrote about the theatre in the 1920's, that doubtful period, Swaffer stood like a vast mountain, immovable and unshakable, and, although he often attacked it, he did the theatre a very great deal of good.

CHAPTER XVI

1928—and The Great Challenge

IN the year 1928 the theatre received the greatest challenge ever hurled at it in the two-thousand-odd years of its existence. Theatrical affairs were greatly upset by the illness of King George V, who caught a chill during the ceremony at the Cenotaph on November 11th. By November 23rd his condition was critical and the Prince of Wales made a lightning journey home from Dar-es-Salaam. An air of impending disaster emptied the theatres and restaurants and damped down all social events, for the King, and his Queen, too, were greatly beloved and respected.

Ernest Truex, the American actor, had gone into management. He had also become so English that he had developed a liking for cricket. He made his essay into management with a quite amusing comedy called *Out Goes She*, which showed his adventures with three wives, English, French and American. This opened at the Criterion Theatre on the very night when the life of King George swayed in the balance. Nobody took much interest in the play —members of the Press present kept going to the telephone for news—and I, who was managing for Truex, had to be busy on a special article which I had been commissioned to write on "The King as a Playgoer." What might have been a comfortable success was killed at the outset. It would never have been a big success, but it might easily have exceeded 100 performances. The King recovered but the play died.

It was one of the most extra ordinary first nights which experienced playgoers and theatre people remember, only equalled by one some years afterwards when, on the first night of Dodie Smith's fine play *Dear Octopus* at the Queen's, we stood on the very brink of war with Hitler, with peace trembling in the balance. During the first act I got news that Chamberlain was flying to Munich, and circulated that news at once. The tension was eased and the people rejoiced. They did not then know that nothing would come of it but a short breathing space. But the play succeeded.

What hit the theatre hardest was not the illness of the King but the challenge already alluded to. Something happened which struck right at the roots of the living theatre; a gauntlet was thrown down but the theatre did not stoop to pick it up. It did nothing about it and took this blow on the chin without retaliation. It did not perhaps understand what it all meant; just a few, a very few, saw the menace.

On the night of September 27th, the film critics went to the Piccadilly Theatre, which had only opened that year, to see a Press Show of a new film. It had been intended as a silent picture, then it was decided to put in some recorded songs while the singers mimed them on the screen. But something more than that happened. Al Jolson was the star and, although the critics admired him in the main, they were a bit allergic to his extremely sentimental methods of putting over songs. That night they heard something more than a mere recorded song; they actually heard Al Jolson speak dialogue. What he said may have been gagged in or it may have been part of the original script, but it was there. They all heard him; there was no doubt about it. A film had spoken. They heard him say: "Say, Ma, listen to this," and, a bit later: "Wait a minute, wait a minute—you ain't heard nothing yet." History had been made, a new epoch opened, and the theatre, which had been able to keep the films at bay while they were silent, although they took heavy toll, was now faced with this new menace which could include actors and actresses who spoke and sang and so challenge it on its own pitch.

The film critics did not seem unduly excited. The theatre was inclined to scoff. Even the astute and opportunist C. B. Cochran said he thought Al Jolson on the films was a very much reduced version of Al Jolson in the flesh. But the Talkies had arrived. The theatre did not realize the danger until *The Singing Fool* hit everybody smack in the eye with Jolson (on celluloid, of course) facing the audience on his knees and singing "Sonny Boy." The Talkies soared to the top of the entertainment tree in a very short time.

Having witnessed that momentous event, Hannen Swaffer stalked into the Duke of York's and told me about it. "The theatre is dead," he remarked in sepulchral tones, "quite dead." "Oh, yes?" I replied. "I have just seen it die," said Swaffer, throwing himself into his accustomed chair. "I expect it will last my lifetime," I said philosophically, for I knew something about theatre history. Swaffer shook his head. "The theatre's dead," he answered; "it's . . . all over." It is not all over, even yet, although the theatre is now a relic of its former self. It will last my lifetime, and a bit beyond. On that night I was the better prophet of the two. Swaffer would not be appeased. He did not mourn the passing of the theatre— that was beneath his dignity—but he probably felt as if some rather distant connection of his, a not too distinguished relative, had passed away and that he must show a little feeling. But he promptly became a film critic as well.

Managers said this talking-picture business was a passing phase. They had said the same about the silent films, they had said the same about radio, which in 1928 was hitting the Theatre hard, and they are saying it in 1959 about television. What the Talkies did was to kill that grand and valuable provincial theatre which was the backbone of the profession. Here was the show with all the stars, just as London and New York saw it—no touring company but the real thing. Only a fragment of the provincial theatre remains today, and television is dealing with that. It was a revolution; it altered the old system of filming, it created stars and new audiences, and the theatre did nothing at all to meet this immense and powerful challenge. It just lay down before it.

Yet, in the West End, amidst bad trade, bad conditions, a most unsettled world, the inroads of radio and now this new competitor, new theatres, were being built. The Carlton has been chronicled. The newcomer in 1928 was the Piccadilly Theatre, and from its almost virgin stage came the Talkie.

The Piccadilly was opened by Edward Laurillard on April 27th 1928, with a new musical play called *Blue Eyes*. He had encountered great difficulties in getting hold of the site, which he overcame by his thick-skinned obstinacy, tenacity and pluck. This was, of course, an essentially modern playhouse; it had no pit, the ground floor was all stalls. There was no gallery in the old sense of the word, and boxes were reduced to a minimum.

The opening night was not auspicious. In order to reach the various parts of the house there seemed to be a lot of staircases and passages to negotiate. Actually, it was all quite simple, but on that first night the place was inadequately staffed by inexperienced people and there was some chaos. The public never helps itself; it drifts, and that caused more trouble. Some of the Press notices said the place would be dangerous in case of fire. All that was quickly put right, but the initial damage was done. Today the Piccadilly is a successful and efficiently run theatre, but it got left badly at the post. Also, its name belied it. It is not in Piccadilly, nor even in Piccadilly Circus, although, if you knew where to look, you could just glimpse a portion of it from there. This nomenclature confused many of the general public, who do not realize the curious way in which theatres are named. Very few managers think it worth while to tell the public where their playhouses are. They themselves know and it is up to the public to find out.

Some of course do proclaim their whereabouts, like the Haymarket, the Aldwych and the Whitehall, which are all actually in the thoroughfares so named. It seems likely that Government Departments were not too pleased when the Whitehall Theatre invaded their august domain. I opened it and applied for the telegraphic address of "Red Tape London." This was immediately turned down.

Blue Eyes, the first play at the Piccadilly, despite its unfortunate opening, managed to run for 276 performances. The music was by Jerome Kern, the book by Guy Bolton and Graham John. An excellent cast included W. H. Berry, Geoffrey Gwyther, George Vollaire, Bertram Wallis, Sylvia Cecil and Evelyn Laye (who looked a vision in the clothes of the period, the days of Bonnie Prince Charlie).

There is no need to delve into the failures of 1928, which were many. In view of the bad times and added competition, the hard core of the theatre managed to put up a pretty brave show. Where a standard of quality and experience reigned, there was success. In those places were found excitement and illusion, the two great drawing cards of the theatre. Plays in those days did not run as long as now; over 200 performances was excellent and over 100 was satisfactory. Costs, although rising, were different. In 1928, four productions topped the three-hundred mark and they were the work of the Older Brigade, Tom Walls, Sir Alfred Butt, Cochran and Basil Dean. Dean achieved the longest run of them all with *Young Woodley*.

At the Aldwych, where policy and consistency reigned, *Plunder*, by Ben Travers, was a big success. It scored 344. All the Aldwych favourites were in it, reinforced on this occasion by that sterling actor, Herbert Waring. In some ways *Plunder* was the best of the Aldwych farces. There was a scene in Scotland Yard, in which Tom Walls was severely grilled by the police but came through it with his cool nonchalance and quick wits. He was made to remain in the room whilst Ralph Lynn was cross-examined. That scene presented two of the best performances the Aldwych, or any other theatre, ever saw. There sat Tom, outwardly calm but inwardly terrified, as Ralph Lynn, in his nice "silly ass" character, was put through it by the relentless "cops." To see Ralph Lynn, friendly, voluble, chatty, but inwardly scared to death, hovering with one foot over a fatal pitfall and recovering himself by a seeming miracle, gazing with assumed interest at a photographic group on the wall but shying away like a frightened horse when he found it composed of policemen, keeping his balance by a miracle like an inexpert skater but coming out on top in the end, was to see fine acting. But the spectacle of Tom, without a word to say, having to keep a still, calm face and yet conveying to the audience his agony of mind, was to see great acting. Only Seymour Hicks could have equalled it. That scene was magnificently written and magnificently played. Theatre prestige stood high at the Aldwych because it was in the hands of people of the theatre.

Two White Arms by a clever writer, Harold Dearden, with Owen Nares, Nigel Bruce, Sydney Fairbrother and Marda Vanne in the cast, ran for 149 nights at the Ambassadors. Edgar Wallace scored a big success at the Apollo with *The Squeaker*, one of the best plays he ever wrote: the scene in the Night Club was as authentic as it was exciting. And he wrote the book of a musical play, too, with score by Vernon Duke, which that master technician of the Theatre, Julian Wylie, produced at the Carlton Theatre. Its title was *The Yellow Mask* and, as its name implies, it was a mystery story. The ancient "Ceremony of the Keys," as performed nightly at the Tower of London, was a feature of this show and Wylie enlisted the co-operation of the Governor of the Tower, which ensured absolute accuracy in the stage presentation. *The Yellow Mask*, which ran for 218 performances, was an exciting, colourful affair in which Bobby Howes made a big personal success, as did Malcolm Keen, Winnie Collins and Phyllis Dare. Julian Wylie was real theatre. The stage obsessed him from his earliest days in Southport, Lancs. He and his brother Lauri presented plays in their toy theatre and sat in the gallery of the local playhouse, watching and learning. Julian was intended for a chartered accountant by his parents, but play-books interested him far more than books of accounts. He went into the profession; he became an agent and an impresario. He staged all sorts of shows. At the age of 21, he was responsible for all the civic entertainments in the City of Manchester to celebrate the accession of King Edward VII, and they were all successful. He never saw one of them; he was ill in bed with the measles. He went in for Magic and was a fine magician. He advertised himself as "The Agent with Ideas" and as such he built up acts for his clients which helped many of them to the very front rank. He had setbacks and difficulties; he knew what is was to have hardly a penny in his pocket, but he worked on. He meant to succeed and he did. He loved work and he loved the theatre; there was nothing else in his world. He was a hard taskmaster to those who did not share his views and give of their best. To him the rehearsals of a show were what mattered most. He adored rehearsing, because it was creative. During his first-night speech, indeed to round it off, he would turn to his company and say: "There will be no rehearsal tomorrow," at which they all cheered, but to him it meant sorrow. He was large, burly and square-looking, with a way of walking with his hands behind him and his chest thrust out, as if to challenge the world. Between his lips was either a cigarette or a cigar in the fag or butt-end stage; he never seemed to light a fresh one. His characteristic gesture was to flick tobacco ash, with his left hand, from the lapel of his coat, whether smoking or not.

He adored sweets of all kinds but especially large "butter nuts"

and "jelly babies," the heads of which he bit off with relish. He
was considered by many to be rough and brusque, not to say rude.
That was really only the "cover up" of a sensitive and shy mind.
Underneath, he was the kindliest and gentlest soul alive and a
staunch friend. He was subject to violent rages, which were often
assumed to scare his company into extra effort—I have known
him throw pennies at them—but the storm was soon over.

He saved pantomime. It had taken a downward plunge and
Julian came to the rescue. He presented pantomime in the traditional
way—splendour and comedy adroitly mixed, beauty fitting in
with slapstick, magic interwoven with romance. Always, for
Julian, the Principal Boy and the story itself were of paramount
importance, overriding the comics. He made pantomime a mixture
which both adults and children could equally enjoy, and he never
allowed anything vulgar or suggestive. I am proud to say that I
worked closely with him for many years—we were very close friends
—and I proclaimed him King of Pantomime, as he undoubtedly
was. Every year he produced a dozen in the great provincial cities
and eventually at Theatre Royal, Drury Lane, itself. That was
when he was proclaimed King, and he told his friends it was "trem-
enjus." He never lost his Lancashire accent. He understood pantomime because he himself had the heart of a child and never really
grew up.

He was always furious when people said he was not "West End"
and not "sophisticated." He did not understand what they meant
by that. And what did it matter? He was real theatre through and
through, and his record of successes at the London Hippodrome
and elsewhere has never been equalled.

He had enemies who were jealous of him and sometimes they
would seem to win, but he would come back and put them to rout by
sheer knowledge and theatrical genius. He was a curious mixture,
just as the theatre is a curious hotch-potch, but he was a great man
and his untimely death took from his profession almost the last
complete and inspired technician. But in 1928 he had many successes
before him.

Daly's Theatre presented *Lady Mary*, a musical play, with book
by Frederick Lonsdale and John Hastings Turner and music by
Philip Charig, and in the cast were George Grossmith, Herbert
Mundin, Paul Cavanagh, Richard Dolman and Helen Gilliland.
It ran for 181 performances.

Drury Lane had an immense success with *Show Boat*, with book
by the ubiquitous Oscar Hammerstein and music by Jerome
Kern. In this, Paul Robeson made a tremendous impact; special
matinées were given, like concerts, at which he sang. Cedric
Hardwicke, Marie Burke (who contributed drama as well as

vocal ability and whose song "Can't Help Loving that Man of Mine" will not be forgotten) and Leslie Sarony (who made a success and later became famous as songwriter, too) were in the cast. Edith Day was the delightful leading lady. To most people *Show Boat* is the same thing as "Old Man River," Paul Robeson's great song in it. It ran for 350 performances.

The once beloved and enchanting Gaiety Theatre was still having a very bad time. A confused sort of show called *Topsy and Eva*, a kind of musical variant on *Uncle Tom's Cabin*, was produced. It featured the Duncan Sisters, Rosetta and Vivien, hailing from America but popular here. It had a very good cast, but surprisingly it was not a success. Gracie Fields, then Queen of the Music Halls and the best loved artiste since Marie Lloyd, went to the rescue. While she was in the cast London flocked to the Gaiety, but she could not stop long, because of contractual liabilities. When she went, much of the glory departed with her, and, shortly after, *Topsy and Eva* were seen no more.

There was a delightful musical play at His Majesty's which deserved a longer run than the 158 it achieved. It was *The Song of the Sea*, with music by Edouard Kunneke and with Stanley Holloway, A. W. Baskcomb, Claude Hulbert, Polly Ward and Lilian Davies in the cast.

Her Cardboard Lover, at the Lyric, played by Leslie Howard, Robert Newton and Tallulah Bankhead, ran for 173 performances.

The firm of Clayton and Waller continued their successful management at the Palace Theatre with *Virginia*, which ran for 228 performances, the cast including George Gee and Emma Haig. "Roll Away, Clouds" is still popular.

Cochran had *This Year of Grace* at the London Pavilion, which ran for 316 performances. Sonnie Hale, Jessie Matthews, Maisie Gay and Tilly Losch were in it. It was a complete Noel Coward show and amazingly good. Everybody remembers "A Room With a View" and "Dance, Little Lady." Maisie Gay had some grand comedy, including a song about the number of women who were perpetually swimming the Channel at the time. Tilly Losch amazed and enchanted London with her "Dance of the Hands" and "Gothic Dance." It was a very big success indeed for the firm of Coward and Cochran.

Young Mr Charles Laughton, who had been making steady progress since the days of *Liliom*, when he was considered worth £2 a week, came right into his own in 1928. Critics and public had spotted him in *The Happy Husband* at the Criterion in 1927, he had been highly praised for his playing as Paul I and Mr Prohack, but in 1928 he really showed what he could do with weird and very sinister parts in *A Man With Red Hair* at the Little

Theatre. It was a masterly performance indeed. He followed that up with a great success in *Alibi*, an adaptation of an Agatha Christie story, and his reputation was made. He completed the year by playing "Mr Pickwick" in a stage version of the immortal *Pickwick Papers*, which Basil Dean staged at the Haymarket. But Charles Laughton was not right as "Mr Pickwick." Still, 1928 was his year, and *Alibi* had run for 250 performances.

Gilbert Miller's battle to keep the St James's Theatre bright with distinction met with success in 1928, when *S.O.S.* by Walter Ellis, was staged. Sir Gerald du Maurier produced it and played in it. It had a star-studded cast including Herbert Marshall, Herbert Waring, George Curzon and Grace Wilson and (a surprising bit of casting for such a place) Gracie Fields. She came from touring revue and music halls to that theatre of distinction. It would have been an ordeal for anybody, but she easily held her own. If she did not make a resounding success, she kept her end up with the celebrated legitimate actors and actresses who surrounded her. *S.O.S.* ran for 188 performances. Perhaps it might not have run so long without Gracie Fields.

There was a most successful musical play at the Prince's, called *Funny Face*, which ran for 263 nights; in the cast were Leslie Henson, at his best, Sydney Howard, giving a vintage performance, and Fred and Adèle Astaire.

Basil Dean, one of the main pillars and upholders of high standards through all the 1920's, produced several plays in 1928. They were *The Happy Husband; Come With Me; Mud and Treacle; The Return of the Soldier; The Moving Finger; The Second Man* (by S. N. Behrman, in which Noel Coward played the lead with distinction); and *Mr Pickwick*. Despite a beautiful production, this was far more stage than vintage Dickens, and perhaps Dean cast Laughton for "Pickwick" because of his success in *The Happy Husband*, but it did not work out.

Dean did another play, *Young Woodley*, by John Van Druten, at the Savoy Theatre. This was the first success by the young author, who died recently to the loss of our theatre, and it was a real success. It had originally been banned by the Censor because it dealt with adolescent love, the love of a schoolboy for his schoolmaster's wife. It was not the blatant sex of so many similar plays which have followed it, but real, imaginative and good theatre. It brought right to the forefront a young actor named Frank Lawton. He had grease-paint in his blood. He had been playing small and moderate parts in all sorts of shows since 1923. He had made a success in 1927 in *Sadie Dupont* at the New, but it remained for *Young Woodley* to reveal his proper talent. He gave a delightful and memorable performance, full of simplicity, never overstressed, but crammed with natural charm and appeal. In the cast, too, were Herbert Mollison, Jack Hawkins (who had now shed the prefix of "Master"), and Frances Doble, who gave a lovely performance. It put both Frank Lawton and John van Druten into a leading place in our theatre. It was exquisitely produced by Basil Dean, with great understanding and restraint—a companion piece to *The Constant Nymph*. It ran for 429 performances and was the Play of the Year.

In 1928 Violet Melnotte sold the Duke of York's, but before doing so she presented a play off her own bat and it happened to be the best thing she had ever done in the theatre. Tom Reynolds, well known producer, and uncle to Binnie and Sonnie Hale, brought me a script and asked me to read it. It was by a dramatist unknown to London, a Glasgow journalist named Robins Millar. It captured me at once. I told Tom Reynolds, a dear friend of mine, that we must try and get Madame Melnotte to present it—not that either of us believed in her but it was a quick way to production and the one which would give us the most power, so we thought. I sang the praises of the play judiciously to the old lady, who was down at her beloved Metropole at Brighton. "Don't take my word for it," I said, "hear what Tom Reynolds has to say. You know him and his reputation. Let him tell you." I stressed the fact that it had only one set of scenery and ten characters (two over her limit, but they were very small parts). I hinted that several managers would be glad of it, but I wanted her to have first nibble. I said I considered it my duty, and anyway the production would not cost much and there was not much in the way of plays looking for a home. I believed in the play and I suggested she should take a little gamble. She agreed to hear it read, so Tom Reynolds and I went down to Brighton and were very graciously received by Madame in a very nice sitting-room facing the sea, which she had taken specially for that afternoon, to impress us. With her was her daughter, Nellie, a charming woman. I was glad to see her. Hers would be a fresh and unbiased view.

Tom Reynolds read the play and read it well. I watched the old lady and her daughter, I saw their interest and I observed that Nellie was affected to tears. I said nothing at all. I just watched the two of them. I loved this play and was anxious to get it produced. In the end, Nellie was crying and even the old be-blued eyes of Madame were dimmed and filled with moisture. She had really been moved. She agreed to do the play. Tom and I returned to London, contacted the author and his agent prepared a contract which he signed. Then Madame returned, to start work.

We were ready for that and had prepared what we considered the ideal cast list. The old lady immediately began to show her power. She vetoed the selection of Mary Jerrold for the part of the mother,

which was hand-made for that wonderful actress, and insisted that
Violet Vanbrugh should have it. She gave as her reason that
Violet's sister Irene had made many successes at the Duke of
York's, so of course Violet must have the part. Of course, Violet
Vanbrugh was too good an actress to be wrong in it—but Mary
Jerrold had absolutely the right quality. The rest of the cast was
agreed.

Then I disclosed my idea for the presentation, which I had worked
out with Tom Reynolds. I wanted a charming light living-room
as the setting. The idea of the play was the return of a dead man,
though it was not really the man you saw, but the memories he
had left in people's minds. I was most anxious to avoid any suggestion
of a ghost; this was the play's great difficulty. But Madame Melnotte,
who only understood one sort of idea about death and that sort
produced ghosts, insisted on a dark, gloomy oak set, the worst
thing possible. She had not the slightest idea what was really in
the author's mind. Of course, she had her way. I wanted a small
but good orchestra, with a harp, and Norman O'Neill to do some
music like that of *Mary Rose*. Madame cut out the orchestra and
refused to have any music at all, even a piano. Then she threw
her bombshell. The production must not cost more than £250,
all in. That was tantamount to murdering a beautiful play.

We faced it. We engaged our cast, Violet Vanbrugh, Fisher
White, Grizelda Hervey, Frank E. Petley, Hilda Bayley, Helene
Pickard, A. S. Homewood and Robert Haslam (a very promising
young actor indeed). We had to hire the scenery. On the morning
of production we waited upon Madame in her office and, on a
silver salver, we handed her 11/-, change out of her £250 production
allowance. She took it and thanked us. She never saw the sarcasm.

She insisted on it being produced on Maundy Thursday, the
worst day in the year; she had done several plays on that date.
I did not kick. I remembered *Tons of Money*, which also was produced
on Maundy Thursday. Despite all the drawbacks the play got
wonderful notices. The critics were unanimous in praise. One of
them said "Better than *Mary Rose*". The name of the play was
Thunder In The Air by Robins Millar. We had to wait until Saturday
morning to get our notices, papers not being published on Good
Friday, but that reference to *Mary Rose* brought Sir James Barrie
to see it at once. He was very kind about it, too, and sent a helpful
telegram which I used for publicity purposes.

Although praised by the press, it was only an artistic success,
doing moderate business but not losing money. Such plays seldom
make really popular successes. James Agate, who praised it in his
notice and who at that time was doing a weekly theatre talk on the
radio, besought the public to flock to see it. Even Madame relented

to the length of saying that, if I liked, I could get a pianist, but I refused and told her she was too late. Then, quite suddenly, she sold the theatre and the play had to come off. But it was a notable play of beauty and imagination in a bleak period. We were all proud of having been connected with it.

Madame Violet Melnotte sold her theatre to one William Hutter, who knew nothing whatever about theatres. He was administering a very large family estate, and bought the theatre as an investment. He was a very nice fellow, a baker and pastry cook by trade. He was also Chairman of the Barnes Urban District Council, which he regarded, and rightly from his own local point of view, as a position of some eminence, but perhaps it was not a good training ground for running a theatre. He took me over with the theatre and Swaffer said immediately that Melnotte had sold out because she had been unable to sack me. Hutter had expected to be able to carry on for a while with *Thunder In the Air* until something new could be found, but Madame was never one to give anybody an easy ride, so she took the play off. I had expected that and had an attraction up my sleeve, a revue by my old friend Archie de Bear called *Many Happy Returns*. So that went on.

It was a good, bright de Bear show full of clever people like Mimi Crawford, Morris Harvey, the New Yorkers, Max Rivers and a pretty chorus. A young girl in it became a star, Jean Colin. It had brilliant ideas but lacked low comedy. It got away well and then it sagged. I knew what it wanted and I had to persuade Archie de Bear, who was a bit temperamental.

Playing an odd week or so in London was a comedian from America whom I had seen once at the Victoria Palace and never forgotten. His name was Herb Williams. I persuaded Archie to go and see him and he fell for him at once. We got together on a publicity campaign, for we knew we must boost this man, who was absolutely new to the West End. We decided he must be called "The Funniest Man on Earth." We knew the risk of that, too, but we also knew that he was so good that a whole lot of people would agree; those who did not—well, they would have paid to find out and that was all right by us. But we wanted to use that slogan as a "quote" from a recognized paper. We got a journalist, a mutual friend, and sent him to see Williams perform. He agreed with us; he wrote that phrase in a "notice," and so it went on the bills— a genuine "quote."

Herb Williams was delighted with everything. He was glad to play in a West End show. We arranged that he should appear on his own in each half of the programme, doing entirely different "stuff" in each. We put him in on a Monday night and we gave him a "Press Night" on the Wednesday; he had had two days and a matinée to "play himself in." The result was a real "rave" press. The box office got busy at once. The week before he appeared, we had only taken £400, below the danger mark. The following week, although the public had only known he was in it for half the week, it rose to £800. It climbed to £1400 a week for the time he was with us. The critics delighted in him; he was quite unique. Some of them came night after night just to see his act. They had a competition as to who could see Herb Williams the most times. Alan Parsons won with 40 visits, and the close runner-up was Ewart Hodgson. Swaffer refused to see anything funny in him at all, but he had to be different. I watched him with joy every night and knew his act by heart. I still remember it. The day was saved and Hutter had a nice entrance into theatreland.

But I had always to look to the future and I knew that, when Herb Williams had to return to the States, that would be the end of *Many Happy Returns*. I had been able, however, to come to terms with one of the greatest box-office draws in the land, Matheson Lang. As soon as Melnotte was out of the way, nobody had any objection to coming to the Duke of York's. Lang had for some years always appeared at the New Theatre, a little way up St Martin's Lane from the Duke of York's. I signed him for three shows, but not to run concurrently, for Lang would not desert the provinces for long. He was wise in that respect. He was to start the autumn season with a play called *Such Men Are Dangerous*. adapted from the original of Alfred Neumann by Ashley Dukes. It was a play about the mad Tsar Paul I; there had been several, but this had, in Count Pahlen, a magnificent part for Lang.

Such Men Are Dangerous opened at the Duke of York's on September 19th, 1928, and did fine business for 125 performances. Lang gave of his best; his splendid appearance and voice, his grand manner and his audience-control all had full scope. He produced the play himself but with him was a young man, rising rapidly as a producer himself, named Reginald Denham, who not only watched and suggested, but really produced Lang.

Isobel Elsom, lovely in looks and in acting too, was the woman in the case, and that amazing actor, Robert Farquharson, was the Mad Tsar. This was an outstanding performance, one of artistic horror but never overdone. He made you detest him and yet he made you see the pitifulness of his madness.

The scene at the end of the second act was vibrant with drama and emotion. Pahlen, which Lang played, knows that for the good of Russia this tyrant must die and he knows that he must kill him. The Tsar wore himself out in a frenzy of insane rage and threw himself on Pahlen's knees, crying and whimpering like a frightened child, hugging the man who knew he must kill him. And Pahlen

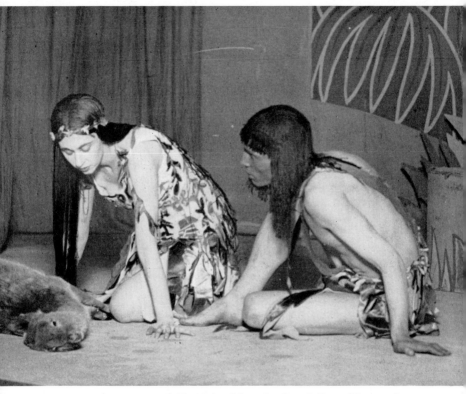

Bernard Shaw's play *Back To Methuselah* at the Royal Court Theatre for the first time in London. One of the scenes in the play showing "Adam" (Keith Johnson) and "Eve" (Gwen Frankcon-Davies).

Vivian Ellis, leading British light composer, who rose to fame in the 1920's.

Basil Dean, whose productions in the 1920's made theatre history.

sat there, with all Russia on his knees and with the full knowledge of what he must do. Lang portrayed it all by subtle means; it was a terrific piece of acting. But Pahlen does not himself fire the fatal shot; he has a servant, a slave, who kills the Tsar at his command. The deed done, Pahlen knows that, although he has freed his country from this monster, he must pay for it with his own life. In a sombre darkened room in the palace, lit only by the red glow of the fire, he and his faithful slave sit waiting for the end. Pahlen has given full instructions. One realized that avengers were almost at the door, when he gave the signal, and the curtain slowly fell. As it touched the stage, a shot rang out. It was over. This was perhaps the only play which ended *after* the curtain had fallen.

A young actor played the slave and gave a memorable performance, making a great impression. His dog-like devotion to his master even to death, his almost exalted actions when he did his dreadful duty—all this was wonderfully expressed. The young actor's name was Donald Wolfit. *Such Men Are Dangerous* was a good play of 1928 and, like all the others mentioned, the work of real men of the theatre.

Other successful plays that year were *Bird in Hand* at the Royalty; *By Candle Light*, a delightful comedy at the Prince of Wales's; *A Damsel In Distress* at the New, in which that excellent actor Basil Foster launched his successful career as actor-manager; *The Flying Squad* at the Lyceum; *The Fourth Wall* at the Haymarket; *Many Waters* at the Ambassadors; *Passing Brompton Road* at the Criterion; *That's a Good Girl* at the Hippodrome, with Jack Buchanan, which reached 363 performances; *So This Is Love* at the Winter Garden; *The Trial of Mary Dugan* at the Queen's, when the whole theatre was turned into the semblance of an American courtroom. Ivor Novello made another successful entrance as a dramatist, and solo this time, with *The Truth Game* at the Globe, and in his cast were Lilian Braithwaite, Viola Tree and Lily Elsie. And the lazy dramatist, Walter Hackett, had a success at the St. Martin's with 77, *Park Lane*.

But . . . the Talkies had arrived.

CHAPTER XVII

Theatre Royal Across the Water and Some Others

OUT of the curiously mixed career of the Coburg Theatre, in the Waterloo Bridge Road, which had been playhouse, music hall and a kind of musical coffee tavern, had gradually emerged a theatre which was to make a big mark on theatrical history and become an institution second to none in the story of British drama. It was to be a kind of National Theatre—in many ways better than such a place, which is likely to be cribbed, cabined and confined by well-meaning but amateur committees and departmental red tape. It is the Old Vic.

Under the direction of an inspired woman named Lilian Baylis, it began to take shape as a theatre where opera and Shakespeare were given to a "popular" public in a manner which they could appreciate and at a price which they could afford, but always in the best possible style in accordance with the finances available, which were slender but seemingly very flexible. At the Old Vic the great British gift of improvisation was in demand. It had grown steadily in prestige and importance since 1914. Established stars would go there to help, established producers gave their services; names like Matheson Lang, Hutin Britton, Andrew Leigh, Estelle Stead, Lady Benson, Mrs Edward Compton and J. Fisher White shine on the scroll.

Then in 1915, that Grand Old Man of the theatre, Ben Greet (to become Sir Philip Ben Greet) went there to take over production. Nobody knew more about Shakespeare than he; he had run his own company for years, second only to that of Benson; he had turned out renowned players by the score, and he did remarkable work in the Waterloo Bridge Road. He did it singlehanded, too, until 1918-1919, when G. R. Foss took over, except for one or two productions by Patrick Kirwan. Greet, however, produced his favourite *Everyman*.

In 1919-1920, productions were staged by Russell Thorndike, Charles Warburton, Betty Potter, Stockwell Hawkins and Ernest Milton. In 1920-1921, Robert Atkins took charge. This experienced and sound actor, who gloried in the Elizabethan tradition, did grand work at the Old Vic. He aimed at an audience beyond the immediate neighbourhood and he began to get it. His energy was fabulous. Between 1920 and 1925 he did every Shakespearean play in the First Folio, except *Cymbeline*. He played in them himself. He did, also, two plays by contemporary authors: Laurence Binyon's *King Arthur*, with music by Sir Edward Elgar, who conducted at the first performance; and *Britain's Daughter* by Gordon Bottomley. Greet did many other exciting things, and took such authors as Barrie and Massinger in his stride.

The fame of the Old Vic went far and wide. Atkins was invited to take the company to Brussels and they went, to represent the British Theatre. But things were not too easy financially; they must expand if they were to continue and there was no money for such expansion. One of the most curious men in the British Theatre suddenly gave them £30,000. It not only saved them, but put the Old Vic on its feet. That man was George Dance, who became Sir George because of this munificence. He had been a writer of music-hall songs, and of libretti for pantomimes and musical comedies. He had developed into the Napoleon of touring companies and made an immense fortune. It is doubtful if he had ever willingly seen a Shakespearean play right through; it is certain he was not interested in the cultural drama (I can testify to that); but he gave that £30,000 to the Old Vic and from that moment its greatness began. Some years before that he had sent me down to Salisbury to buy Stonehenge, but it was not for sale. I marvelled at that job, for I could not see what he wanted with it, I could not understand how it could be sent on tour. But when that knighthood was given him for helping the Old Vic, a great light shone. It is doubtful if Dance had ever seen Stonehenge either.

To give in detail all that happened at the Old Vic in the 1920's is beyond the scope of this volume and has been ably dealt with elsewhere. All that is necessary is that its work is woven into the texture of that period. It had already taken its place as the training ground for youth, as the Benson and Ben Greet companies had been previously. Experienced players were glad to go there to broaden their scope and acquire something not to be found in the highly commercialized West End theatres of that time. from which Shakespeare was notably absent.

Robert Atkins got wonderful results at very small cost. He also got fine casts. In a most effective production of *Henry VIII* in 1923, he played Wolsey, Ion Swinley played Buckingham, and Hay Petrie made a big success in the small part of the Porter. Petrie was destined to become one of the best Shakespearean clowns of his time and he learnt much at the Old Vic. Some of the others who played there at this period were George Hayes, Austin Trevor, Francis L. Sullivan, Hilton Edwards, John Laurie, Marie Ney,

Florence Buckton, Dorice Fordred and Jane Bacon. Ernest Milton was often there and helped greatly.

Perhaps the most notable production of all was *Peer Gynt*, the first performance of this Ibsen masterpiece on the British stage. Russell Thorndike played Peer and Robert Atkins produced.

Atkins carried on until 1924/5 and wrote his name in letters of gold in the Old Vic saga. He was succeeded by Andrew Leigh, who saw the decade out. The names which embellish it during the 1920's apart from those, already mentioned, include Elizabeth Allan, Heather Angel, William Armstrong, Mary Barton, Eric Bloom, Douglas Burbidge, Olivia Burleigh, Nell Carter, Sir Lewis Casson, Esmé Church, George Coulouris, Neil Curtis, Adèle Dixon, Dame Edith Evans, Barbara Everest, Jean Forbes-Robertson, Leslie French, John Garside, Sir John Gielgud, Baliol Holloway, Esmond Knight, Victor Lewisohn, Marie Lohr, Cavan O'Connor, Helena Pickard, Arnold Pilbeam, Margaret Rutherford, Horace Sequeira, Eric Spear, Dame Sybil Thorndike, Wendy Toye, Ralph Truman, Frank Vosper, Wilfrid Walter, Sir Donald Wolfit, Henry Wolston, Leslie Woodgate, Maxwell Wray and John Wyse. That list gives some idea of the activity of the place and of the work it was doing for the newcomers and established actors and actresses alike. It was to come to full bloom during the 1930's but the bud was swelling in the 1920's. John Gielgud had made his début there in 1921, as the Herald in *Henry V*. In 1929 he went back there and played a tremendous round of parts, and there London saw his superb Hamlet for the first time. During 1925 and 1926 Dame Edith Evans did marvellous work there, playing all sorts of roles from Portia to the Nurse in *Romeo and Juliet*, from Cleopatra to "Mistress Page" in *The Merry Wives of Windsor*, not forgetting Rosalind, Beatrice, and many more. In the 1920's the Old Vic was steadily building up a tradition to replace, to some extent, that destroyed during the First World War.

Other theatres doing fine work outside the western central district at this time were the Embassy, which was opened by Herbert Jay and Sybil Arundale; the Golders Green Hippodrome, a music hall which became a theatre in 1923; The "Q" Theatre, largely used as a "tryout;" and Streatham Hill, which opened in 1929. But a very bright light of the 1920's was the rise of the Old Vic, which had begun to earn the status of a Theatre Royal, even if it never received a Patent.

There were some men who did magnificent work in the period and who must be given a place in this story. One of them never owned a theatre but he presented a variety of good plays and always provided first-class quality. His name was Alban B. Limpus; he may be hardly remembered today but he was prominent in the 1920's. He looked far more like an admiral than a theatrical manager and with very good cause, for he had been educated on H.M.S. *Worcester*, the famous training ship, and from 1892 until 1899 had followed the sea. He served in sailing ships, on tramp steamers and finally with P & O. When the Boer War broke out, he took to the land and served with Paget's Horse with distinction. Perhaps the perils of the ocean and of Boer shot and shell were a good training for the dangers of the theatrical profession, which he entered in 1905, in a managerial capacity in the F. R. Benson company. He remained with Benson until 1909, when he went into management on his own account. At the beginning he operated on tour and did well. When the First World War broke out, he went to sea again, as a Lieutenant-Commander in the R.N.V.R., and saw much service with the Dover Patrol and the 10th Cruiser Squadron, neither particularly inactive or safe jobs. But he came through. He returned to the theatre. He was responsible for backing, either wholly or in part, and for presenting some excellent plays n the 1920's. They included *Mr Pim Passes By* and *Mis' Nell of New Orleans*, both in association with Dion Boucicault. That was in 1921. In the following year came *If Four Walls Told*; in 1923 *Trespassers;* in 1924 *Collusion* in association with T. C. Dagnall; and he was behind *The Blue Peter* (with Charles Kenyon) and *The Vortex*, the Noel Coward play. In 1925 came *Hay Fever* (Noel Coward) and *The Scarlet Lady*. In 1927 he did yet another Coward play, *The Marquise*, and also *A Spot on the Son*. *The Masque of Venice* and *Passing Brompton Road* came in 1928, and *Her Shop*, and that great success, *The First Mrs Fraser*, in 1929, both with Marie Tempest in the lead. He was a most charming man whose word was his bond and who believed in quality. Any production with which he had to do was presented in first-rate style. He was a link between Church and Stage, for his father was Canon Henry Francis Limpus. Alban Brownlow Limpus, who died in 1941, was a manager of the school of the actor-managers and kept a standard when others failed to do so. He deserves remembrance in the ephemeral world of the theatre.

T. C. Dagnall, who has been mentioned, was a civil engineer who married a charming actress and went into the theatre. He had wonderful luck and maybe his wife's judgement helped him, for she became afterwards a successful play-broker. Among T. C. Dagnall's successful productions were *Ambrose Applejohn's Adventure* and *Lord Richard in The Pantry*. He died in 1926 when only 46 years old.

The other outstanding man of the 1920's had already appeared in this chronicle. He was not a manager in the approved sense of the word, although on occasion he did present plays in that capacity. It was as actor, dramatist and producer, especially in the latter capacity, that he rose to fame in the 1920's. He still flourishes today, although he mostly operates in America. He is Reginald Denham. He had started his career before the 'twenties dawned. He was originally intended for music and singing and won scholarships in both subjects. Then he became interested in acting and won another scholarship, at the Guildhall School of Music and Acting. There he was lucky enough to study under Cairns James, who was such an expert that he nearly belied the truth that acting cannot be taught. The stage got Reginald Denham. He started right at the bottom and worked his way up. He did all sorts of things in all sorts of places and he learnt his trade. His first professional job was "walking on" at His Majesty's Theatre in Sir Herbert Tree's great production of *Joseph and His Brethren* in 1913. Then he joined Benson but, when the First World War broke out, he went into the army. He did a lot of amateur productions while he was serving and, when the war was over and he was demobilised, he, like so many more, was out of work. This is no place to give the details of Reginald Denham's career; he has done that himself in his own life story, as good a theatrical book as any written.

When the 1920's were under way he had made acting a secondary consideration and had become a producer, or director as they are called nowadays. As the decade progressed, he became one of the outstanding producers of the period and was still a very young man. He was interested in every branch of the theatre, active in the Play Producing Societies which sprang up, and especially interested in the Repertory Players, for whom and with whom he did such yeoman service. He produced Edward Percy's *If Four Walls Told* with great success. He got much renown out of his production of *Fata Morgana*. He was one of the successes of the 1920's. But then he is a practical man of the theatre and knows every department of it. He is also artistic and sensitive to a degree but without any affectation or loss of practicability. He has music in his soul and it shows itself in his work. His imaginative mind produces things of great beauty; yet he has a terrific sense of humour, which does not stop at pracical jokes. Above all that, he has tremendous determination and an inflexible will. His face shows it—that pugnacious nose and set chin, his habit of drawing back his head, as if poised to strike, like a serpent. He has wit, which can be kindly, charming and bitter according to need and mood. He does not know the meaning of the word defeat. Although he has tremendous self-confidence, there is no "side" and no conceit. He can always laugh at himself and the man who can do that can do most things. He made his own way. Well educated, well bred, cultured and quick-brained, he gave the tapestry of the 1920's some very glowing patches. Next to Basil Dean's, his work as producer stands out clearly. He had not Basil Dean's resources.

He had his failures, he had his successes, he knew bad times. He wrote plays as well as producing them; he took the films in his stride and made many. He has a touch of his own which puts something vital into any play he rehearses, and quality is always to be found in his work. He had very little really good luck, things never went the easy way, but he never missed an opportunity. What he has done—and he has done much with still plenty more to do—he accomplished by himself. He is a most important product of the 1920's. Indeed, one single piece of work he did therein —out of many—would serve to write his name high in the Scroll of the Theatre: that was his production of a play called *Rope*.

Musician, actor, dramatist, stage producer, film director— he is all those things, but perhaps he is happiest of all in another and unprofessional capacity, that of bird-watcher. For that is Reggie Denham's great joy.

CHAPTER XVIII

Last Scene of All

WITH the arrival of 1929, the last scene of all the strange eventful history of the theatre during that decade was reached, although in some respects it bore a resemblance to Shakespeare's "lean and slippered pantaloon" of the Sixth Age, it did not fulfil the Seventh and die "sans teeth, sans eyes, sans taste, sans everything," nor was it mere oblivion. There were some very good and successful plays during its last twelve months, although theatre business in general was not good at all. As had been the case all through the 1920's, outside influences were against it. Conditions of life in general were greatly disturbed, and there was the tremendous and growing power of the Talkies.

But, despite all that, the theatre had begun to rally a bit. There were many failures but some long runs. Three new theatres opened their doors, two in the West End and one in the suburbs. They were the Dominion, standing on the site of Meux's Brewery, for so long a London landmark, at the corner of Tottenham Court Road and New Oxford Street, near a bus stop known as "The Horseshoe" because of the public house adjoining the Dominion; the Duchess, in Catherine Street, Strand, (almost opposite Theatre Royal, Drury Lane, and right opposite the Strand Theatre), which was a much smaller and more intimate theatre than the Dominion, the latter holding 2800 as against barely 500 at the Duchess; and Streatham Hill Theatre, an excellent modern playhouse with a capacity of about 2700.

The Dominion opened on October 3rd, 1929, with an American musical play, *Follow Through*, a memory of which is a delightful little dancer named Ada May. The Duchess opened on November 25th, 1929, under the management of J. & D. de Lion, with a war play called *Tunnel Trench*. Streatham Hill had as its opening attraction (it existed for touring companies, naturally) the Cochran revue, *Wake Up and Dream*. Both Streatham Hill and Golders Green would get London companies just after the West End run and sometimes prior thereto.

There were plays in 1929 which, if not epoch-making, were better than many in the preceding years of the decade. There is no space for mention of many of them but some must go into the record. They will revive playgoers memories.

Sir Alfred Butt presented *Canaries Sometimes Sing* by Frederick Lonsdale, outstanding dramatist of the period, at the Globe Theatre, in which Ronald Squire made a great personal success. This extremely polished actor, with the most expressive hands on the stage, and the gift of using his eyes and face in the manner of Sir Charles Hawtrey, whose successor he was in comedy roles, left a great gap in the ranks of actors when he died in 1958. He had talent and charm, a combination seldom met with, an ease and poise all his own, and a most wicked but attractive chuckle, which spoke volumes. *Canaries Sometimes Sing* ran for 144 performances.

Edgar Wallace continued his successful career as a dramatist with *The Calendar* (Wyndham's, 220 performances), in which Owen Nares played the lead, a most unusual character for him, for it represented a man in trouble with the Jockey Club Stewards. Owen Nares had been doomed to be a matinée idol for a great part of his career, but he was a much better character actor than many people realized. He was a curious man, lonely by nature, far more interested in things than in people, and with an odd habit of stripping completely nude in his dressing-room, and sitting with his feet in the wash basin. He never betrayed the slightest self-consciousness and his charming smile seemed to cover him like a cloak. He liked all sorts of old-fashioned eighteenth-century card games like Piquet, Écarté etc. in preference to Bridge. And he usually had a couple of rather bad-tempered Jock Russell terriers with him. He was not a good conversationalist but a fine listener, or seemed to be. In reply to some interesting information of a sensational nature, his only comment would be: "Oh, really?" with that smile accompanying it. He was one of the few people in the theatre who called me by my Christian name of "Walter;" to multitudes I am "Popie."

It was very difficult for Edgar Wallace to make money out of a success; his overwhelming and somewhat ostentatious generosity prevented it. If he got a success, he promptly presented the leading players with gold cigar or cigarette boxes or jewellery, and often doubled salaries.

A revival of *Dear Brutus*, also at Wyndham's, notched 108 performances.

The not-long-established Arts Theatre Club, now most popular and with one of the best restaurants in London, did some very good work. It sent *The Lady With a Lamp* to the Garrick to run for 176 performances. It was by Reginald Berkeley and, as its name implied, about Florence Nightingale. That part was beautifully played by Gwen Ffrangcon-Davies, one of the outstanding actresses of the period, and in it were Leslie Banks, Eille Norwood, an actor given to inventions which did not work too well, and Edith Evans. From the same source came *The Lake* (176 performances) and *The Infinite Shoeblack* (156) by Norman Macowan.

Other plays of some note were *The Matriarch* at the Royalty, (229) with Mrs Patrick Campbell; *Merry, Merry*, a musical play at the Carlton (131); *Murder on the Second Floor* at the Lyric (167); *Her Past* at the Shaftesbury (149); *Fame* at the St. James's, which had a run of 108 performances and was presented jointly by Gilbert Miller and Sir Gerald du Maurier. It was by Audrey and Waveney Carten, two clever young women representative of the generation of the 1920's, who had a considerable flair for the stage and were very popular socially. A distinguished cast included Sir Gerald himself, Cathleen Nesbitt, Nigel Bruce, Nora Swinburne, Frank Vosper, Walter Fitzgerald, Una Venning, Dorothy Monkman and Naomi Jacob.

Baa-Baa, Black Sheep at the New, by Ian Hay and P. G. Wodehouse, ran for 115 nights; the amazing *Co-optimists* had a successful season at the Vaudeville; and the Palace had two musical plays, *Dear Love* (132) and *Hold Everything* (173). Owen Nares was in the latter but it did not suit him; this essentially English gentleman did not fit in, and he left after a short while. His second son Geoffrey (who was killed in the Second World War), a very frank lad at the time, announced to all his friends: "Father's got the sack from the Palace. No holiday for us this year."

The Five O'Clock Girl at the London Hippodrome only lasted for 122 performances. This was a musical play and it was not helped by poor publicity. The leading lady was Jean Colin, who was announced and bally-hooed as "The New June"—June herself was a big star at the time. In stage affairs there cannot be a "new" or a "second" anybody. If that were possible, the original would not have achieved greatness. Miss Colin, who had scored a success in Archie de Bear's *Many Happy Returns* and in other shows, has plenty of talent and personality of her own, requiring no such comparison. In *The Five O'Clock Girl*, too, was that small American actor, Ernest Truex. He found the big spaces of the Hippodrome stage a little difficult for "timing" and had to trot about instead of walking. I wonder how he overcame—perhaps he did not—his dislike of hearing his own footsteps on the stage. In *Good Morning, Bill* at the Duke of York's, we had used, at his request, extra stage cloths and a double carpet down a flight of stairs, because he could not bear to hear himself walk. But he put up a brave show in *The Five O'Clock Girl*.

The Gaiety had a welcome success with a home-made musical play called *Love Lies*, written by Stanley Lupino and that fine

music hall comedian and actor, Arthur Rigby, with music by Hal
Brody and others. It will be remembered because of a song in it
which Stanley Lupino sang "I lift Up My Finger and I say Tweet-
Tweet."

The Middle Watch at the Shaftesbury, by Ian Hay and Stephen
King-Hall, was the presentation of Basil Foster as actor-manager,
and that excellent actor (and member of the famous cricketing
family of Worcestershire) played very well in it, with Clive Currie,
Reginald Purdell and Olive Blakeney. It ran for 387 performances
and deserved every bit of it. The expert team of Jack Hulbert and
Cicely Courtneidge did *The House that Jack Built* at the Adelphi, a
revue (270). *Rose Marie* was revived at Drury Lane for 100 performances.

An excellent revival of *The School for Scandal* was played 121 times
at the Kingsway, with Frank Cellier as Sir Peter, Henry Hewitt as
Charles Surface, and Angela Baddeley, that excellent actress, as
Lady Teazle. The Victoria Palace staged *The Show's The Thing*
(292), and a wholly delightful version of *La Via Parisienne*, by A. P.
Herbert, ran for 224 performances at the Lyric, Hammersmith.
A Warm Corner filled the Prince's comfortably 238 times. It was a
musical play and in it were W. H. Berry, Austin Melford, Heather
Thatcher and Connie Ediss, a great performer. who had for so
long been a pillar of the Gaiety.

The offering at the Aldwych was *A Cup of Kindness* by Ben Travers.
This ran for 291 performances with the full team, and was specially
noteworthy for a magnificent "old man" performance by Tom
Walls. His scene with a bottle of wine was a triumph of comic
acting.

The Sacred Flame, by Somerset Maugham and very good indeed,
with Gladys Cooper in the lead, was at the Playhouse for 209
performances. *Sorry You've Been Troubled,* by Walter Hackett, lasted
for 157 nights at the St Martin's. Basil Dean produced four plays:
The Circle of Chalk; The Black Ace; The Roof (Galsworthy's last
play and hardly a success, but with Madeline Carroll and Eric
Portman, a rising young actor then with Old Vic successes to his
credit, in the cast); and his major effort, a dramatized version of
the best-selling novel *Beau Geste,* at His Majesty's. This was a most
elaborate production, but the story did not seem so sincere and
credible on the stage as it had done between the covers of a book.
There were some remarkable "crowd" scenes, notably during a
fight in a barrack room, and a lively scrap with Arabs from the
battlements of a desert fortress. In both these, Dean showed his
mastery of stage craft. There were some notable performances by
Edmund Willard (who looked so fierce on stage and was so gentle
off) as a brutal sergeant; Frank Cochran as a queer and half-

crazy little legionary nick-named "The Grasshopper." Jack
Hawkins, Madeline Carroll, and that fine actress, Marie Lohr.
The title role was played by a young actor named Laurence Olivier,
who made an impression. That was a busy year for him as he also
played in *The Circle of Chalk*, *The Stranger Within*, and *Paris Bound*,
and paid his first visit to America in *Murder on the Second Floor*.
Then, in the December, he was at the Fortune Theatre, under the
management of Tom Walls, and made a big success in a play called
The Last Enemy. This was a psychic play written by Frank Harvey, a
first class actor-dramatist. It deserved a far better result than it
got, but psychic plays seldom really succeed. It looked like failing
completely. I invoked the aid of my friend Hannen Swaffer who,
since the death of Sir Arthur Conan Doyle, had been the leading
Spiritualist. He liked *The Last Enemy* in his critical capacity and he
wrote for us a large poster which was plastered all over London and
which sent the business up for some weeks. It showed Swaffer's
power at that time. Laurence Olivier played a wild, impetuous
young man who came back from the dead. His entrance, straight
through a seemingly solid door, was a big thrill and was backed by
a fine performance. He was in another play in 1929, which comes into
the story later.

Ivor Novello was climbing steadily to the top. He was neglecting
his music but concentrating on acting and writing plays. His contribution in 1929 was *A Symphony in Two Flats*. Lilian Braithwaite,
Benita Hume, and Minnie Rayner, who became Ivor's mascot, were
in the cast and he gave himself a part with a touch of tragedy in it—
a composer who was going blind. The play ran for 153 performances
at the Apollo. Ivor was building up his theatre reputation, and
busy on the films, too.

Even if failures were many, 1929 produced some vintage plays.
One of them was Bernard Shaw's *The Apple Cart*. It opened at
Malvern as the bedrock of the Festival there. The critics were
taken down to see it on a Sunday, and left Paddington early in the
morning on an excursion train which ambled through the country-
side while they got hungrier and hungrier. I went along, too, by
invitation of my friend the late Roy Limbert, the manager of the
Malvern Theatre and with Barry Jackson, the originator of the
Malvern Festival. It was a most amusing railway journey. In the
carriage were Swaffer, Henry Oscar, Golding Bright, the astute
playbroker, artists' representative, and sleepy first-nighter, and
Macdonnell of the B.B.C. Philip Snowden, on behalf of the Labour
Government, had given some debtor powers a good wigging at
The Hague, and Swaffer the Socialist was jubilant. He kept leaning
out of the window at wayside stations and astonishing the porters
and passengers by his wild appearance and his yells of "Keep the

Socialist Out!" I ran a scare through the critics on the train by spreading the rumour that the lunch at Malvern to which we were invited was to be a vegetarian one out of compliment to Shaw. This caused alarm and despondency to all except Jack Bergel of the *Evening News*, who of course knew all about vegetarianism and discoursed learnedly on calories and the like, things not generally understood even then. When the lovely town of Malvern was reached the inhabitants had turned up at the station in force to see the great critics from London. Inadequate transport had been laid on, but I got the critics to fall into line and, led by the mighty Swaffer with a mien of immense dignity and a faraway look, we marched through the town to the theatre. The inhabitants were most impressed. We were received at the theatre—where Shaw, who always pretended to detest publicity, was in great perturbation over our late arrival —and ushered into lunch. It was not a vegetarian lunch but a very good one. There was an orchestra in attendance which discoursed light classical music. Swaffer, who was now in holiday mood, wanted it to play "Sonny Boy," the Al Jolson Talkie song then all the rage. He wrote a note on a piece of paper and had it sen⁺ to the conductor. The note said: "Mr Ashton Hargreaves of the *Manchester Guardian* requests that the orchestra will play "Sonny Boy." This caused some dismay, for music on a Sunday was something of a novelty in respectable Malvern in those days, and this song . . .? The conductor did not see his way to refuse the Press; he consulted with his leader and with obvious reluctance they were preparing to "vamp it," for they had no copies, when George W. Bishop of the *Daily Telegraph* rose to speak. So Malvern did not hear "Sonny Boy." Now maybe this does not sound the right frame of mind in which critics should approach such a serious undertaking as a new play by Shaw, but remember they had travelled by excursion train. Very late, they went into the theatre. There is no need to describe *The Apple Cart* now. It is a classic. Cedric Hardwicke played King Magnus and Edith Evans was Orinthia. It was received with acclamation by all the critics except Hannen Swaffer, who reckoned he must be in reverse. He attacked Shaw and the play. Shaw answered back. It was fine publicity for everybody. *The Apple Cart* came to the Queen's Theatre on September 17th, and ran for 285 performances. Afterwards, as was the custom, it visited Golders Green and Streatham Hill. At Golders Green something happened which shows how much success and publicity registers with the ordinary public. A gentleman went round to see Cedric Hardwicke, who naturally asked him what he thought of the play. The man looked a bit serious. "Well," he said, "you were very good, of course, and so were the other actors and actresses, but take my tip, old man. Don't take this play into the

West End. It won't do any good there." It had just run for 285 performances.

Cochran presented *Wake Up and Dream* at the London Pavilion. This was a revue with words and music by Cole Porter and two of the numbers at least have lived on: "What is this thing called Love?" and "Let's Do It." Jessie Matthews and Sonnie Hale were in the show and Sonnie gave a remarkable impersonation of Sir Thomas Beecham. That year, Cochran had some failures which deserved success: *Porgy* at His Majesty's; *Paris Bound* at the Lyric, with Edna Best and Herbert Marshall, two real attractions; and *Caprice* at the St James's, which brought the Lunts to London. He had brought to London also a play by an Irish author named Sean O'Casey, in which Charles Laughton made a big success. This was *The Silver Tassie*. Raymond Massie produced it for Cochran. Controversy ran high; some thought it wonderful, others heartily condemned it. Augustus John had designed a wonderful scene depicting war. The play was before its time. But he had a success which made up for all disappointments. This was *Bitter Sweet*, Noel Coward's romantic masterpiece. This opened first in Manchester and was a sweeping success. The principals were Peggy Wood, the great American prima donna and actress, George Metaxas, Ivy St Helier, Austin Trevor and Clifford Heatherley, with a brilliant cast behind them. Noel Coward wrote, composed and produced it, and that genius in her own line, Gladys Calthrop, did the décor. It came to His Majesty's on July 18th, 1929. Unlike its reception at Manchester, the first night was anything but encouraging, as were the critics. Many of them did not like "The Green Carnation" number which was reminiscent of the decadence of Aubrey Beardsley, Oscar Wilde and the days of *The Yellow Book*. It gave offence. Indeed, two eminent critics, Hannen Swaffer and Ewart Hodgson, were accused by Cochran of "guying" the show from the back of the circle. He wrote complaining to their editors. In the case of Swaffer, naturally nothing was done; how could it be? But Ewart Hodgson got into real trouble and there was a revolution in Fleet Street about it. Swaffer had the mortification of seeing his printed forecast of a run of about three months proved utterly wrong, but he probably did not care much. Despite the slow start, the general public, not for the first time and not for the only time in that year either, proved the critics wrong. Noel Coward's human story of sentiment—not sentimentality—and his delightful melody had their way. *Bitter Sweet* ran for 673 performances. During the run, Evelyn Laye replaced Peggy Wood, who had to return to America. Miss Laye had been the first choice but could not accept owing to other contracts. But *Bitter Sweet*, by breaking tradition, had scared

Cochran's right-hand man, Frank Collins, who did such splendid work in staging the shows. He was frightened because in this story the hero was killed in a duel quite early on, and there was not the conventional happy ending. For both Cochran and Coward, who had been having bad luck, *Bitter Sweet* proved in its own words that "Spring Breaks Through Again." One person who seldom got any credit for her work on the musical side, in this and so many other Cochran and Coward productions, should have a line in this book. That person was Elsie April, a little genius, a tiny, wraithlike person whose knowledge was amazing and who never seemed to stop working.

There was another great musical play in 1929 and a home-made one, too. That was *Mr Cinders*. It had a book by Clifford Grey and Greatrex Newman, with music by Vivian Ellis and Richard Myers. It was produced by Julian Wylie. He was determined to get back into the London Hippodrome with this show, which was his spiritual home, but from which, on account of one failure amidst many successes, he had been turned out. He designed *Mr Cinders* on Hippodrome lines. With that flair of his for casting, he engaged and teamed up Binnie Hale and Bobby Howes. He considered them an ideal stage team and he was right. He put every penny he had into the play and was heavily overdrawn at the Bank when it was produced in Blackpool. It was a great success. He hoped the Hippodrome would snap it up. They did not. He toured the country, playing to capacity everywhere, but you cannot recoup the enormous expense of a big musical production in a few weeks and he needed money. The great Australian firm of Williamson's saw the show and liked it; they were invading London and here was a fine card to play. Against his will Wylie had to sell them an option. Up to the last minute he hoped for a move from the Hippodrome but it never came. Williamson's secured the show. Wylie saw his favourite creation slip from his grasp. Williamson's took the play to the Adelphi and Wylie was not even asked to produce it. He was told again that he was not "West End." He became a sad, depressed man, his pride hurt, his hopes humbled. J. A. E. Malone produced *Mr Cinders*, with many alterations, for the Adelphi where it opened on February 11th, 1929. It was one of the coldest nights for many years and some of that frigidity got into the audience and into the critics. Yet the merits of the show were fully apparent. Binnie Hale and Bobby Howes were ideal; the story was good, a variant on the never failing Cinderella theme; the music was delightful, and one of Vivian Ellis's best numbers "Spread a Little Happiness" has become a classic. Yet, somehow, the show hung fire. Archie de Bear, in charge of publicity, worked wonders. The "throwaway" which advertised the play bore on its cover a cartoon of Hannen Swaffer, drawn by Binnie Hale, who is as brilliant a cartoonist as she is a mimic. The Williamson firm decided that some magic had gone from the show. They told Malone they were going to call back Julian Wylie to put it back into its original form. Malone was enraged. "That man enters this theatre only over my dead body," he shouted . . . and a few hours later he was dead. Wylie went back, restored his magic touch, West End or not, and *Mr Cinders* soared to success and, what is more, finished its run of 528 performances at the Hippodrome. It was one of the romances of the 1920's.

Reginald Denham really began to come into his own in 1929. He had broken in with *If Four Walls Told* by E. P. Smith, a Mincing Lane broker and "amateur" of the theatre. Denham had produced this for the Repertory Players and an association began between him and E. P. Smith which lasted for a long time; and the friendship still remains. E. P. Smith not only succeeded in his business but also became an M.P. and a successful playwright. He and Denham wrote plays together. Denham had first really attracted notice in 1926 when he had managed and also produced *To What Red Hell?* at Wyndham's, a play by Percy Robinson. In 1929 he did two plays at the Ambassadors which proved him to belong to the front rank of producers—*Rope* and *The Misdoings of Charley Peace. Rope* was what must be called for want of a better name a psychological thriller. It had all the thrills of an ordinary bloodcurdler but it showed not so much the desire for crime, as such, but the workings of a man's mind and what it led to. It was written by Patrick Hamilton, a famous author today. It has been revived, filmed and televised, but nothing has ever recaptured the real thrill which it gave to playgoers in 1929. This was due to Denham's almost uncanny interpretation of Patrick Hamilton's real meaning, and achieved by some marvellous tricks of lighting which in his own book *Stars in My Hair* he attributes modestly to what he learnt under Tree. Basically that may be true but, as the whole opening of the play is supposed to be performed in darkness, Denham's gift of technique came into its own. It did really seem to be played in the dark, and yet it was not. In *Rope* three major performances were given, too, by Ernest Milton, Brian Ahearne and Anthony Ireland. Gilbert Miller of the St James's paid Denham a great compliment concerning his work on this play. *Rope* ran for 131 performances; today it would have run for a couple of years.

The other Denham production at the Ambassadors was the play about Charlie Peace. This was written by E. P. Smith, who now dropped, for purposes of the theatre, his surname and be-

A scene in *The Beloved Vagabond* at the Duke of York's Theatre. Frederick Ranalow as Paragot and Lilian Davies as Joanna Rushworth.

A scene from *Young Woodley* at the Savoy Theatre. This play, written by John van Druten, was a sensational success. Frances Dabole, David Horne and Frank Lawton.

Basil Foster, leading man,
sportsman and distin-
guished actor-manager.

Henry Ainley as *Hassan* at
His Majesty's Theatre. A
great production of that
period.

came Edward Percy, his two Christian names. It was an expert
piece of criminology about a popular—if that phrase is allowable
—criminal. There were many difficulties to overcome in the
presentation of this play: seventeen changes of scene on a tiny
stage, difficult lighting and the selection of an actor to play Peace.
Denham asked du Maurier to play it, who was first insulted,
then intrigued, but was prevented finally by a previous contract. Robert Farquharson, an ideal choice, fell ill during rehearsals. Denham gave the part to the man he had engaged to
understudy it, Oswald Dale Roberts. On the first night this unknown actor "stole the show," and got amazing notices, but the
play died after five weeks. Poor Roberts took this to heart, he said
he was to blame, nobody knew him and that was the cause of
the failure. He was quite wrong, but it became an obsession with
him and brought about his tragic death not long afterwards.
There was a real hoodoo on that play—there are such things in
the theatre—but it got further laurels for Denham.

A really magnificent success was scored at the Haymarket
with *The First Mrs Fraser* by that leading critic and dramatist,
St John Ervine. This production was of the greatest interest to
the public, for it brought back to the stage Henry Ainley, who had
been away a long time owing to ill health and an unfortunate
failing. He took this "come back" with both hands. He had a part
which fitted him like a glove, he was in the theatre in which he
had scored such a success in *Quinney's*, and he was playing opposite
Marie Tempest at her best. This was a high spot of 1929 acting.
In the cast were Robert Andrews, W. Graham Browne, Marie
Tempest's husband (a good actor and producer, too), and Ursula
Jeans. The play ran for 632 performances.

In the January of 1929 there had come to the Savoy a play which
made the greatest impact of that year. It was *Journey's End*, by
R. C. Sheriff, an unknown dramatist then engaged in the world
of insurance. This play had been sent round to all the managers
and been rejected by all. Reginald Denham was one of the re-
jectors. He did not believe in the picture of war which it presented;
others thought that war was an unpopular subject; and others
veered off because it was an all-male play. Also, up to then no
war play had met with much success. Nobody can blame any
of those people, who were relying on their judgment and their
experience as to what the public wants. However, there is in the
theatre a psychological moment when views as to subjects and
manner of acting undergo a change, and that moment had come
with regard to war plays, eleven years after the war was over.
Journey's End marked that change. Eventually the Stage Society
produced it on a Sunday night. Denham was offered the job of

producing it, but refused. James Whale undertook it. The production took place in the December of 1928 and the leading part of Captain Stanhope was played at that performance by Laurence Olivier. Those critics who were present raved about the play; James Agate sang its praises over the radio. Still the managers held aloof. An actor named Maurice Browne stepped into the breach. He had only been before the London public since 1927, and had made a big success in *The Unknown Warrior*. Maybe it was that part which drew him to *Journey's End*. As actor-manager he took the Savoy and launched the play. In that production Colin Clive played Captain Stanhope, and others in the cast were George Zucco, David Horne, Alexander Field, Maurice Evans and Robert Speight, all of whom made big successes. The play got a wonderful Press, then, like so many others, hovered awhile but eventually ran for 594 performances. Touring companies took it all over the world. It is now a classic of the theatre.

The actor who dominated the stage of 1929 was Matheson Lang. He did two seasons in London that year, both at the Duke of York's. The first play was *The Chinese Bungalow*, of which he was part author and with which he had been most successful on tour. In this, he played a Chinaman. His outstanding success had been in a Chinese character, Mr Wu, his Othello and many others notwithstanding. The public liked him as a Chinaman, although he did infinitely better things. His Mr Wu captured public imagination and it was certainly a terrific piece of acting, the sort of thing which seems beyond the compass of most actors today. He acted with every bit of himself. In Mr Wu his silent, expressionless, motionless figure standing over his erring daughter seemed to grow in stature and become an avenging outraged God as you watched, hearing in the background the rustle of the wings of the Angel of Death. He achieved all that without a single movement, gesture or facial expression.

In *The Chinese Bungalow* he played a rich Chinese merchant whose English wife was unfaithful to him. He knew it and had his revenge in his own way. It was melodrama at its best. Lang's Yuan Sing was a marvellous exposition of the Oriental mind. He betrayed nothing of his knowledge or feelings, yet he built up around him an atmosphere of fear and suspense, as if a cyclone was gathering to break the offending parties. And he did it by acting, by mental suggestion. He never tried to evoke the sympathy of the audience which lay, quite wrongly, with the guilty couple and the wife's sister, an accomplice. Lang played against his audience, and won them over with his gentleness and courtesy to everyone, his seeming tenderness to the two girls, of whose guilt he knew, when, standing like a mountain between them he said:

"Come, my chelly blossom—and you, my heart of jade, two clystal souls" . . . as he led them to the house, they being ignorant that he saw right through that crystal. In the end he faced the lover. It was death for one of them. There were two glasses; in one the wine was poisoned, in the other it was pure. The lover was made to choose and drank first; then Lang drank from the other glass. The lover departed. Lang ascended a great throne chair on a dais. He sat quite still and was then racked with a paroxysm of pain. He had drunk the poison. He played his death scene in that chair, his life slowly ebbing from him in bursts of agony until finally, in unbearable torment, he leapt to his feet and fell headlong down the steps, crashing to the floor.

Lang excelled in death scenes. Sometimes, like Charles II, he was a long time dying, but as a spectacle of acting every moment of it was worth while. In *The Chinese Bungalow* you would have sworn that he died before your very eyes. I only saw two other actors who got near him in this line, Forbes-Robertson and William Haviland. *The Chinese Bungalow* has been filmed and televised, but in those forms it never achieved the stature given it by that magnificent actor.

Lang was essentially of the theatre and had many of its superstitions. He never spoke the "tag" line at rehearsals; he would say "The Colleen Bawn" instead. He liked to have that legendary actor "Walter Plinge" in his company—that odd stage name which hides a "double." In *The Chinese Bungalow* there was a remarkable bronze Buddha, a massive affair lent him by a collector of such things. Lang was warned by him that, if he wanted luck, he himself must cover that idol's face each night with a piece of rich material. Lang did that religiously. No stage hand was ever allowed to do it. He himself covered that idol's face every night with a piece of rich cloth of gold. There was a Siamese cat in the play too, called Sybilla. She was of a very fierce nature and would allow only two people to touch her, Matheson Lang and myself. The property man often got mauled. But, with Lang and me, Sybilla was gentle, sweet and obedient, even allowing flashlight photos to be taken of her. And, if either of us put her there, she would sit on the idol's shoulder as good as gold, but not for anybody else.

That play was produced in the middle of a terrible winter, the same that saw the production of *Mr Cinders*. The Duke of York's in those days had a most primitive heating system, just two large gas radiators down in the stalls. One would observe the anomaly of the stalls patrons, muffled up and overcoated, crouching and shivering around those radiators, while on the stage the players lay about, fanning themselves and complaining of the terrible heat, knowing that the very wash-basins in their dressing-rooms were frozen hard. *The Chinese Bungalow* ran for 109 performances. In it with Lang were Frances Doble, Marjorie Mars, Austin Trevor, and Donald Wolfit, playing the small part of a Malay.

Matheson Lang's second production at the Duke of York's was *Jew Süss*, which Ashley Dukes had dramatized from the best-selling novel of Lion Feuchtwanger. The announcement, made a year before production, that Lang was to play it brought an immediate rush to the box office, and an enormous first-night application. For a whole year prior to the production I kept anticipation alive by publicity and the excitement grew and grew. Lang tried it out at Blackpool and there was no doubt as to its success. He had with him, as assistant producer and producer of himself, Reginald Denham, and in appreciation of Denham's work he put on the programmes the line "The Play Produced by Matheson Lang and Reginald Denham."

There had been difficulties in casting. The major trouble was the part of the Duke Karl Alexander, the villain of the play. Lang and I had grown very friendly, a friendship which lasted until his death. One day I ran into Henry Ainley, just out of his nursing home and looking for work. I rushed to Lang and suggested Ainley, the very man and of great publicity value. Lang was aware of this and also of the box office value of Ainley, too, but in spite of all I could do he would not have Ainley. I found out later that there was a very old feud between the two men. The part was eventually given to Frank Harvey. The other difficulty was the part of Naomi, the Jew's daughter, whom the lascivious Duke drives to death. This was a difficult role to cast. The girl who would fit it must have beauty and at the same time an appearance of absolute innocence and virginity. She has been kept in entire seclusion from the world, about which she knows nothing. Yet she must be capable of showing deep feeling, great emotion and tragic power. Such people are hard to come by, but we found a girl and took a chance. She was 22 at that time and had been on the stage a bare three years, beginning like so many other young players, at the Birmingham Repertory Theatre. Most of her experience had been on tour, in small outlying theatres and at the Arts Theatre. She got that coveted part and I take great pride in having had something to do with it. For that girl is Peggy Ashcroft.

Lang gave *Jew Süss* a truly beautiful production. No money was spared and miracles were performed on the moderate-sized stage, because practical men were in charge.

In the cast, besides Lang and Peggy Ashcroft, were A. Bromley Davenport, Felix Aylmer, Frank Harvey, Veronica Turleigh, Philip Desborough, Lewin Mannering, Joan Maude, Mary

Sheridan and many others. There was a ballet, danced by Pearl Argyle and Harold Turner, who became one of our leading male dancers; and conducting the orchestra was a young man who had also composed the ballet and was that night at the outset of his brilliant but tragically short career, Constant Lambert.

There was a brilliant first-night audience, anxious to see how this famous novel would take the stage. Almost from the very beginning there was great enthusiasm. The fine prose of Ashley Dukes, the superb costumes, scenery and acting made an instant effect. Frank Harvey as the Duke made a big success. A. Bromley Davenport as General Remchingen provided what comedy there was, and Felix Aylmer was the shrewd and foxy Councillor Weissensee of the imagination. There was not a square peg; the pattern was perfect. Lewin Mannering as Rabbi Gabriel, with a touch of the Wandering Jew about him, set the atmosphere for the scene of stark tragedy in which Naomi lost her life. It was the only scene in which Peggy Ashcroft appeared, but it was vital; it was the hub of the play. To say that she played it magnificently is to understate. That young girl dominated the audience and held them spellbound. Her emotions and feelings came from her like chords from a harp. It was something of great beauty such as seldom comes in the theatre. She had no name with which to hold her audience; she did it by sheer talent and power. That night, indeed, a star was born; a great actress took the stage. It was a performance which will always light the memory like a beacon. Her acclamation at the end was remarkable even for those days, when audiences had not forgotten how to applaud. Today she stands at the pinnacle of her profession and is a Dame of the British Empire. That night of September 19th, 1929, at the Duke of York's saw her start. There should be a plaque there to record it.

Lang himself gave a performance which ranked with anything he had ever done before, even his "Othello;" in one scene he transcended all his previous triumphs. That was the scene at the end of Act 4, when he is alone with his dead daughter, she who had been his great treasure, outclassing all his immense riches, his beloved of beloveds, his ambition, his whole life. The man seemed to crumble before one's eyes in his grief and agony as he crouched there over the corpse in his arms. It was the whole tragedy of the universe caught and held for a few fleeting seconds, silent, terrific, terrible. The curtain fell in deep silence—it was nearly a minute before the storm of applause broke forth—the greatest tribute any actor can win.

Nor was he less amazing in the scene at the end when, as a prisoner knowing that a dreadful death awaits him and quite fearless of it, he derides and curses the vile Duke. Standing before the slaughterer of his child, his tremendous power and hatred —once again he seemed to grow in stature and size—drives the duke into the fit which kills him and leaves the Jew triumphant and his daughter avenged. His own burning at the stake was almost an anti-climax, but here he showed his joy and absolute disregard of this world. He was the agent of the God of Vengeance and the flames were welcome; they would reunite him with his beloved Naomi.

The scenes of enthusiasm at the end were quite remarkable. The play ran for 211 performances. It was one of the occasions during the 1920's when the footlights burnt steady and clear. In this book, as the curtain falls on the mixed, curious patchwork of the period, good and bad—it is fitting that one of its very greatest actors, almost the last of the old tradition, the last of the possessors of the grand manner, a pillar of the theatre, should stand upon the stage alone in the person of Alexander Matheson Lang.

CHAPTER XIX

Curtain Speech

CURTAIN speeches, made at the end of a performance on a first night by the leading player, producer or, more rarely, by the author, are not so frequent as they were in the 1920's, although it became customary a bit later for some popular figures to make curtain speeches nearly every night. In the 1920's it was the custom of a first-night audience to demand such a speech and to get it. Sometimes those speeches did good, sometimes they did harm. It depended on who made them and how they were delivered. Some leading actors needed little or no encouragement; others—and Matheson Lang was a notable example—would hold off until the last minute, thereby making the audience more and more insistent.

In those speeches it was customary to give thanks to those people who had helped the production in an unseen capacity and whose names were not even included in the "Credits" on the programme; and, naturally, to draw attention to the talent which had been in full view, thereby gaining further applause. Some actor-managers had reduced the first-night speech to a fine art. Seymour Hicks knew all about it, and also how to sneak "curtains;" both he and Lang were adepts at this, and why not? It is all part of the game. Sir Gerald du Maurier would be serious and sincere, clutching his heart while he was speaking. It was all so very natural and spontaneous . . . and so carefully thought out!

This last chapter must serve as a curtain speech to this humble attempt of mine to catch and confine the drama and theatre of the 1920's within the narrow spaces of a book. Much has had to be omitted because of the limitations of space, but at least it is a chronicle at first hand. There are one or two things and credits which must be stressed in this curtain speech.

The theatre, like the world around it, had been deprived of the solid and stable backbone which the actor-managers had provided. It wavered in the chilly wind which rushed in to fill the vacuum created by the end of the First World War and which had not been replaced by any blessing or prosperity engendered by Peace. This was a period of transition and such times are always difficult.

A generation had been mown down and a new one had not yet

had time to grow up. The old way of life had gone. Values had changed, standards of living had altered, the people of this country, on whom the theatre had to rely, were seething in the melting pot. The ship of the theatre was blown hither and thither, sometimes almost submerged, sometimes bravely riding the storm. That it survived as it did shows the tremendous tenacity that the living theatre possesses.

New forces were arrayed against it. Speed was revolutionizing the world; the mastery of the internal combustion engine had begun. Social revolutions were in progress; those who had been rich found themselves considerably poorer, and many of those who had been poor had become rich. The theatre is considered to be cultural. The years of the 1920's showed little cultural advancement, if any. They were too violent and hectic for that. They have been called gay, but most certainly they were not gay at all. A few wild and irresponsible young people behaved in a crazy manner which spread a thin veneer of spurious gaiety over a very small section of society. It was more bad manners than gaiety. People danced and danced and danced, but that had become more of a habit, like smoking or drug-taking, rather than an expression of gaiety. Most people danced because it was the fashion, not because it made them gay. The Music Halls which, in their older form, had really been gay, had received their death blow. The public which had made them had passed away with the older way of life and the drop in the purchasing power of money. The individualists who had made the Halls succumbed to Revue and Dance Bands became "Top of the Bill." Cabaret came into vogue, and this meant that Music Hall, which had started on the floor of public houses rather less than a century previously, went back to that location, but the pubs were now smart hotels.

Night Clubs sprang up everywhere and, if anyone thinks they were gay places, they must know very little about them. One or two were bright and amusing, but the majority were haunts which battened on the new idea which had grown up during the War of freedom from old convention, whereby one could find somewhere other than one's home to go to, where one could drink after regular hours and pay through the nose for the privilege. But it became fashionable to go to them.

The good manners and formality of the old order, as regards hospitality, were almost extinguished. Parties became minor riots where nobody stopped long; they drifted from one to another and "gate crashing" was quite usual. Cocktails now took the places of the more solid food and drink previously served at parties, which had been called "At Homes." America was already exerting power over a war-weary country anxious to forget its sufferings and privations. For many people were blinded for a while by the false, shrill gaiety of the night hours to the bogies of falling trade, restricted credit, heavy taxation, rising prices and labour unrest.

Radio had become very popular. Films got bigger and bigger and drew greater crowds. All those things took the public away from the theatre, but two of the deadliest blows against the theatrical profession were dealt by itself. Many actors and actresses spent more and more time making pictures. That meant they spent less time in the theatre or, if doing both jobs at once, gave rather tired and lethargic performances. It filled their pockets, of course, but it reduced their appeal, for they were now seen by the public far too often and, in the case of the films, at cheaper prices. The theatre was no longer a full-time job, served by experts and specialists. And, inside it, conditions were changing. The mystery of illusion, its greatest asset, was going down before the glare of publicity and the rise to power of press representatives and publicity men. Far too much was known about the people of the stage, and often it was phoney. But even worse than that was the change of social conditions in the theatre. Players became acutely society-conscious. Actors and actresses became "ladies and gentlemen." That did them infinite harm.

Prior to the First World War they had been people apart. They did not "mix" with their public; they kept themselves to themselves; they used their own clubs and pubs and restaurants. They dressed rather differently, looking what they were, the descendants of the old time rogues and vagabonds, social outcasts, and therefore intriguing. Ordinary people did not invite them to their houses, and they did not want to go. They were not considered respectable, and that delighted them. They were sensible folk and they knew that there is little or no interest in respectability, there being so much of it about. But those outside the pale had a compelling interest for people of ordinary life, so they preferred to keep aloof and be the people of illusion. It made the public pay to see them and that pleased everybody.

All that was going swiftly in the 1920's. Professionals began to dress and behave just like ordinary folk. They went everywhere and met everybody. Their illusion was gone, for mostly they are very ordinary folk outside their proper place, the theatre. The stage was no longer a "profession" to which a lady or gentleman could not belong. Public Schools and Universities sent recruits to the stage. It became as respectable a calling as commerce, banks, insurance companies, the law, medicine, the Church or the Services. And none of that was really any good to the theatre. The common tongues of the profession, rhyming slang and back slang, were discarded. When actors and actresses became ladies and gentlemen, it did not interfere with their talent, but it destroyed their romance.

Nor were managements giving good measure. Rising costs were met not by endeavouring to give better value, but by economies. The delightful little theatre orchestras were dropped, as being too expensive; gramophones ground out mechanized music in their places—that was becoming general in the 1920's. The "curtain raiser," such a valuable thing, had gone. But the enthusiastic playgoers of the pit and gallery were still there to give audible dissent or warm applause. The design of the new theatres, without pits and galleries of the old kind, showed them that they were on their way out, even if they did not fully recognize it.

Still, to go to a theatre was an event, even in the 1920's, and evening dress was still worn, especially at first nights. It was still "an evening out." Nowadays there is every inducement to spend an "evening in," and the radio was sowing the seeds of that in the 1920's.

The Talkies, as has been shown, arrived late in the period. They were destined to speedily destroy that magnificent provincial theatre, wherein the players learnt their job in the only possible manner. There was still quite a bit of touring, of course, in the 1920's, although already many theatres had become cinemas. When the Talkies really got going, the change-over became a landslide.

This book has endeavoured to show how, during that transition period, the success and maintenance of real standards had been achieved by practical people, and how eventually the commercial adventurer who had rushed in discovered that theatreland was not a business, but something they would never understand— governed by an unknown quantity, public taste and caprice. But those practical people were getting fewer and, as yet, the younger generation was unable to fill the gap. However, the men who were to become the twin pillars of the 1930's and 1940's, and later, too, were already in full view—Noel Coward and Ivor Novello, with Coward the more prominent in the 1920's.

The bright spots of the 1920's were the Aldwych farces, the musical plays and revues of Grossmith and Laurillard, (afterwards Grossmith and Malone), Sir Alfred Butt, Clayton and Waller, Archie de Bear, Albert de Courville, Julian Wylie and André Charlot. The musical entertainments of the 1920's were excellent. They still had melody, even if syncopated, and the melodies of the 1920's, derived from those shows, have a delightful nostalgic appeal today. C. B. Cochran was, of course, outstanding right through the period, and Nigel Playfair did excellent work, both "straight" and musical, at the Lyric, Hammersmith. But much of the music in general came from across the Atlantic. However, there was Vivian Ellis coming to the fore, with Noel Gay and some others, and there were the melodies of Noel Coward. The theatre had to wait until the 1930's to have Novello in his prime, although he had made a good start.

On the straight side, Frank Curzon and Sir Gerald du Maurier carried on a tradition, as did Gladys Cooper, too; also Gilbert Miller, Bronson Albery and Howard Wyndham ran their theatres as theatres should be run and the Haymarket retained its belief in policy. Some of the mighty figures were still there, overlapping from the older days: Sir Charles Hawtrey, Fred Terry and Julia Neilson, Sir John Martin-Harvey and Matheson Lang, although most of them spent a great deal of time in the provinces; they fought against the cinema and they won. H. M. Harwood did splendid work at the Ambassadors, and amongst the producers, who were becoming more and more important, Reginald Denham had arisen to do real service. But, so far as the 1920's are concerned, the palm must go to Basil Dean, first for that St Martin's management of ReandeaN with Alec Rea, and later on his own account as "Basil Dean Productions."

Dean gave beauty and craftsmanship, artistic value and new blood. During the 1920's he produced no less than fifty-two plays, all of them of value and many of them great successes. He introduced new players to the stage who learnt much under his guidance and are now "stars." He gave a first chance to new dramatists. The list of players and dramatists with whom he worked during the 1920's is not even surpassed by that wonderful Vedrenne-Barker management in the 1900's. He is a pillar of our theatre and he held aloft the torch of quality during the darkest hours of the 1920's. He is worthy of a foremost place in theatre history.

Salute should be given also, to the fine achievements of the Repertory Companies notably those of Birmingham and Liverpool, both of which owed much to Dean. Sir Barry Jackson stands like a beacon, not to be dimmed whilst our theatre lasts. From the Birmingham Repertory came so many people destined for fame, and he was not afraid to invade the West End with new ideas. He it was who, during the 1920's, gave us the plays of Bernard Shaw. William Armstrong did yeoman service at Liverpool, too. He had taken over directorship there in 1922. There were other valuable Repertory companies, more than can be mentioned here, whose work became of even more value as the years went on. The Little Theatres were growing up all over the country like fortalices where the living drama might defend itself against the onslaught of mechanisation. And tribute should be paid to such undertakings as The Arts Theatre Club and the play producing societies like the Stage Society and the Repertory Players and others.

Of course, many dramatists of the pre-1920 vintage were still active—Shaw, Galsworthy, Barrie, Maugham, Besier, Arnold Bennett, Sutro etc., and there were still many of the players who had been spokes on the wheels whereof the actor-managers were the hubs. Many have been mentioned but there were others who deserve a remembrance, like C. V. France, H. R. Hignett, Arthur Wontner, A. E. George, John Deverell, Lyn Harding, Basil Gill, George Tully, Ellis Jeffreys, Sydney Fairbrother, Hilda Trevelyan, Norman McKinnel, Dennis Eadie, Horace Hodges, Mary Jerrold, Dawson Milward, Lyall Swete, Ethel Irving, Henry Wenman, O. B. Clarence, Henrietta Watson, Nina Boucicault, Arthur Whitby and so many more. There was nothing the matter with individual acting in the 1920's by old-timers or newcomers alike. What had happened was the departure of firm and intimate control, and expert knowledge in the part of managerial high command. Not all the pre-1920 managements were good; there was Violet Melnotte, who has been dealt with, and she was not alone in her methods.

In the 1920's there was still humanity in the theatre, and new playhouses were being built, but the running of theatres had become a "headache" because of taxation, rising costs and falling receipts. And yet the full sweep of mechanical competition had still to be felt. The theatre was still the Aristocrat. It still lead the way. It did not take its stars second-hand from films or radio; it made them itself. The microphone had not invaded stages, the players still relied on their voices, and audiences still had the vitality and interest to punish players whom they could not hear. The "teen-agers" had not been invented but the "flappers" chose their heart-throbs from amongst actors—John Gielgud's photo was to occupy a frame in many a girl's bedroom, but the film stars were beginning to usurp such places, notably Rudolph Valentino. Theatre-going still had some excitement left, and the acting was still virile enough to cause excitement. Above all, playgoers had not lost their ability to applaud, which, as the years advanced, their constant devotion to the Talkies diminished and now slavery to the "Telly" has almost entirely eradicated.

The theatre, as the 1920's closed, had come through a bad phase and was fighting back. It was to strike a worst phase in the 1930's, but it did not know that yet.

Although in a far lesser degree than formerly, it was still the home of illusion, and the first business of the theatre is to create illusion. That detestable phrase "Show Business' had not been invented, to bring down the theatre to the level of the booth and fairground.

Despite its lack of order, its failures, its heartbreaks and tragedies, some bright beacons flared. Maybe their memories still glow and will flame afresh for those who have had the patience and tenacity to read this chronicle of the days already nearly forty years ago, when the footlights flickered . . . but never went out.

Index of Names

Ahearne, Brian, 131, 224
Ainley, Henry, 27, 44, 70, 73, 90, 106–7, 116, 126, 139, 148, 157, 225, 228
Albanesi, Meggie, 28, 41, 45, 85, 90, 104, 107, 133
Albery, Bronson, Sir, 23, 26, 144, 235
Alexander, Sir George, 18, 25, 92, 118, 145
Allan, Elizabeth, 212
Allen, Adrianne, 181
Alleyn, Edward, 134
Anderson, Mary, 45
Andrews, Bobbie, 71, 73, 225
Angel, Heather, 212
Anthony, Ellis, 92
April, Elsie, 223
Argyle, Pearl, 229
Arkell, Reginald, 98, 135, 184
Arlen, Michael, 139
Arliss, George, 109
Armstrong, William, 212, 235
Arnaud, Yvonne, 52, 95, 142, 158
Arnold, Tom, 149
Arthur, Paul, 73
Arundale, Jay, 212
Arundale, Sybil, 149, 212
Asche, Oscar, 22, 76–7, 116, 144
Ashcroft, Peggy, 228–9
Ashton and Mitchell, 138
Ashton, Winifred, 85
Ashwell, Dame Lena, 18
Astaire, Adele, 111, 161, 204
Astaire, Fred, 111, 161, 204
Atkins, Robert, 210–12
Austin, Charles, 56, 100
Austin, Frederick, 54, 159
Aylmer, Felix, 228–9
Aynesworth, Allan, 90, 156, 184

Bach, Reginald, 92
Bacon, Jane, 212
Baddeley, Angela, 182, 219
Baddeley, Hermione, 107, 162, 183
Bairnsfather, Bruce, 91

Baldestone, John L., 158
Balieff, 77
Bancroft, Lady, 17
Bancroft, Sir Squire, 17, 26
Bankhead, Tullulah, 109, 127, 134, 139, 147, 157–8, 183, 203
Banks, Leslie, 73, 159, 218
Bannerman, Margaret, 72, 76, 106, 157
Barker, Eric, 34
Barrett, George, 95
Barrie, Sir J. M., 44, 91–2, 103–4, 107, 206, 211, 236
Barrington, Rutland, 52
Barrymore, John, 147
Barton, Mary, 212
Baskcomb, A. W., 162, 203
Bates, Thorpe, 74–5
Baughan, E. A., 34
Bayley, Hilda, 206
Baylis, Lilian, 210
Beardsley, Aubrey, 222
Bedells, Phyllis, 57
Beecham, Adrian, 97
Beecham, Sir Thomas, 222
Behrman, S. N., 204
Belasco, David, 74
Beldon, Eileen, 128
Bellew, Kyrle, 26, 73
Benson, Sir Frank, 20, 210–11
Benson, Lady, 210
Bennett, Arnold, 44, 130, 236
Bennett, Mavis, 134
Berkeley, Reginald, 184, 217
Berlioz, 118
Bernhardt, Sarah, 73, 100, 101
Berry, W. H., 52, 74, 98, 109, 119, 135, 144, 200, 219
Besier, Rudolph, 94, 103, 236
Best, Edna, 37, 73, 89, 104, 147, 157, 222
Billing, Pemberton, 92
Binyon, Laurence, 211
Bird, Golding, 31
Bird, Richard, 107, 130
Birkenhead, Lord, 56

Blakeney, Olive (Mrs. Nedell), 159, 219
Blaney, Norah, 111-2, 129, 184
Blore, Eric, 80, 212
Bloom, Leslie, 31
Blow, Sydney, 108
Bolton, Guy, 200
Boote, Rosie, 29
Bottomley, Gordon, 211
Boucicault, Dion, 27, 72, 213
Boucicault, Nina, 179, 236
Bourchier, Arthur, 26, 73, 92, 173
Bourchier, Chili, 129
Boughton, Rutland, 100
Bower, Marion, 92
Braham, Philip, 110, 148
Braithwaite, Lilian, 85, 132, 209, 220
Brandon, Dorothy, 109
Brayton, Lily, 76, 116
Breon, Edmond, 180
Bright, Golding, 30, 220
Brisson, Carl, 110, 135, 183
Britton, Hutin, 44, 210
Brook, Clive, 83
Browne, Graham, 142, 175-6, 225
Browne, Irene, 124
Browne, Louise, 183
Browne, Maurice, 226
Brough, Mary, 95
Brody, Hal, 219
Bruce, Nigel, 201, 218
Buchanan, Jack, 32, 75, 79, 100, 136, 144, 162, 164, 167-72, 208
Buckton, Florence, 212
Burbidge, Douglas, 212
Burke, Marie, 202
Burleigh, Olivia, 212
Burrows, Arthur, 88
Butt, Sir Alfred, 22-3, 26, 28, 49, 51, 58, 66, 89, 107, 129-30, 143-44, 200, 217, 234
Butterworth, Clara, 75
Byng, Douglas, 148
Byrne, Cecily, 184

Cadell, Jean, 182
Calthrop, Donald, 73
Calthrop, Gladys, 222
Calvert, Louis, 70
Campbell, Mrs. Patrick, 28, 218
Capek, Brothers, 108
Carey, Joyce, 41
Carlton, Billy, 79

Carpenter, Edward Charles, 126
Carr, J. Comyns, 116
Carroll, Madeline, 219-20
Carroll, Sydney, 149
Carten, Audrey, 218
Carten, Waveney, 218
Carter, Nell, 212
Casson, Lewis, 45, 73, 93, 131, 157, 212
Cathcart, Countess, 157
Cavanagh, Paul, 181, 202
Cecil, Sylvia, 200
Cellier, Frank, 157, 175-6, 180, 219
Chapin, Harold, 85
Charig, Philip, 202
Charlot, André, 22, 26, 39, 79-80, 110-11, 234
Charlton, Randal, 33
Chekov, 145
Chester, Betty, 135, 164
Chevalier, Maurice, 181
Chisholm, Robert, 149
Christie, Agatha, 203
Church, Esmé, 212
Churchill, Winston, 153
Clare, Mary, 45, 86, 131
Clarence, O. B., 96, 236
Clark, Holman, 29
Clarke, George, 160
Clarke-Smith, D. A., 158
Clarkson, Willy, 58
Cliff, Laddie, 80, 135
Clayton and Waller, 149, 184, 203, 234
Clift, E. P., 83, 158
Clive, Colin, 226
Clunes, Alec, 148
Cochran, Charles B., 26, 54, 78, 80, 99, 100, 112, 124, 148, 162, 174, 178, 182-3, 198, 200, 203, 216, 222-3, 234
Cochrane, Frank, 107, 219
Coffin, Hayden, 75
Cohen, Edgar, 30
Cohen, Harry I., 150
Cohen, Madeline, 30
Colefax, Lady, 29
Colin, Jean, 207, 218
Collier, Constance, 41, 106, 132, 158-9
Collins, Arthur, 26, 45, 104-5, 129
Collins, Frank, 54, 223
Collins, José, 54, 75, 98, 111, 135, 149, 181
Collins, Winnie, 201

Compton, Fay, 44, 94, 106, 147, 155–7
Compton, Mrs. Edward, 210
Cooper, Gladys, 71, 73, 92, 108, 124–5, 139, 183, 219, 235
Cooper, William, 49
Cortis, Diana, 85
Coulouris, George, 212
Courtneidge, Cicely, 142, 161, 174, 219
Courtneidge, Robert, 18, 73, 158
Cowan, Lawrence, 34
Coward, Noel, 44, 73, 110–12, 132, 142, 147–8, 155, 157, 176–9, 203–4, 213, 222–5.
Cowie, Laura, 107
Cowl, Jane, 155
Coyne, Joseph, 100, 111, 149, 162
Crawford, Mimi, 99, 162, 182, 207
Cray, David, 157
Croft, Anne, 135, 164
Crosby, Bing, 170
Curzon, Frank, 18, 23, 26, 108, 124, 139, 173, 235
Curzon, George, 154, 179, 204
Currie, Clive, 219
Curtis, Neil, 212

Dagnall, T. C., 213
Dainton, Marie, 159
Dance, George, 50, 211
Dane, Clemence, 85–6, 133
Dare, Phyllis, 79, 98, 135, 161, 201
Darlington, W. A., 34, 131
Darragh, 82
Davenport, A. Bromley, 228–9
"David L'Estrange," 132
Davies, Lilian, 99, 144, 179, 203
Davies, "Hoppy," 29
Dawes, W. H. (Billy), 56
Day, Edith, 58–9, 97, 143, 181, 203
Dean, Basil, 23, 37, 44–5, 82–7, 90–1, 104, 107, 129–30, 132–3, 145, 149, 157–8, 177, 179, 200, 204–5, 215, 219, 235
Dearden, Harold, 201
de Bear, Archie, 39, 108, 129, 162, 207, 218, 223–4
Debenham, Cecily, 184
de Casalis, Jeane, 73, 125, 181
de Courville, Albert, 22, 26, 54, 75, 77, 111, 135–6, 149, 234
de Lion, J. & D., 216
Delius, 106
Dell, Ethel M., 72, 89

Delysia, Alice, 148
Denham, Reginald, 43, 125, 148, 208, 214, 225, 228, 235
Denny, Ernest, 83
Desborough, Philip, 228
Deslys, Gaby, 174
de Valois, Ninette, 110
Deverell, John, 236
Dickson, Dorothy, 80, 100, 112, 135, 159, 162, 170, 176
Disher, M. Willson, 33
Dixon, Adele, 212
Doble, Frances, 128, 177, 205, 228
Dolin, Anton, 160, 162, 181
Dolly, Eddie, 164
Dolly Sisters, 78–9, 164
Dolman, Richard, 202
Donat, Robert, 126
Doyle, Sir Arthur Conan, 220
Draper, Ruth, 176, 180
Drayton, Alfred, 106, 184
Drew, Philip Yale, 72
Drinkwater, John, 106–8
Druten, John van, 204–5
Dukes, Ashley, 147, 208, 228–9
Duke, Vernon, 201
du Maurier, Sir Gerald, 18, 26, 72, 109, 133, 149, 151, 159, 184, 218, 225, 231, 235
Duncan Sisters, 203
Dunn, Bobbie, 175
Dunsany, Lord, 72
Dyall, Franklyn, 131

Eadie, Dennis, 92, 236
Edginton, May, 94
Ediss, Connie, 219
Edlin, Tubby, 110
Edwards, George, 18, 27, 50, 52, 54, 75, 79–80, 96
Edwards, Hilton, 211
Edwin, Grace, 142
Elgar, Sir Edward, 211
Eliott, Gertrude, 149
Elliott, Madge, 176
Ellis, Anthony, 155
Ellis, Edith, 148
Ellis, Vivian, 97, 142, 160, 163, 223, 235
Ellis, Walter, 203
Elsie, Lily, 184, 209
Elsom, Isobel, 69, 109, 208
Emerson, John, 158
Emery, Winifred, 71
Emm, Andrew, 134

Ervine, St John, 44, 84, 189, 225
Esmond-Moore, Jill, 156
Evans, Edith, 71, 73, 90, 130, 212, 218, 221
Evans, Maurice, 226
Evans, Will, 94
Everest, Barbara, 212
Evett, Robert, 27, 54, 98–9, 111, 135

Faber, Leslie, 73, 91, 109, 141, 159
Fagan, J. Bernard, 69–70, 89, 158
Fairbrother, Sydney, 41, 201, 236
Fall, Leo, 110
Farjeon, Herbert, 112
Farjeon, J. Jefferson, 148
Farquarson, Robert, 208, 225
Farquhar, Lord, 29
Farrar, Gwen, 111–2, 129, 181
Feuchtwanger, Lion, 228
Ffrangcon-Davies, Gwen, 100, 130, 146, 217
Field, Alexander, 226
Fields, Gracie, 203–4
Filippi, Rosina, 116
Fillis, Frank, 62
Finck, Herman, 55, 89, 97, 99, 154
Fitton, Mary, 86
Fitzgerald, Walter, 218
Flecker, James Elroy, 106
Fleming, Brandon, 149
Fleming, Ian, 142
Fletcher, Percy, 76, 144
Forbes, Norman, 72, 124
Forbes-Robertson, Jean, 212
Forbes-Robertson, Sir Johnston, 18, 20, 71, 173, 227
Forder, Frank, 108
Fordred, Dorice, 212
Foss, G. R., 210
Foster, Basil S., 72, 133, 208, 219
France, C. V., 131, 236
Fraser, Lovat, 54
Fraser-Simpson, H., 135, 140
Fratellini Brothers, 78–9
Freeman, Frank, 104
French, Harold, 84
French, Leslie, 179, 212
Friml, Rudolf, 111, 184
Frohman, Charles, 18, 118
Fry, Horace, 49
Furber, Douglas, 80

Galsworthy, John, 45, 85, 91, 93, 102, 130, 132, 134, 149, 154, 219
Garside, John, 212

Gaunt, William, 49, 52, 74, 180
Gay, 99
Gay, Maisie, 110–11, 135, 181, 203
Gay, Noel, 235
Gee, George, 181, 203
George, A. E., 236
George, Lloyd, 24
Gerrard, Gene, 181
Gershwin, George, 136, 150, 181
Gielgud, John, 108, 150, 212, 236
Gilbert, Jean, 98
Gill, Basil, 45, 107, 119, 157, 236
Gilliland, Helen, 111, 139, 202
Glass, Dudley, 179
Gleason, James, 154
Glenville, Shaun, 183
Glynne, Mary, 183
Gogol, 161
Goolden, Richard, 159
Gordon, Leon, 131
Graham, Harry, 55
Grant, William, 138
Granville-Barker, H., 142
Graves, George, 54, 110
Green, Harry, 72
Greenwald, Joseph, 175
Greet, Sir Philip Ben, 20, 210–11
Grein, J. T., 34, 92–3
Grey, Clifford, 223
Grey, Sir Edward, 17
Grieg, 109
Grossmith, 22
Grossmith and Laurillard, 22–3, 26, 50, 56, 74, 80, 136, 234
Grossmith and Malone, 234
Grossmith, George, 52, 80, 95, 100, 106–7, 112, 149, 167, 202
Grossmith, Lawrence, 149, 176, 180
Guitrys, 93
Guitry, Sacha, 158, 161
Gulliver, Charles, 26
Gunning, 37
Gwenn, Edmund, 45, 91, 105, 158
Gwyther, Geoffrey, 135, 200

Hackett, James, 41
Hackett, Raymond, 108
Hackett, Walter, 27–8, 30, 36, 70, 125, 133, 140, 142, 209, 219
Haddon, Archibald, 33, 68–70
Haddon, Peter, 135
Haig, 183, 203
Hale, Binnie, 56, 75, 89, 111, 136, 149, 162, 205, 223–4

Hale, Robert, 58, 75, 129, 162
Hale, Sonnie, 129, 162, 203, 205, 222
Hall, Thurstan, 89
Hamilton, Cecily, 147
Hamilton, Patrick, 224
Hammerstein II, Oscar, 143, 161–2, 181–2, 202
Hampton, Louise, 92, 142
Handley, Tommy, 135
Hannen, Nicholas, 125, 130
Harbach, Otto, 143, 161–2
Harben, Hubert, 182
Harding, Lyn, 74, 134, 236
Hardwicke, Cedric, 128–9, 157, 181, 202, 221
Hardy, Thomas, 146
Hare, Sir John, 18
Hare, J. Robertson, 95, 97, 140
Harker, Gordon, 159
Harker, Joseph and Phil, 46
Harris, Sir Augustus, 129
Harris, George W., 83–4, 86
Harris, Robert, 130, 176
Harrison, Frederick, 23, 26
Hart, L., 176
Harvey, Frank, 220, 228–9
Harvey, Morris, 135, 207
Harwood, H. M., 41, 125, 235
Haslam, Robert, 206
Hastings, Patrick, 158
Hawkes, Sylvia, 136
Haviland, William, 227
Hawkins, Master Jack, 131, 157
Hawkins, Jack, 205, 220
Hawkins, Stockwell, 210
Hawtrey, Sir Charles, 18, 26, 44, 69–70, 217, 235
Hay, Ian, 73, 105, 133, 218–9
Haye, Helen, 45, 126, 154
Hayes, George, 211
Headford, Marchioness of, 29
Heatherley, Clifford, 222
Henley, 33
Henry, Charles, 100
Henry, Leonard, 135
Henson, Leslie, 51, 56, 80, 94–5, 100, 112, 136, 150, 162, 176, 203
Henson, Mrs. Leslie, 95
Herbert, A. P., 159, 219
Herbert, Victor, 98
Hervey, Grizelda, 155, 206
Hewitt, Henry, 219
Hibbert, H. G., 34
Hicks, Lady, 158

Hicks, Sir Seymour, 18, 27, 55, 90, 108, 158, 185, 200, 231
Highley, Reginald, 94
Hignet, H. R., 236
Higson, 29
Hishin, Bernard, 56–7
Hitchens, Robert, 45
Hoare, C. Douglas, 108
Hodges, Horace, 131, 236
Hodgson, Ewart, 207
Hoffe, Monckton, 70
Holloway, Baliol, 212
Holloway, Stanley, 56, 203
Homewood, A. S., 206
Hopwood, Avery, 157
Horne, David, 226
Horniman, Roy, 71
Horsnell, Horace, 112
Howard, Bannister, 94
Howard, Leslie, 27, 203
Howard, Sydney, 158, 182, 204
Howes, Bobby, 144, 184, 201, 223
Hudd, Walter, 142
Hulbert, Claude, 203
Hulbert, Jack, 55, 142, 174, 181, 219
Hume, Benita, 220
Hunt, Martita, 181
Hunter, Ian, 91, 184
Huntly, G. P., 160
Huntley, Raymond, 128, 179
Hurgon, Austen, 97
Hurlbutt, W. J., 74
Hutchinson, A. S. M., 108
Hutchinson, Ernest, 43
Hutter, William, 207
Hyson, Carl, 80
Hylton, Jack, 95

Ibsen, 93, 102, 149, 212
Ireland, Anthony, 224
Irving, Ethel, 41, 236
Irving, Henry, 17–8, 20, 100, 115
Irving, Laurence, 114

Jackson, Sir Barry, 128, 220, 235
Jacob, Naomi, 113, 218
James, Cairns, 214
Janis, Elsie, 55, 135, 174
Janis, Mrs., 55
Jay, Isobel, 118
Jeans, Ronald, 110
Jeans, Ursula, 225
Jeffreys, Ellis, 42, 154, 180, 236
Jennings, Gertrude, 41, 85, 106
Jerome, Jerome Klapka, 173

Jerrold, Mary, 142, 184, 205-6, 236
Jesse, F. Tennyson, 89, 125
Joel, Jack, 29
Jolson, Al, 198
John, Augustus, 222
John, Graham, 163, 200
Johns, Mervyn, 113
Johnson, Dr., 102
Jones, Amy, 34
Jones, Henry Arthur, 108
June, 99

Kalman, Emmerlich, 55, 79
Kean, Edmund, 104, 133
Keen, Malcolm, 45, 84-5, 107, 201
Keith-Johnson, Colin, 128, 147
Kelly, Renee, 28, 43
Kendal, Henry, 43, 73, 135
Kendal, Mrs., 18
Kennedy, Margaret, 157
Kent, 41, 131, 157
Kenyon, Charles, 82, 213
Kern, Jerome, 112, 162, 200, 202
Kerr, Fred, 184
Kershaw, Willette, 72
King-Hall, Stephen, 219
Kingston, Gertrude, 184
Kirby, John, 148, 160
Kirwan, Patrick, 210
Knight, Esmond, 212
Knoblock, Edward, 130, 134
Komisarjevsky, 145, 155
Kunneke, 98, 203

Lambert, Constant, 229
Landi, Elissa, 125
Lane, Grace, 108, 148
Lang, Matheson, 18, 20, 44, 71-2,
    91, 107, 148, 208, 210, 226-31,
    235
Langtry, Mrs., 109
Lauder, Harry, 65, 160
Laughton, Charles, 107, 146, 155,
    161, 176, 203-4, 222
Laurillard, 22
Laurillard, Edward, 123-4, 199
Laurie, John, 211
Laurier, Jay, 99
La Verne, Lucille, 150
Lawrence, Gertrude, 79, 100, 110-
    11, 181-2
Lawton, Frank, 184, 204
Laye, Evelyn, 78-9, 99, 110, 135,
    143, 154, 185, 200, 222
Layton and Johnson, 136

Lee, Norman, 148
Lehar, Franz, 134, 149, 150, 176
Lehmann, Beatrix, 140
Lehmann, Liza, 109
Leigh, Andrew, 210, 212
Le Sage, Sir John M., 34
Leslie, Lew, 162, 181
Leslie, Sylvia, 74
Lester, Alfred, 75, 111, 129
L'Estrange, Davis, 158
Lever, Lady (Arthur), 37
Levey, Ethel, 56, 144
Levy, Benn W., 157
Lewes, Miriam, 183
Lewisohn, Victor, 212
Leycester, Laura, 108
Lillie, Beatrice, 70, 79, 99, 170
Limbert, Roy, 220
Limpus, Alban B., 212
Limpus, Canon Henry Francis, 213
Lindo, Olga, 126, 154
Lion, Leon M., 70, 92-3
Lister, Francis, 70, 89, 126
Littlewood, S. R., 34
Livesey, Roger, 92
Livesey, Sam, 158, 179
Lloyd, Marie, 100-1, 203
Lohr, Marie, 27, 43, 90, 116, 212,
    220
Lonsdale, Frederick, 98, 103, 106,
    110, 125, 135, 149, 180, 184, 202, 217
Loos, Anita, 158
Lopokova, Lydia, 110
Loraine, Robert, 73, 106, 130
Lorne, Marion, 28
Losch, Tilly, 203
Lotinga, Ernie, 149
Luigi, 29
Lunts, 222
Lupino, Stanley, 99, 136, 218
Lurgan, Lord, 29
Lynn, Ralph, 75, 79, 94-5, 125, 140,
    154, 200
Lynn, Sydney, 95

Macdermott, 68
Macgill, Moyna, 84, 86, 92
MacOwan, Norman, 37, 218
Maeterlinck, 71
Malleson, Miles, 175
Malone, J. A. E., 80, 94, 100, 107,
    112, 223
Mann, Charlton, 37
Mannering, Lewin, 228-9
Margetson, Arthur, 179, 184

Marlowe, Christopher, 86
Marlowe, Thomas, 30
Marriott-Watson, Nan, 92
Marshall, Herbert, 125, 184, 204, 222
Mars, Marjorie, 155, 228
Martin-Harvey, Sir John, 18, 20, 235
Mason, A. E. W., 26, 29, 94
Mason, Ena, 95
Massey, Raymond, 113, 131, 222
Massine, Leonide, 110
Massinger, 211
Matthews, A. E., 149, 176
Matthews, Jessie, 162, 182, 203, 222
Maturin, Eric, 127, 183
Maude, Cyril, 18, 26, 74, 89, 181
Maude, Joan, 228
Maugham, Somerset, 72, 90, 102, 106, 118, 134, 145, 148, 183, 219, 236
Mawdesley, Robert, 124
May, Ada, 216
Mayer, Joseph, 154
Mayne, Clarice, 100
McCarthy, Lilian, 44
McEvoy, Charles, 107
McKinnel, Norman, 72, 130, 236
Megrue, Roi Cooper, 125
Melford, Austin, 219
Melnotte, Violet, 26, 37–8, 40, 110, 146, 156, 176, 178, 180, 205–8, 236
Melville, A., 134
Melville, Winnie, 184
Merivale, Philip, 86
Merson, Billy, 99, 143, 160, 163–6, 168
Mextaxas, George, 222
Michaelis, Robert, 74
Middleton, Edgar C., 181
Millar, Robins, 205–6
Miller, Gilbert, 27, 30, 44, 184, 203, 218, 224, 235
Miller, David, 164
Miller, Ruby, 71
Mills, Florence, 112, 162
Milne, A. A., 27, 72, 90, 106–7, 133
Milton, Billy, 181
Milton, Ernest, 210, 212, 224
Milward, Dawson, 124, 236
Minto, Dorothy, 180
Mite, Tiny, 160
Molesworth, Ida, 131, 134
Mollison, Clifford, 73, 91, 157, 205

Molnar, Ferene, 155
Monkhouse, Alan, 133
Monkman, Dorothy, 218
Monkman, Phyllis, 135
Montgomery, James, 58
Moore, C. Barnard, 184
Moore, Eva, 183
Moore, Hilda, 184
Moore, Mary, 18, 26
Morrison, 34
Morton, Leon, 52
Moscovitch, Maurice, 43, 104
Mundin, Herbert, 111, 162, 202
Munro, C. K., 125
Murray, Paul, 174
Myers, Richard, 223
Myrio, 135

Nares, Owen, 27, 29, 36, 41, 43, 85, 89, 107–9, 124, 126, 149, 154, 201, 217–8
Nathan, Winifred, 134
Nattova, 135
Neagle, Anna, 143
Nedell, Bernard J., 159
Neilson, Julia, 18, 20, 183, 235
Neilson-Terry, Dennis, 183
Nesbitt, Cathleen, 107, 218
Neumann, Alfred, 208
Newman, Greatrex, 162, 176, 223
Newton, H. Chance, 34
Newton, Robert, 203
New Yorkers, 207
Ney, Marie, 211
Northcliffe, Lord, 90
Norton, Frederick, 76
Norwood, Eille, 108, 218
Novello, Ivor, 46, 51, 73–4, 79, 86, 93, 98, 108, 132, 135–6, 139, 145, 155–6, 158–9, 170–1, 177, 209, 220, 234–5
O'Casey, Sean, 222
O'Connor, Cavan, 212
Old Bill, M.P., 91
Oldham, Derek, 110, 143, 184
Olivier, Laurence, 144, 220, 226
O'Neill, Eugene, 109, 142
O'Neill, Norman, 44, 162, 206
O'Neill, Peggy, 43, 106, 148
Oscar, Henry, 181, 220

Page, Norman, 182
Page, Philip, 34
Palmer, Rex, 103
Parker, Cecil, 157

Parker, Louis N., 93, 135
Parsons, Alan, 208
Parsons, Hubert, 109
Passmore, Walter, 75
Pavola, 113, 176
Pearce, Vera, 135, 164
Peisley, Frederick, 92
Pepys, Samuel, 158
Percy, Edward, 92, 132, 214, 225
Percy, Esme, 107
Perrins, Leslie, 113
Petley, Frank E., 206
Petrie, Hay, 211
Phelps, Samuel, 34
Phillips, Montague, 75
Phillips, Stephen, 116
Phillpotts, Adelaide, 157
Phillpotts, Eden, 128, 157
Pickard, Helen, 206, 212
Pilbeam, Arnold, 212
Pinero, 75, 93, 102, 139
Pink, Wal, 54
Pirandello, 150
Pitts, Zasu, 28
Playfair, Nigel, 27, 44, 54, 159, 234
Pollock, Channing, 73, 126
Pollock, Elizabeth, 125
Ponsonby, "Scrubby," 30
Porter, Cole, 222
Portman, Eric, 219
Potter, Betty, 210
Potter, Mrs. Brown, 116
Pounds, Courtice, 100
Pounds, Lorna and Toots, 56, 100, 160
Pounds, Toots, 160
Powell, Templer, 131
Power, Hartley, 159
Printempts, Yvonne, 161
Purdell, Reginald, 219

Quartermaine, Leon, 107, 157

Raikes, Charles S. M., 109
Rains, Claud, 73, 86
Ranalow, Frederick, 179
Randolph, Elsie, 162
Randolph, June and Elsie, 144
Ranevsky, Boris, 124–5
Raphael, John N., 41
Rayner, Minnie, 220
Rea, Alec, 44, 82–3, 87, 235
Rea, M.P., Rt. Hon. Russell, 82
Rea, William J., 106
Read, Carol, 144, 183

Rees, Sir Milsom, 29
Reeve, Ada, 56
Relph, George, 179
Reynolds, Alfred, 159
Reynolds, Tom, 58–9, 205
Richardson, Ralph, 157
Ridgeway, Philip, 145, 155–6, 161, 183
Ridley, Arnold, 150
Rigby, Arthur, 219
Riscoe, Arthur, 43
Ritchard, Cyril, 176
Rivers, Max, 207
Roberts, Arthur, 78, 99
Roberts, Florence, 34
Roberts, J. H., 84
Roberts, Oswald Dale, 225
Robertson, Tom, 17, 102
Robeson, Paul, 142, 202
Robey, George, 54, 57, 89, 99, 110, 135
Robinson, Lennox, 41
Robinson, Percy, 224
Robson, Flora, 86, 125
Rodgers, Richard, 156, 161, 176, 182–3
Rohmer, Sax, 99
Romberg, Sigmund, 161
Ronald, Sir Landon, 45
Rooks, Irene, 86
Rose, Arthur, 108
Rosmer, Milton, 132
Rosetta and Vivien, 203
Royston, Roy, 144
Russell, Mabel, 179
Rutherford, Margaret, 212

Sacks, Joseph Leopold, 23, 27, 58–9, 60–7, 89, 123–4, 144, 180
St Helier, Ivy, 135, 222
St John, Lily, 52
Saintbury, H. A., 104, 184
Sammons, Albert, 48
"Sapper," 72
Sardou, 124
Sarony, Leslie, 203
Saunders, Madge, 95
Savoir, Alfred, 92
Schletter, Annie, 124
Schubert, Franz, 99
Scott, Tom, 32
Sealby, Mabel, 176
Sedger, Horace, 51
Selfridge, Gordon, 29
Selton, Morton, 126, 154

Sequiera, Horace, 212
Seyler, Athene, 130
Shakespeare, 21, 82, 86, 102, 119, 130, 144, 165, 210, 216
Sharland, Reginald, 135, 164
Shaw, George Bernard, 69, 102, 128, 130–1, 220–1, 235–6
Shelley, 34
Shepherd, Firth, 75, 176
Sheridan, Mary, 229
Sheridan, Richard Brinsley, 27
Sheriff, R. C., 225
Shillingford, Osmond, 155
Shine, Wilfred, 183
Shotter, Winifred, 112, 136
Sissie, 110
Sissie and Blake, 110
Smith, Aubrey, 73, 85, 106, 127
Smith, Bruce, 46
Smith, Clay, 79, 135
Smith, Dodie, 197
Smith, E. P., 224
Sokolova, Lydia, 110
Spear, Eric, 212
Speight, Robert, 226
Spence, E. F., 34
Spinelly, 162
Squire, Ronald, 72, 180, 217
Stacpoole, H. de Vere, 37
Stamp-Taylor, Enid, 100
Stayton, Frank, 142
Stead, Estelle, 210
Sterlin, Louis, 31
Stewart, Athole, 45
Stock, Ralph, 176
Stoll, Sir Oswald, 22–3, 26
Stolz, Robert, 184
Straus, Oscar, 98, 143, 163
Stuart, Aimee, 155
Stuart, Leslie, 160–1
Stuart, Philip, 155
Suffolk, Countess of, 99
Sullivan, Francis L., 211
Sunderland, Scott, 128
Sutro, Alfred, 90, 134, 151, 236
Swaffer, Hannen, 34–5
Swete, Lyall, 236
Swinburne, Nora, 218
Swinley, Ian, 146, 211

Tate, Harry, 90
Tate, James, W., 99
Taylor, Coleridge, 118
Taylor, Enid, 100
Taylor, Valerie, 180

Tchaikowsky, 111
Tearle, Godfrey, 45–6, 70–1, 73, 89–90, 104, 114–22, 125, 131, 149, 154, 158
Tearle, Osmund, 114
Tempest, Dame Marie, 18, 26, 37, 112, 135, 142, 155, 175–6, 213, 225
Tennyson, 137
Terriss, Ellaline, 158
Terry, Fred, 18, 20, 183, 235
Terry, J. E. Harold, 108, 125
Thatcher, Heather, 52, 136, 219
Thesiger, Ernest, 148
Thompson, Beatrix, 107
Thorndike, Russell, 73, 210, 212
Thorndike, Sybil, 45, 68, 93, 108, 112, 131, 144, 157, 212
Thurston, E. Temple, 104
Tierney, Harry, 58
Titheradge, Dion, 184
Titheradge, Madge, 45, 73, 116, 133, 149, 155, 157, 176, 179
Titterton, W. R., 33
Tours, Frank E., 58
Toye, Wendy, 212
Travers, Ben, 89, 141, 154, 175, 200, 219
Tree, Sir Herbert, 18, 20–2, 24–5, 29, 70, 82, 107, 116–18, 173, 214
Tree, Lady, 124, 175
Tree, Mr., 114–5
Tree, Viola, 70, 209
Tresmand, Ivy, 144
Trevelyan, Hilda, 236
Trevor, Austin, 146–7, 211, 222, 228
"Trini," 78, 99
Trix Sisters, 79, 142
Trouncer, Cecil, 134
Truex, Ernest, 154, 180, 197, 218
Truman, Ralph, 212
Tully, George, 73, 236
Turleigh, Veronica, 228
Turnbull, "Tiny," 31
Turner, Harold, 229
Turner, John Hastings, 104, 140, 154, 175, 202

"Uncle Rex," 103

Vachell, Horace Annesley, 106, 134
Va ja, Ernest, 125
"Valentine," 94
Valentino, Rudolph, 236

Vanbrugh, Irene, 27, 71–2, 118, 156, 206
Vanbrugh, Violet, 26, 72, 90, 206
Vane, Sutton, 112
Vanne, Marda, 179, 201
Vedrenne, J. E., 30
Vedrenne-Barker, 93, 235
Veness, Amy, 128
Venning, Una, 71, 218
Verne, Jules, 99
Vollaire, George, 200
Vosper, Frank, 41, 157, 212, 218

Wakefield, Hugh, 92
Walkley, A. B., 34
Wall, Harry, 130
Wall, Max, 154
Wallace, Edgar, 54, 111, 136, 159, 183, 201, 217
Waller, Lewis, 18, 119
Wallis, Bertram, 98, 110–11, 200
Wallis, Lewis, 18
Walls and Henson Ltd., 94
Walls, Tom, 94–7, 125, 140–1, 154, 175, 180, 200, 219–20
Walter, Wilfrid, 130, 212
Warburton, Charles, 210
Ward, Dorothy, 183
Ward, Polly, 203
Ward, Ronald, 113
Warde, Willie, 95
Waring, Herbert, 184, 200, 204
Warrender, Harold, 162
Watson, Henrietta, 179, 236
Watson, Horace, 26
Watson, Malcolm, 34
Weaver, Wyn, 108
Webster, Tom, 129
Welchman, Harry, 56, 75, 98, 135, 139, 181
Weldon, Ben, 158
Wells, H. G., 84
Wenman, Henry, 236
Western, George, 162
Western, Kenneth, 162

Whale, James, 226
Whitby, Arthur, 86, 236
White, Fisher, 206, 210
White, James, 27, 29, 54, 56, 98, 110, 142, 174, 176
White, Lee, 79, 135
White, Pearl, 148
Wilde, Oscar, 92, 222
Wilks, Allan Tupper, 127
Willard, Edmund, 107, 219
Williams, Emlyn, 120–1
Williams, Herb., 207–8
Williams, Walter, 79, 99
Wills, Drusilla, 146
Wilshin, Sunday, 162
Wilson, Grace, 204
Wimperis, Arthur, 92, 97
Winn, Godfrey, 134, 157, 176
Winston, Bruce, 45
Wodehouse, P. G., 112, 180, 218
Woizikowsky, Leon, 110
Wolfit, Sir Donald, 148, 209, 212, 228
Wolston, Henry, 212
Wontner, Arthur, 72, 135, 236
Wood, Peggy, 222
Woodgate, Leslie, 212
Woodhouse, Vernon, 125
Woods, Tom, 179
Wray, Maxwell, 212
Wright, Haidee, 86
Wright, Huntley. 75
Wyatt, Frank Gunning, 37–8
Wylie, Julian, 57, 77–9, 99, 135, 148, 201–2, 223–4, 234
Wylie, Lauri, 160, 201
Wyndham, Sir Charles, 18, 25
Wyndham, Howard, 23, 26, 235
Wyse, John, 212

Yetta, Powlowski, 150
Youmans, Vincent, 149, 161, 182

Zucco, George, 226

Index of Titles

Abie's Irish Rose, 175
Abraham Lincoln, 73
Adam and Eva, 150
Advertising April, 112
Aladdin, 79
Alf's Button, 131
Alibi, 204
Alice in Wonderland, 93
All the King's Horses, 156
Aloma, 154
A Man with Red Hair, 203
Ambrose Applejohn's Adventure, 70, 92, 213
Ambush, 106
A Midsummer Night's Dream, 57, 130
And So To Bed, 158
Angel Face, 94, 98
Angelo, 104, 113
A Night Out, 56
Antony and Cleopatra, 120
Anyhouse, 150
Apache, The, 183
Apple Cart, The, 220–1
Arcadians, The, 75
Aren't We All, 106
A Roof and Four Walls, 104
Ashes, 157
Ask Beccles, 156
As You Like It, 54, 116
At Mrs Beam's, 108, 113
A to Z, 79, 168
At the Villa Rose, 26
Attila, 116
Audacious Mr Squires, The, 129
Aviator, The, 65
A Warm Corner, 219

Baa-Baa, Black Sheep, 218
Babes in the Wood, 79
Bachelor Husbands, 134
Back to Methuselah, 128
Bad Man, The, 107
Balkan Princess, The, 118
Battling Butler, 100
Beau Geste, 219

Beauty Prize, The, 112
Beaux Stratagem, The, 183
Beggar on Horseback, 149
Beggar's Opera, The, 54, 99
Belle of New York, The, 149
Bells, The, 17
Beloved Vagabond, The, 179
Berkeley Square, 158
Best People, The, 157
Betrothal, The, 71
Better Days, 148
Betty in Mayfair, 140
Bill of Divorcement, A 85–6
Bing Boys, The, 57
Bird in Hand, 209
Bird of Paradise, The, 154
Bitter Sweet, 222–3
Black Ace, The, 219
Black Birds, 162, 181
Blessed Are The Rich, 150
Blinkers, 134
Blood and Sand, 72
Bluebird's Eighth Wife, 92
Blue Bird, The, 71
Blue Eyes, 199, 200
Blue Kitten, 144
Blue Lagoon, 37, 83–5
Blue Mazurka, 176
Blue Peter, 213
Blue Skies, 184
Blue Train, 184
Boodle, 144
Boy Friend, The, 183
Britain's Daughter, 211
Broadway, 158
Broken Wing, The, 89
Brown Sugar, 37
Bruce Bairnsfather Revue, 150
Bull-Dog Drummond, 72
Buzz Buzz, 79
By Candle Light, 209
By the Way, 142, 161

Cabaret Girl, The, 100, 136
Caesar and Cleopatra, 147
Cairo, 76

Calendar, The, 217
Camel's Back, The, 134
Canaries Sometimes Sing, 217
Candida, 45
Caprice, 222
Careless Rapture, 47
Carnival, 44, 148
Carousel, 156
Carry On Sergeant, 150
Cartoons, 129
Cat and the Canary, The, 92
Catherine, 111
Cat's Cradle, The, 155
Charlot's Revue, 135
Charlot's Revue 1924, 182
Charlot's Show of 1926, 162
Charm School, The, 41
Cheep, 79
Cherry Orchard, The, 146
Chinese Bungalow, The, 226-8
Chinese Honeymoon, A, 159
Chu Chin Chow, 22, 76-7
Cinderella Man, The, 28, 126
Cinema Lady, The, 74
Circle, The, 72
Circle of Chalk, The, 219-20
Civilian Clothes, 113
Claimant, The, 133
Clo-Clo, 150
Cleopatra, 143
Clowns in Clover, 174-5
Cochran Revue, The, 1926, 162
Collusion, 125, 213
Come In, 134-5
Come Out of the Kitchen, 43
Come With Me, 204
Conchita, 134
Conquering Hero, The, 133
Constant Nymph, The, 157, 205
Count X, 74
Courting, 150
Cousin from Nowhere, The, 111
Creaking Chair, The, 126
Crest of the Wave, 47
Crime, 184
Cristalinda, 150
Crooked Billet, The, 184
Crooked Friday, The, 150
Cuckoo in the Nest, The, 141
Cup of Kindness, A, 219
Curate's Egg, The, 97
Cymbeline, 108, 211

Daisy, The, 155
Damsel in Distress, A, 208

Dancers, The, 109
Dancing Mothers, The, 149
Daniel, 73-4
Daredevil, The, 134
Dear Brutus, 92, 217
Dear Love, 218
Dear Octopus, 197
Deburau, 73
Decameron Nights, 89
Dede, 100
De Luxe Annie, 150
Desert Song, The, 181
Desire for Change, The, 150
Destruction, 94
Diplomacy, 72, 124-5, 154
Dippers, The, 89
Dollar Princess, The, 142
Don, 103
Don Q, 73
Dorothy, 100
Double Dan, 183
Dover Road, The, 90
Dover Street to Dixie, 112
Downhill, 158
Dracula, 178
Dr Fu Manchu, 99
Duenna, The, 135
Dulcy, 113

East of Suez, 90
Easy Money, 149
Easy Virtue, 155
Edge of Beyond, The, 71
Elopement, The, 113
Elsie Janis at Home, 136
Emma, 74
Emperor Jones, The, 142
Enchanted Cottage, The, 93
Enter Kiki, 108
Escape, 154
Everyman, 210
Exploits of Elaine, The, 148

Fairy Tale, The, 134
Faithful Heart, The, 70-1, 119
Fake, The, 125
Fallen Angels, 147
Fall Guy, The, 154
Falling Leaves, 134
Fame, 218
Fanatics, The, 175
Fantasia, 80
Far Above Rubies, 134
Farmer's Wife, The, 128, 147, 157
Fata Morgana, 125, 129, 214
Faust, 116

Faust on Toast, 69, 75
Fedora, 43
Firebrand, The, 159
First and the Last, The, 85
First Kiss, The, 134
First Mrs Fraser, The, 213, 225
First Year, The, 154–5
Five O'Clock Girl, The, 218
Flag Lieutenant, The, 119
Flame, The, 134
Flying Squad, The, 208
Fol de Rols, 162
Folies Bergere Revue, The, 149
Follow Through, 216
Forest, The, 132
Fourth Wall, The, 208
Frasquita, 149
French Leave, 42–3
Fulfilling of the Law, The, 74
Fun of the Fayre, 78
Funny Face, 204

Garden of Allah, The, 45–6, 48, 71, 89, 106, 119, 183
Gay Lord Quex, The, 106–7
Gentleman in Waiting, The, 150
Ghost Goes West, The, 126
Ghost Train, The, 150
Gilbert and Sullivan Operas, 136
Gipsy Princess, The, 79
Girl Friend, The, 183
Girl From Cooks, The, 180
Glamorous Night, 47
Glamour, 113
Gloriana, 150
Going Up, 59, 65–7
Gold Diggers, The, 157
Golden Moth, The, 75
Gondoliers, The, 37
Good Gracious Annabelle! 112–13
Good Luck, 105–6, 129
Good Morning, Bill, 180, 218
Good Old Days, The, 144
Gorilla, The, 148
Government Inspector, The, 146, 161
Grain of Mustard Seed, The, 41, 125
Great Adventure, The, 130
Great Big World, The, 71
Great Broxupp, The, 107
Great Lover, The, 43
Great Well, The, 92
Green Cord, The, 92
Green Goddess, The, 109

Green Hat, The, 139
Grounds for Divorce, 149
Growing Pains, 150
Gruach, 132
Guardsman, The, 150

Hamlet, 147
Hanky Panky John, 74
Happy Husband, The, 176, 203–4
Hassan, 83, 106–7
Havoc, 130
Hay Fever, 142, 213
Head Over Heels, 109
Heartbreak House, 69, 71, 128
Heart of a Child, 74
Heiress, The, 119
Henry IV, 70
Henry V, 212
Henry VIII, 211
Her Cardboard Lover, 203
Her Market Price, 134
Her Past, 218
Her Shop, 213
High Road, The, 184
His Lady Friends, 43
Hit the Deck, 182
Hold Everything, 218
Home Chat, 177, 179
Hotel Mouse, The, 74
Hour and the Man, The, 74, 134
House of Peril, The, 28
House that Jack Built, The, 219
Hunky Dory, 74
Husbands Are a Problem, 94
Hullo America, 164
Hypocrite, The, 116

If, 72
If Four Walls Told, 92, 213–14, 224
If I Were King, 184
I'll Leave It To You, 44
Immortal Hour, The, 100
Importance of Being Earnest, 106
In Dahomey, 162
Inevitable, The, 113
Infinite Shoeblack, The, 218
In Nelson's Day, 94
Insect Play, The, 108
Interference, 184
In the Next Room, 132
Irene, 58–9, 67
Iris, 139
Island King, The, 98
Isobel, Edward and Anne, 106
Is Zat So? 154

It Pays To Advertise, 125, 140
It's All Wrong, 55–6, 139
Ivanoff, 146

Jane Clegg, 145
Jane O'Day from Broadway, 58
Jenny, 97
Jew Suss, 228
Jig-Saw, 54
John Bull's Other Island, 71
John Ferguson, 44, 54
Johnny Jones, 75
Johnny Jones and his Sister Sue, 57
Joseph and His Brethren, 214
Journey's End, 225–6
Julius Caesar, 44, 182
Jumble Sale, 56
Just a Kin, 150
Just Fancy, 56
Justice, 93
Just Like Judy, 83

Kate, 134
Katinka, 111
Katja the Dancer, 144
Kid Boots, 162
King Arthur, 211
King Fu, 65–6
King Lear, 120
King's Rhapsody, 170
Kismet, 150
Knave of Diamonds, The, 71

Lady Be Good, 161, 176
Lady Luck, 176
Lady Mary, 202
Lady of Lyons, The, 37
Lady of the Rose, The, 98
Lady With a Lamp, 217
Lake, The, 218
Land of Promise, The, 118, 120
Lass O'Laughter, 92
Last Enemy, The, 220
Last of Mrs Cheyney, The, 149
Last Waltz, 98
La Tosca, 41
Laughing Lady, The, 90
£ s. d., 150
Lavender Ladies, 142
League of Nations, The, 78
Leap Year, 135
Letter, The, 183
Le Vie Parisienne, 219
Lido Lady, 161
Lie, The, 108

Lightin' 149
Light of Heart, The, 120–1
Likes of 'er, The, 107
Lilac Domino, The, 59, 65–6, 75
Lilac Time, 100
Lilies of the Field, The, 104, 140
Liliom, 155–6, 203
Listening In, 97
Little Dutch Girl, The, 55
Little Girl in Red, The, 75
Little Minister, The, 107
Little Miss Bluebeard, 151
London Calling, 110–11
London Life, 130
London, Paris and New York, 54, 80
London Revue, The, 148
Lonely Lady, 73
Lord Richard in the Pantry, 26, 213
Looking Glass, The, 136
Lord of Creation, 134
Love, 74
Love Adrift, 161
Love Among the Paint Pots, 85
Love Lies, 218
Love's Awakening, 97
Love's Prisoner, 139
Loyalties, 91

Macbeth, 157, 165
Madame Pompadour, 110, 143
Madras House, The, 142
Magda, 108
Magdalen's Husband, A, 132
Magic Crystal, The, 134
Maid of the Mountains, The, 54
Man from Hong Kong, The, 150
Man In Dress Clothes, The, 90
Man With a Heart, The, 151
Man With a Load of Mischief, The, 147
Many Happy Returns, 207–8, 218
Many Waters, 208
Marigold, 181–2
Marquise, The, 176, 213
Marriage by Instalments, 113
Marriage of Kitty, The, 112
Mary, 79
Mary, Queen of Scots, 116
Mary Rose, 44, 206
Mask and the Face, The, 129
Masque of Venice, The, 213
Matriarch, The, 218
Mayor of Casterbridge, The, 146
Meddlers, The, 150
Medea, 45

Medorah, 56
Melloney Holtspur, 107
Mercenary Mary, 148
Merchant of Venice, 97
Merely Molly, 154
Merrys, Merrys, 218
Merry Widow, The, 135
Merry Wives of Windsor, The, 212
Merton of the Movies, 113
Middle Watch, The, 219
Midnight Frolics, The, 79
Midsummer Madness, 135
Misdoings of Charley Peace, 224
Miss Nell of New Orleans, 71, 213
Miss Thompson, 145
Mixed Doubles, 142
Mr Cinders, 223–4, 227
"Mr Garrick," 93
Mr Malatesta, 70
Mr Pim Passes By, 27, 213
Mr Todd's Experiment, 33, 35–6, 43, 279
Mr What's His Name, 185
Mr Wu, 91
M'Lady, 74
Money for Nothing, 79
Moon and Sixpence, The, 148
Morals, 134
Moving Finger, The, 204
Mud and Treacle, 204
Murder on the Second Floor, 218, 220
Music Box, The, 111
My Niece, 75
My Son, 94
My Son John, 165

Naughty Princess, The, 50, 52, 54
Ned Kean of Old Drury, 104
New Clown, The, 144
New Morality, The, 85, 147
Nicolette, 150
Night Night, 74
Nighty Night, 94
9.45, 142
Nine O'Clock Revue, The, 99
None But The Brave, 156
No, No, Nanette, 139, 149
Now and Then, 80
No. 17, 148
Nuts in May, 94

Odd Spot, The, 136
Oh, Julie! 56
Oh, Kay, 181

Oklahoma, 143
Old Adam, The, 147
Old English, 130, 134
Old Heidelberg, 145, 161
Old Woman, The, 73
Oliver Cromwell, 106
Omar Khayyam, 109
On Approval, 180
One Dam Thing After Another, 182–3
On With the Dance, 148
Ordeal, 150
Othello, 44, 71, 114–6
Other Mr Gibbs, The, 134
Our Betters, 106
Our Nell, 135
Out Goes She, 197
Outsider, The, 109
Out to Win, 73
Outward Bound, 112, 129
Over Sunday, 83

Paddy The Next Best Thing, 43, 92
Palladium Pleasures, 160
Pansy's Arabian Night, 133
Paris Bound, 220, 222
Partners Again, 106
Passing Brompton Road, 208, 213
Passing of the Third Floor Back, The, 173
Patricia, 135
Peace and Quiet, 113
Peep Show, The, 77
Peer Gynt, 212
Peggy-Anne, 176
Peg Of My Heart, 31
Pelican, The, 125
Perfect Fit, The, 134
Persevering Pat, 150
Peter Ibbetson, 41
Peter Pan, 19, 118, 180
Phi-Phi, 99, 100
Piccadilly Puritan, The, 113
Pigeon, The, 93
Pilgrim of Eternity, 74
Pins and Needles, 75
Playbox, The, 133
Playboy of the Western World, The, 70
Plunder, 200
Plus Fours, 106
Polly, 99
Polly Preferred, 134
Polly With a Past, 73
Pomp and Circumstance, 94

Poppy, 135
Porgy, 222
Potash and Perlmutter, 51
Pot Luck, 80
Potiphar's Wife, 180
Pretty Peggy, 56
Primrose, 136
Prince and the Beggar Maid, The, 118
Prince Fazil, 157
Princess Charming, 184
Prisoner of War, The, 150
Prisoner of Zenda, The, 106
Prodigal Daughter, A, 94
Punch Bowl, The, 129
Puppets, 136
Puss Puss, 80
Put and Take, 80

Quality Street, 72
Quarantine, 89
Queen High, 162
Queen Was in the Parlour, The, 155, 158
Quest, 176
Quinney's, 119, 225

Rabbi and the Priest, The, 93
Rain, 145, 149
Rainbow, The, 111
Rat, The, 132, 158
Rats, 111-2
Rebel Maid, The, 75
Reckless Reggie, 113
Return of Sherlock Holmes, The, 108
Return of the Soldier, The, 204
Richard III, 115, 165
Right to Strike, The, 43
Riki-Tiki, 161
Ringer, The, 159
Ring O'Bells, The, 150
Rising Generation, The, 108
Riverside Nights, 159
Robert E. Lee, 108
Robert Macaire, 75
Robey en Casserole, 75
Rockets, 100
Romeo and Juliet, 140, 212
Roof, The, 219
Rookery Nook, 154
Rope, 215, 224
Rose and the Ring, The, 113
Rose Marie, 139, 143-4, 160, 163, 165, 181, 219

Round in Fifty, 99
Round Table, The, 151
Round the World in Eighty Days, 99
R.S.V.P., 162
Running Water, 94
R.U.R., 107, 113

Sacred and Profane Love, 83
Sacred Flame, The, 219
Sadie Dupont, 204
Safety Match, A, 73
St Joan, 45, 131
Sally, 80
Salome, 92
Salomy Jane, 150
Sarah of Soho, 94
Savage and the Woman, The, 72
Scarlet Lady, The, 213
School for Scandal, The, 118, 219
Scotch Mist, 158
Seagull, The, 148
Sea Urchins, The, 150
Second Little Revue, The, 135
Second Man, The, 204
Second Mrs Tanqueray, The, 92
Secret Agent, The, 94
Secrets, 94, 103
77, Park Lane, 209
Shall We Join the Ladies? 91
Shanghai, 66
Shepherds' Pie, 73
She Stoops to Conquer, 71
Show, The, 149
Showboat, 202-3
Show Off, The, 134
Showroom, The, 45
Show's The Thing, The, 219
Signal, The, 150
Sign on the Door, The, 73
Silver Box, The, 93, 149
Silver Tassie, The, 222
Silver Wings, 89
Singing Fool, The, 198
Sinners, 134
Sirocco, 176-8, 180
Skin Game, The, 44, 84
Sky High, 149
Sleeping Partners, 158
Smith Family, The, 90
Snap, 100
Social Convenience, A, 74
Soldier of Fortune, A, 115
Some, 79
Sometimes, 150
Song of the Sea, The, 203

Sorry You've Been Troubled, 219
S.O.S., 204
So This is London, 108
So This is Love, 209
Southern Maid, The, 54
Spring Cleaning, 149
Squeaker, The, 201
Speckled Band, The, 74
Sport of Kings, The, 133
Spot on the Sun, A, 175, 213
Still Dancing, 148
Stop Flirting! 111, 136
Storm, 125
Stranger Within, The, 220
Street Singer, The, 135
Strife, 45
Student Prince, The, 161
Sweet William, 74
Success, 106
Such Men Are Dangerous, 208–9
Sunny, 161
Sunshine of the World, The, 58
Sun Up, 150
Sybil, 75
Symphony in Two Flats, A, 220

Tabs, 79
Taming of the Shrew, The, 118
Tancred, 113
Tarnish, 142
Tartan Peril, 74
Tell Me More, 150
Tempest, The, 70
Terror, The, 183
Tess of the D'Urbevilles, 145–6
Thark, 175
That's A Good Girl, 209
Theodore & Co., 51
They Knew What They Wanted, 158
Thing That Matters, The, 74
This Marriage, 134
This Woman Business, 157
This Year of Grace, 203
Threads, 74
Three Birds, 113
Three Cheers, 65
Three Graces, The, 134
Three Sisters, The, 146
Thunder In The Air, 206–7
Tiger Cats, 130
Timothy, 74
Tina, 119
Tip Toes, 162
To Have the Honour, 133

Tom Trouble, 45
Toni, 136
Tonight's The Night, 51, 136
Tons of Money, 94–5, 97, 125, 206
Topsy and Eva, 203
To What Red Hell? 224
Treasure Island, 92, 173
Trelawny of the Wells, 157
Trespassers, 113, 213
Trial of Mary Dugan, The, 209
Tricks, 142
Trojan Woman, The, 45
Trump Card, The, 74
Trust Emily, 113
Truth About Blayds, The, 72
Truth About the Russian Ballet, The, 158
Truth Game, The, 209
Tunnel Trench, 216
Turandot, 118
Two Jacks and a Jill, 74
Two White Arms, 201
Tyrant, The, 148

Uncle Tom's Cabin, 203
Uncle Vanya, 146
Under His Protection, 134
Unfair Sex, The, 150
Unknown Warrior, The, 226
Up In Mabel's Room, 69, 74

Vagabond King, The, 184
Vaudeville Matinees, 162
Very Idea, The, 134
Virginia, 203
Vortex, The, 132, 150, 213

Wake Up and Dream, 216, 222
Wandering Jew, The, 44
Way of an Eagle, The, 89
Way of the World, The, 130
Way Things Happen, The, 133
Welcome Stranger, 72
What Every Woman Knows, 104, 119
Wheel, The, 89
When Crummles Played, 183
When Knights Were Bold, 93, 134
Where the Rainbow Ends, 24
Whip, The, 105–6
White Birds, 181
White Cargo, 119, 131, 134
White Chateau, The, 184
Whirl of the World, The, 135
Whirled Into Happiness, 99

Whiteheaded Boy, The, 41
Whole Town's Talking, The, 158
Wicked Earl, The, 181
Widowers Houses, 93
Wild Duck, The, 149
Wildflower, 161
Will, The, 107
Will Shakespeare, 73, 83, 86
Windows, 93
Woman to Woman, 72
Wonderful Visit, The, 84–5

Wrecker, The, 183
Wrong Number, The, 73

Yellow Mask, The, 201
Yellow Sands, 157
Yoicks, 135
You'd Be Surprised, 110
Young Idea, The, 112
Young Person in Pink, 41–2
Young Visiters, The, 41
Young Woodley, 200, 204

Index of Theatres

Abbey Theatre, 41, 157
Adelphi, 26, 47, 50, 52, 57, 74, 89,
    93, 98, 109, 113, 119, 124, 133,
    135, 139, 150, 154, 174–5, 219,
    223
Aldwych, 41, 47, 70, 75, 83, 85, 93–
    4, 96, 113, 125, 133, 140–1, 154,
    175, 199–200, 219
Alexandra Palace, 139
Alhambra, 26, 47, 56–7, 75, 110, 113
Ambassadors, 47, 72–3, 93–4, 104,
    113, 125, 133, 142, 150, 154, 159,
    175, 201, 208, 224
Apollo, 42, 47, 50, 73–4, 89, 93, 97,
    104, 113, 125, 133–4, 142, 154,
    175, 201, 220
Arts Theatre Club, 217

Barnes Theatre, 155
Birmingham Repertory Company,
    100
Birmingham Repertory Theatre, 82,
    84, 228, 235

Carlton, 176, 201, 218
Coliseum, 26
Comedy, 41, 47, 70, 89, 93–4, 113,
    126, 133–4, 142, 150
Court, 41, 47, 69, 70, 92–3, 102, 109,
    113, 128–9, 133
Criterion, 26, 70, 89, 93, 112–3, 125,
    129, 133, 142, 144, 155, 176, 197,
    203, 208

Daly's, 18, 27, 47, 54, 75, 93, 98,
    110, 113, 135, 142, 144, 163, 174,
    176, 202
Dominion, 216
Duchess, 216
Duke of York's, 18, 27, 37, 40, 47,
    71, 73, 89, 93–4, 97, 110–13, 129,
    148, 150, 155, 158, 176–80, 182,
    198, 205, 208

Embassy, 112, 212
Empire, 26, 47, 56–8, 66, 75, 90, 93,
    97, 111, 113, 124, 133, 135, 144,
    150, 161
Everyman, 68, 132

Fortune, 133–4, 150, 176, 180, 220

Gaiety, 18, 26, 29, 47, 50–2, 66, 69,
    71, 75, 95, 97–8, 111, 113, 126,
    133, 135–6, 144, 161, 164, 167,
    180, 203, 218–9
Gaiety, Manchester, 82
Garrick, 26, 37, 43, 47, 71–2, 74, 90,
    100, 106, 108, 112–13, 132–34,
    145–6, 149–50, 156, 173, 176
Globe, 26–7, 42–3, 47, 66, 72, 74,
    90, 92–3, 106, 113, 136, 147, 156,
    180, 217
Golders Green Hippodrome, 212,
    216, 221
Grand, Croydon, 145

Haymarket, 26, 41, 44, 47, 72, 74, 90, 93, 106, 113, 119, 130, 133, 147, 157, 199, 208, 225, 235

Hippodrome, 26, 48, 54, 57, 77, 79, 93, 99, 133, 135, 148, 161, 182, 208, 218, 223–4

His Majesty's, 22, 27, 29, 50, 76, 82, 90–1, 93, 106, 113, 116–7, 133–5, 161, 173, 181, 203, 214, 219, 222

Holborn Empire, 45, 144

Kelly's Theatre, 82

Kingsway, 47, 74–5, 93, 99, 113, 133–5, 147, 155, 181, 219

King's Theatre, Hammersmith, 116

Liverpool Repertory Theatre, 82, 84

Lincoln's Inn Theatre, 54

Little, 47, 73, 93, 99, 113, 127, 133–6, 148, 150, 178, 203

London Pavilion, 48, 54, 78, 80, 93, 99–100, 112–13, 148, 162, 182–3, 203, 222

Lyceum, 48, 72–3, 91, 93, 100, 113, 118, 133–4, 148, 183, 208

Lyric, 43, 55, 76, 93, 99, 133, 135, 150, 154, 157, 183, 203, 218, 222

Lyric, Hammersmith, 27, 44, 48, 54, 130, 133, 135, 159, 183, 219, 235

Middlesex Music Hall, 52

Moss Empires, 26

New, 26–7, 44, 48, 72, 91, 93, 107, 113, 130, 133–4, 144, 148, 152, 179, 183, 204, 208, 218, 226–7, 229

New Oxford, 93

Old Vic, 210–12, 219

Oxford, 48, 100, 133–4, 148, 150

Oxford Music Hall, 78

Palace, 26, 55, 89, 111, 113, 133, 135, 137, 149, 164, 183–4, 203, 218

Palladium, 26, 93, 100, 133, 135, 149, 160, 164

Piccadilly, 120, 198–9, 200

Plane Street Theatre, 62, 63

Playhouse, 26, 48, 69, 74, 91–3, 108, 113, 131, 133–4, 150, 156, 183, 219

Prince of Wales, 37, 48, 74, 79–80, 83–4, 108, 113, 118, 131–3, 135, 157, 162, 179, 184, 208

Princes, 48, 56, 72–3, 93, 108, 113, 131, 133, 136, 149–50, 157, 203, 219

Queen's, 26, 27–8, 33, 36, 41, 43, 48, 51, 55, 57, 74, 79–80, 92–3, 107, 111, 113, 126, 133–5, 139, 149–50, 158, 162, 175

Regent, 93, 100, 108, 113, 133

Royal Opera House, 46, 110, 112, 176

Royalty, 48, 74, 80, 92–4, 108, 113, 125, 132–4, 156, 184, 209, 218

Sadler's Wells, 34

St James's, 27, 30, 44, 48, 74, 93, 109, 113, 118, 133, 149–50, 161, 184, 203, 218, 222, 224

St Martins, 44–5, 48, 83–4, 90–1, 93, 107, 113, 132–3, 145, 149–50, 155, 158, 184, 209, 219

Savoy, 41, 43, 48, 92–4, 99, 108, 112–13, 133–4, 150, 158, 181, 183, 204, 225–6

Scala, 48, 73, 113, 133–4, 157

Shaftesbury, 43, 48, 50, 56, 65, 73–4, 86, 92, 94–5, 108, 111, 113, 133–4, 136, 142, 149–50, 161–5, 184, 218–19

Strand, 26, 43, 48, 73–4, 79, 92, 94, 109, 113, 130, 133–4, 150, 158, 173, 216

Streatham Hill, 212, 216, 221

Theatre Royal, Brighton, 132

Theatre Royal, Drury Lane, 26, 45, 47, 66, 85, 89, 93, 104–5, 113, 119, 126, 129–30, 132–3, 143, 156, 163, 177, 181, 202, 216, 219

Theatre Royal, Nottingham, 56

Vaudeville, 48, 56, 79–80, 93, 100, 111–13, 127, 133, 136, 150, 162, 184, 218

Victoria Palace, 26, 68, 207, 219

Whitehall, 199

Winter Garden, 48, 50, 52, 56, 80, 93, 100, 112–13, 133, 136, 150, 162, 184, 209

Wyndhams, 26, 48, 72, 92–3, 109, 113, 133–4, 149, 159, 185, 217, 224